The diplomacy of ideas

U.S. foreign policy and cultural relations, 1938 – 1950

The diplomacy of ideas

U.S. foreign policy and
cultural relations, 1938–1950

FRANK A. NINKOVICH

CAMBRIDGE UNIVERSITY PRESS
Cambridge
London   New York   New Rochelle
Melbourne   Sydney

Published by the Press Syndicate of the University of Cambridge
The Pitt Building, Trumpington Street, Cambridge CB2 IRP
32 East 57th Street, New York, NY 10022, USA
296 Beaconsfield Parade, Middle Park, Melbourne 3206, Australia

First published 1981

Printed in the United States of America

Typeset by David E. Seham Associates Inc., Metuchen, New Jersey
Printed and bound by the Murray Printing Company, Westford, Massachusetts

Library of Congress Cataloging in Publication Data
Ninkovich, Frank A. 1944–
The diplomacy of ideas.
Bibliography: p.
Includes index.
1. United States–Foreign relations–1933–1945.
2. United States–Foreign relations–1945–1953.
3. United States–Relations (general) with foreign countries.
I. Title.
E804.N56   327.73   80-13388
ISBN 0 521 23241 4

Contents

v

To Carol

Preface

It is frequently true of intellectual life that interests and researches are governed as much by accidental discoveries and unpredictable detours as by planning and foresight. When I began my graduate studies in U.S. foreign policy, any thoughts of culture or cultural relations were far beyond my intellectual horizon. My initiation into such concerns was purely fortuitous, sparked by what started out as an almost whimsical inquiry into an interesting if seemingly inconsequential literary squabble that briefly exercised the Cold War America of the late 1940s. I was soon surprised to discover that this incident (concerning the writing of poetry, of all things) reverberated with internationalist and nativist sentiments that resembled traditional American attitudes toward foreign policy proper, and as a historian of foreign relations I began to wonder why this should be so. Only slowly did it dawn on me that controversies centering on matters of so-called high culture were dual phenomena: They were symbolic in the abstract aesthetic sense that critics make it their business to interpret; but their logical and institutional designs were also shaped in more concrete fashion by cultural patterns common to the entire society, to the interpretation of which literary critics bring no special skills or wisdom. I thought that if these events were part of the very reality they mirrored rather than merely society's intellectual adornments, then perhaps an investigation of the cultural side of American diplomacy would be worthwhile if it helped to illuminate the larger world of foreign policy.

As I became enmeshed in the topic, I became dissatisfied with existing treatments of culture and cultural relations and resolved to strike out on my own. But it was not long before I became unsure of my intellectual footing, for the study of cultural matters, and especially one's own culture, is basically an unnatural activity. As culture is ubiquitous, it is a problem merely to distinguish its

vii

presence, much less to puzzle out its importance, and this no doubt is why anthropology is a comparative discipline. Questions of culture's social manifestations aside, its subjective intellectual features proved especially vexing. Because culture structures the way we think about and perceive the world, it requires no small degree of intellectual detachment before one can hope to conceptualize it adequately. An understanding of culture is inherently problematic, for it entails the objectification and questioning of deeply ingrained beliefs and received truths whose power is so great that one's inquiry is always in danger of being subverted by the objects of one's study. Moreover, contrary to idealistic assumptions concerning the transcendence of intellect, one must face up to a troubling paradox: The study of culture requires emancipation from cultural fetters at the same time that it is manifestly impossible for intellect to proceed independently of this bondage. If one comes from a liberal society and a liberal intellectual tradition whose ideology unendingly trumpets the possibilities of freedom and transcendence in every sphere of life – in short, from a culture whose biases are profoundly anticultural – such problems are difficult to admit, much less to address. Given these built-in tendencies toward parochialism, it was tempting to conclude that those most deeply immersed in a given cultural milieu are the least qualified to study it.

Despite these paradoxes, there was much to be said in favor of an "insider's" study. It is probably true, from a dispassionate scientific point of view, that cultural peculiarities can more easily be cataloged by an observant outsider. But without derogating the virtues of objective knowledge, it is fair to observe that science provides neither an exclusive nor an inherently superior form of understanding. The humanities, too, history among them, have a rightful claim to our attention and they possess their own subjective methods, results, and validity. One of their peculiarities is that the vitality of humanistic learning and understanding may depend as much on a painful process of unlearning as on an efficient aggrandizement of new data. When viewed in this light, the acquisition of humanistic knowledge can actually benefit from a prior baptism in the culture rather than automatically suffer from such an immersion. The possession of a stock of cultural preconceptions, to be shed only as they are outgrown, can lead to a form of understanding that grows out of and is therefore a part of the culture rather than something external to it. Thus, from a humanistic perspective, propositions about the culture are all the more meaningful to the degree that they possess cultural resonance. Some of our finest national history has been written from such an orientation and, despite the compelling claims of those who favor a social scientific or internationalist approach, the need for such history will remain so long as cultural uniqueness is a fact of life.

As it turned out, then, my doubts about the feasibility of this study proved to be minor in the end because the justifications for the internal study of culture are in their essentials little different from the consoling arguments that historians have always offered in defense of their subjectively uncertain craft. For all the accidental and problematic aspects of my intellectual interests, they led straight back to history and expanded my primitive understanding of what doing history was all about. One really can't ask for much more from one's work.

Any historian is necessarily dependent upon the labors of others for his results. Fortunately, the archivists at the Butler Library of Columbia University, the Institute of International Education, the Library of Congress Manuscript Division, the Harry S Truman Library, the U.S. National Archives, the University of Chicago's Regenstein Library, and the University of Illinois Archives were all extremely helpful in guiding my way.

Special thanks are also due to the following: to Mr. Charles Benton and Ms. Louise Benton, for going to a good deal of trouble to make available the private papers of the late Senator William Benton; to Mr. Ben Cherrington and Mrs. Dorothea Blair, for responding to some difficult written questions; to Mr. J. Manuel Espinosa of the Department of State's Bureau of Educational and Cultural Affairs, for sharing his sources and providing valuable research suggestions; to Mrs. Wilma Fairbank, for never losing patience with my arguments; to Irv Gellman, for generously sharing the results of his extensive researches; to Ray Harvey, of what was then the USIA, for making available his files; to Dorothy Greene Johnson, for her recollections and judicious comments; to Dean Richard McKeon, for his reminiscences of the early days of

UNESCO; to Professors John U. Nef and Edward Shils, for granting access to manuscript collections; to Mr. Howland Sargeant and Mrs. Louise Wright, for searching their memories.

I am especially grateful to the Edward W. Hazen Foundation for a timely grant that allowed me to concentrate without interruption on an early version of the manuscript. Despite advance warning of my contrary views, they acted in the finest tradition of intellectual liberalism.

To my dissertation advisers at the University of Chicago, Akira Iriye, Barry Karl, and William McNeill, I shall owe a lasting intellectual debt. I cannot recall the point at which I came to understand that my intellectual prowess was not so self-determined as I had imagined, but my chagrin at this discovery has since been replaced by the realization that innovation in the humanities must be solidly grounded in prior intellectual efforts. One could do no better in this regard than to have these men for one's progenitors.

Most of all, credit should go to my wife, Carol, not only for the many hours that she put into this work, but more importantly for her steadying confidence in my abilities. This faith in itself made the undertaking worthwhile.

FRANK A. NINKOVICH

August, 1980

Introduction

Cultural relations can be thought of as two different yet related processes. For students of diplomacy, they are first and foremost a specialized form of statecraft concerned with the management of intellectual influences in international politics. This intellectual diplomacy has deep historical roots. The pharaohs of Egypt, to take only one example from antiquity, demanded young aristocratic hostages of their vanquished foes, not so much as guarantees of good behavior as to inculcate these future leaders with an Egyptian outlook and style of life. Despite an impressive historical pedigree, however, the cultural zone of foreign policy has always remained a fringe area of diplomatic activity and historians have been satisfied by and large to concentrate on the political, economic, and military aspects of foreign policy. In the United States, with which this study is concerned, cultural relations have repeated this pattern of diplomatic marginality and scholarly indifference.

This neglect, if not justifiable, is at least understandable. The U.S. Department of State's programs in cultural relations have been a minor cog in the gearbox of foreign policy. Major questions of "high policy" or even more mundane foreign policy concerns – in other words, the usual stuff of diplomatic history – were not debated, much less decided, by cultural officers. True, over the years the cultural programs have increased greatly in size and, if for no other reason, in importance. Nevertheless, they have continued to occupy a lowly position in the diplomatic pecking order. Given this relatively inconsequential status, it might seem only sensible to view the study of cultural relations as a scholarly analog of the "tertiary recovery" procedures employed by oil producers–that is, as a marginal supplement to played-out political and economic modes of analysis. Be that as it may, this study's aim goes beyond an incremental extension of our knowledge of the

I

policymaking process or the addition of an extra "dimension" to our understanding of U.S. foreign policy.

Although cultural relations are a minor form of diplomacy, at the same time the entire foreign policy process is itself subordinate to larger cultural dynamics. Going beyond the fixation with transnational intellectual contacts, from a macroanthropological perspective cultural relations can be viewed as no less than the totality of relations between cultures. Here one confronts the truly grand processes of diffusion and acculturation that, when viewed as a whole, form a global pattern of intercultural interaction and adaptation. The study of such contacts and their effects provides a lofty conceptual perch from which to survey the dynamics of world history. From such a theoretical height, diplomatic relations of every stripe, the cultural included, constitute but a fraction of all intercultural transactions and exercise a relatively modest influence in the overall scheme of things. By this standard, a nation's foreign policy is only an expression of powerful cultural forces beyond its grasp.

To study one form of cultural relations is inevitably to confront the other, for the diplomatic pursuit of cultural influence is obviously conditioned by its cultural environment. Unfortunately for the study of international relations, the anthropological conception is at present little more than a blunt instrument, well suited only to world-historical speculations. For the elucidation of specific foreign policies, it must give way to more restrained concepts and to more sharply defined choices of subject matter. It is here that the study of cultural diplomacy, traditionally perceived as too narrow to be of much value to students of foreign policy, can serve as a peephole affording at least a partial glimpse of broader vistas. Acknowledging beforehand its inability to penetrate to the source of cultural processes, such a study can at least explore particular visions of those dynamics. It might also shed some indirect light on the nature of cultural influences, internal and external, upon foreign policy.

There are a number of reasons why this should be so. First, the founders of the American cultural programs and their successors possessed a weighty anthropological sense of their task, though it was less than sophisticated in terms of theory. Their conceptions possessed an amazing degree of elasticity, beginning with an elitist fixation on the virtues of intellectual exchanges and expanding in later years to embrace the manipulation of mass education and technological diffusion, but they were always informed by a belief that diplomacy was only a small part of a larger, more fundamental, and ultimately benevolent dynamic of historical change. It was their objective not only to work in harmony with this process by becoming its allies, but also to expedite its self-realization. By the very nature of their concerns, the cultural personnel were forced to confront, if not traditional foreign policy issues, the assumptions underlying those issues. Their consignment to the diplomatic basement, so to speak, gave them access to the foundations of U.S. foreign policy.

There is another point at which this study embraces larger concerns. Culture involves more than patterns of ideas, for ideas are always intimately connected to technological forms and to social structures; that is, they are part of a social geography. The State Department's policies in cultural relations were an organic development, not simply an intellectual response, rooted in an institutional and social environment that mirrored the fundamental values of the larger society. The same was true of the other nations to undertake cultural diplomacy in the twentieth century. With a circularity that inheres in the topic, each nation attempted to shape the factors that were in turn shaping it, each in accordance with its traditions. The point is that these peculiarities of "national character" make the cultural programs good material for studying in some detail the influence of domestic factors in the foreign policy process. In particular, the U.S. programs, where tradition played a prominent part, provide an opportunity to study an evolving relationship between ideas and institutions in the context of a rapidly changing international environment. In this way, the study of the cultural programs can illuminate suggestively some of the connections between foreign policy ideas and their social underpinnings.

Finally, the fact that the cultural programs were relatively unburdened by the day-to-day complexities of foreign policy makes them an excellent vehicle for tracing in outline changes in the basic patterns of U.S. foreign policy, patterns that are normally obscured in the study of more intricate diplomatic topics. If the traditional matter of foreign policy is here lacking, its form is enhanced. Even a narrow study of the cultural programs would have been impossible without some inquiry into the major shifts in the conduct and structure of American foreign policy caused by the nation's absorption into the mainstream of international politics. It would be too much to claim that the programs formed a microcosm of U.S. foreign policy. Their development might more usefully be viewed as a metaphor or trope than as a literal model for other policy developments. In addition to providing a general survey of the cultural programs, this history has kept such a larger interpretive purpose in mind.

The programs, then, have a dual significance: as part of the policy process and as symbols of the larger cultural forces at work upon policy. Consequently, the scope of this work is both narrow and broad, modest and ambitious. It is narrow in the sense that it confines itself to a relatively obscure subdivision of the diplomatic community, treating it for a brief time span. It is broad because the events treated herein have a significance that transcends their modest bureaucratic horizons. It is a study of cultural relations, and of culture at work. Considerations of manageability and professional competence dictated restricting the study to a form of cultural relations that is but a pale shadow of the grand anthropological process; but this acknowledgment of limits coexists with a recognition that the resemblance, even though a poor caricature, nonetheless illustrates important features of foreign policy too long neglected. This dualism comes with the topic. Indeed, it is the reason for my fascination with it as well as the source of any importance that it might possess.

Having said this much, I am obliged to make a few remarks on the meaning of that slippery term, "culture." Obviously, it would be presumptuous as well as foolhardy for a historian to tackle a concept that has puzzled generations of anthropologists. Nevertheless, because the word will be repeated until it might come to appear drained of meaning altogether, some comment is in order. The temptation is to make do with some minimally acceptable definition of culture, such as the truism that it is learned behavior or that it represents social heredity. It is, of course, both of these. But this study assumes more than that. I am among those who hold that culture and culture change are more than simply intellectual or mental phenomena. From the standpoint of the study of diplomacy, material and institutional factors need to be taken into account, if only because power, which lies at the core of international relations, assumes at bottom a palpable form. Thus in the debate over the nature of culture that still rages in anthropological circles, I would ultimately, if only halfheartedly, take my stand with the so-called cultural materialists.[1] By contrast, the cultural enthusiasts of whom I write were zealous proponents of a cultural idealism, an outlook dependent ultimately upon idealistic metaphysical premises concerning the nature of reality. Employing a reductionist logic more often found among materialist thinkers, they viewed the large process of cultural relations as being a function of intellectual relations.[2]

Their views coincided nicely with the anthropological theory of the day. Admittedly, the cultural personnel within the State Department never discarded the crude nineteenth-century evolutionism that had been discredited by Franz Boas and his disciples, a view that saw cultures evolving from primitive, irrational forms into modern liberal-rational entities. Despite the widespread scholarly acceptance of a nonnormative cultural relativism, they preferred to retain their faith in the ultimate triumph of rationality and progress.[3] For the most part, though, their thinking paralleled the mentalist, psychological outlook then enjoying great popularity in American anthropological circles. The American school of historical ethnology, according to one of its prominent practitioners, conceived of cultural diffusion as "a process psychological in essence." This emphasis on psychological factors elevated the role of individually transmitted ideas to supreme importance in explaining externally induced culture change or acculturation. Diffusion came to be perceived largely in terms of the transmission of abstract "culture traits." Consistent with this idealist orientation, the scholars of the Boas school displayed little interest in the material or economic aspects of culture. There is no evidence, however, to suggest that the State Department's cultural personnel were deeply affected by anthropologists' dogmas; more likely both reflected dominant American cultural values and assumptions.[4]

There is no denying the obvious fact that culture is transmitted by individuals or that ideas play a significant role in the processes of diffusion and acculturation. But there is strong reason to question whether the overall workings of intercultural change are dominated by intellectual and individual processes to the exclusion of material and systemic factors. One way of looking at the matter is to conceive of cultures as possessing a permeability gradient that allows material goods and technologies to penetrate their barriers far more rapidly and readily than new ideas. That is why military power ranks first in the concern of nations (and cultural affairs last, usually); it is also the reason why intellectual penetration follows only in the wake of demonstrations of military-economic superiority, and even then to only a limited extent. Where the introduction of new intellectual outlooks appears to precede technologically powered diffusion – the so-called reverse cultural lag – it is usually because of a prior understanding of the concrete power of modern technological forms and a desire to more readily acquire them for domestic use.

This is not an argument for a straightforwardly materialist interpretation of culture and culture change. To say that material forms penetrate more readily is only to point to the strongest feature of culture – its systematic symbolic function. The wisest statesmen have long recognized that military power was of only limited use in dealing with flourishing cultural traditions. China's long history of sinicizing its conquerors provides perhaps the strongest example of the tendency toward cultural inertia. Although one can point to instances of cultural extirpation caused by outside contact, foreign ideas and technologies usually end up adjusting to the limitations imposed by local traditions. Cultures are especially resistant to new patterns of thought, so much so that the introduction of new ideas usually comes to resemble domestication rather than assimilation. The implantation of ideas might make sense from an individual perspective, but it is problematic at best if cultures are viewed as systems.[5]

Thus the arguments for culture as a symbolic organizing medium are well taken, as far as they go.[6] But I think that the symbolic nature of culture is best understood, from an international perspective at least, by jettisoning the idealist view of culture change. To my mind, the crude idealism of the cultural enthusiasts does not provide a tenable historical perspective. Philosophically, the gap between us yawns wide. However, as the foregoing remarks were intended to indicate, I have no wish to deny the significance of ideas or ideals in history; quite to the contrary, this study confirms their importance although it denies their exclusive sway. I shall not further pursue these points for, among other things, this history is also an extended argument for my point of view.

CHAPTER I

Philanthropic origins of cultural policy

Until the advent of large-scale institutional philanthropy in the twentieth century, cultural relations were a private activity, guided by the ubiquitous Invisible Hand. This is not to suggest that those engaged in intercultural contact – traders, missionaries, military personnel, tourists, and an assortment of emerging international types bred by industrialism – had only a blind self-interest as their immediate compass; for frequently they saw themselves as instruments of a higher purpose, be it called Providence, Civilization, or simply Progress. Nor is it to imply that such activities were unrelated to foreign policy; quite to the contrary, private initiatives were often viewed as liberal antidotes to the baleful effects of formal diplomacy.[1] But it was only with the formation of the Carnegie Endowment for International Peace in 1910 that cultural relations were institutionalized and tied, however tentatively, to foreign policy objectives. From this point, a philanthropic structure was gradually erected as a halfway house between cultural laissez faire and governmental entrance into policymaking.

The reasoning behind steel magnate Andrew Carnegie's decision to create the endowment was almost childlike in its innocence. Central to his expectation that a philanthropic tonic could stimulate peace was a belief that international conflicts were caused by diplomatic misunderstandings. At the dedication of the Pan American Union, one of the many peace "palaces" for which he donated the construction funds, Carnegie claimed that war was the result of a lack of mutual confidence among diplomats. As statesmen tended to be strangers, they were a "naturally and mutually suspicious" lot. Consequently, when strangers quarreled, the usual result was strife. But when two friends differed, Carnegie concluded that the probable result was "peaceful settlement either by themselves, or, failing that, by arbitration of friends, and the two friends become dearer to each other for life." Friendship, accommodation, peace – the whole of international politics was reduced to a problem of interpersonal relations. Built upon the assumption that policy was determined exclusively within the narrow confines of traditional cabinet diplomacy, Carnegie's palace was intended to serve as a sort of hemispheric fraternity house in which diplomats could comfortably cement the bonds of their clubbish brotherhood. The purpose behind the endowment was not very different, except that it was intended to promote friendship and understanding on a broader scale.[2]

The men to whom Carnegie entrusted the administration of his foundation were not so naive about the ease with which war could be abolished. In appointing the endowment's board of trustees, Carnegie largely ignored the advanced pacifist element who had acted as midwives at its birth, choosing instead to rely heavily upon members of the Eastern legal and financial establishment. The foundation was put in the hands of practical "men of affairs" who were more attuned to a recognition of the frequently decisive role of power in international relations. Yet, as the eyes of the trustees surveyed the broader panorama of the international scene, their national narrowness was dispersed in the solvent of a more liberal spirit; for the men in charge were ultimately optimists, fervid believers in peace, prosperity, and progress as the inevitable blessings of Western civilization.[3]

The dominant personality in charting the endowment's course in its formative years was Elihu Root, its first president and chairman of the board of trustees. Root had pursued a distinguished career, first in private life as an eminent New York City corporation lawyer, then with successive posts as secretary of war and secretary of state, and ending with a term as the Republican senator from New York. Until his death in 1937, he was generally regarded as one of the nation's few authentic elder statesmen. Carnegie valued his judgment highly, and it was Root who persuaded the tycoon to point the endowment in the direction of a "scientific and thorough study of the causes of war and the remedy which can be applied to the causes, rather than merely the treatment of symptoms." This statement made the endowment's mandate appear to be more open-minded than it actually was, for Root had strong and rather unscientific convictions regarding both symptoms and remedies. As a leader in the movement for the spread and codification of international law and as the recipient of the Nobel Peace Prize in 1913, Root was a prominent advocate of judicial settlement of international disputes.[4]

Underlying his legalistic approach to international affairs was an acceptance of the primacy of the nation-state, an awareness of the role of national power, and an acknowledgment of the inevitability of conflicts of interest among nations. He was also far less sanguine than Carnegie regarding the immediate prospects for permanent peace. But his views were tempered by the conviction that "moral influences" were anterior to power factors and, as part of the progressive evolution of civilization, were "gradually, steadily in the course of centuries taking the place of brute force in the control of the affairs of men." Ultimately, Root believed that political conflict stemmed from cultural differences. It followed that any system of international law – with or without sanctions – would need to be undergirded by a supportive framework of public opinion. This implied the need for an international communion of ideas and sympathies. Thus Root was unashamed to preach "the gospel of fraternization" as a means of spreading that sentiment that was to become the moral tissue of a legal global community.[5]

The endowment's second-in-command and Root's successor following his retirement from the presidency in 1925 was the austere and forbidding Nicholas Murray Butler. It was Butler who had first broached the idea of an International Institute to Carnegie, and of the various sponsors of the idea, he was the only one to be appointed to the board of trustees. As president of Columbia University and through his close connections to the peace movement, Butler had pioneered in the development of institutional cultural exchanges. In his position as head of the American branch of the Association for International Conciliation, a French-based peace organization founded in 1905, Butler began to promote the visits of eminent personages and "men of good will" as a means of strengthening transnational friendships. With endowment funds at his disposal, Butler would expand upon and systematize these initial explorations in cultural relations.[6]

Butler has traditionally been portrayed as the epitome of a mossback conservative. But as one of his closest colleagues has noted, "Butler's conservatism was that of the nineteenth century liberal," and his views on foreign policy derived from a tradition that would have won the unstinting approval of a Herder or a Mazzini. Like Root, Butler accepted the existence of nations and patriotism as necessary parts of the international system. He ridiculed as "hopelessly impractical," "misleading," and "harmful," what he called "colloidal internationalism," a concept favored by those in the peace movement who exalted the supranational brotherhood of man and looked forward to a global community cleansed of nationalism. Instead, Butler advocated what he called a "crystalline internationalism," in which "the strength and beauty of the whole international structure when completed . . . would depend upon and reflect the beauty of each of its national elements." This did not mean that international peace would result from the strengthening of nationalism; quite to the contrary, international harmony was the precondition of a tranquil national existence.[7]

Although Butler rejected communitarian internationalism, he was no friend of the traditional "European" theory of balance of power, which bowed before the nation-state as the ne plus ultra of world politics. As an alternative to militant nationalism, Butler prescribed the development of what he called the "International Mind," which, given the adoption of a universal set of values, would function as an international superego. To a large degree, moral transformation would be achieved through transnational contacts, with cultural relations serving as the vehicle of reeducation. But, as Butler once remarked, "Ideas travel by slow freight." He believed along with Root that the causes of war were buried "deep down in human nature" and that the process of imbuing public opinion with a new set of values would be "a long and arduous one." What values and what ideas? His answer to this question was unabashedly elitist. Butler operated on the basis of a trickle-down theory of cultural change that envisaged the eventual widespread adoption of genteel values. Peering down from the rarefied altitude of Morningside Heights, he declared that in order for the United States to play its proper role in world politics, "the American public and Congress must be educated to behave like gentlemen." And so with other nations. Once civilized men came to agree that war was no longer socially acceptable it would, like dueling, go the way of other atavisms.[8]

This belief in an impending transvaluation of values appeared to reflect the objective workings of the historical process. Although Root and Butler rejected the notion of an organic world community as utopian, they did possess a less mystical conception of global interdependence that was consistent with a continuing trend toward international intellectual cooperation then taking place on a functional basis. In effect, the process resembled the extension to the international plane of the American enthusiasm for voluntary association noted by de Tocqueville. Beginning with the holding of an International Statistical Congress in Brussels in 1853, a wide array of contacts had been institutionalized in the form of specialized international unions. Typically, the pattern called for the holding of an international congress to discuss matters of common concern, followed by the formation of a permanent federative association. The body could be either public, as in the case of the International Postal Union or the Berne Copyright Union, or private, as in the case of the numerous scholarly organizations that had come into being. By 1911 there were already in existence 150 private international unions and 45 public international bodies, and by 1913 the movement had progressed to the point that one enthusiastic analyst could declare international organization to be "an accomplished fact." Just as the process of world trade and quickened communications were forging a unitary, interdependent global economy, so the functional movement appeared to be creating the structural basis for an international consciousness. The Carnegie Endowment would base its programs on the belief that such contacts were "elemental and constructive forces in bringing to pass the International Mind."[9]

In its first few years, the endowment pioneered in arranging interchanges of important personages in the attempt to create more cordial relationships between national elites, especially with Latin America and the Far East. In the process, it established what was to become the standard repertory of cultural relations: exchanges of professors and students, exchanges of publications, stimulation of translations and the book trade, the teaching of English, exchanges of leaders from every walk of life – all of these were to become the stock-in-trade of future governmental programs. But the endowment's first love was Europe and the outbreak of war in 1914 had caused it to suspend its Continental ambitions. It did not sit on the sidelines, however. Butler and

Root were convinced that the universal spread of democratic institutions was "the first and most far-reaching change that must be
effected in order to secure reasonably permanent international
peace." Thus the endowment, while its programs were frustrated,
called for the prosecution of the war "to final victory for democracy."[10]

Meanwhile, the government was beginning to experiment with
a host of new activities, including cultural relations. Aggressive
agents of the Committee on Public Information, the ad hoc propaganda organ run by George Creel, set up embryonic cultural programs in places like France, Italy, and Mexico. But the short duration of American belligerence prevented an elaboration of the
CPI's tentative efforts or the synchronization of cultural activities
with the efforts of the private sector. Although the war had a na-
tionalizing effect in many areas, especially upon the economy, cultural activities were left uncoordinated at the fringes of a hectic
wartime experimentation. Afterward, the guillotinelike sudden-
ness with which Congress abolished the CPI ruled out any possibility of following up on wartime cultural initiatives.[11]

The action of Congress faithfully mirrored the general distrust
of the centralization of power brought about by the war. The fear
of governmental meddling, not very far from the surface in all of
American politics, turned out to be even more relevant in the case
of cultural policy, for a commitment to private planning and organization lay at the very core of the principles around which the
nascent cultural programs came to be organized. The motives
were complex and interrelated: An old-line liberal distrust of statist meddling in intellectual affairs, a complementary faith in the
superior virtue of grass-roots involvement, and the belief in the
practical potential of functional internationalism provided an interlocking conceptual system.

Butler and his colleagues were firmly convinced of the propriety of private control and they drew a sharp distinction between
peoples and governments. Butler believed that a government, although representing the will of the people in a mechanical sense,
could not possibly give expression to a nation's soul. Only the
voluntary, spontaneous activity of the people themselves – as expressed in their art, literature, science, education, and religion –
could adequately provide a complete cultural portrait. The fact

that cultural relations were perceived as being anterior to politics added to the antigovernmental animus and fortified the image of a world order based on the functional integration of common interests. Whereas reliance upon state control was characteristic of European methods and smacked of realpolitik, the American way called for the primacy of private initiative. In Butler's favorite phrase, cultural relations belonged "in the sphere of Liberty." As Paul Reinsch argued in his book, *Public International Unions,* the beauty of the liberal historical process lay in the fact that it was "not a thing imposed from above by force, or dictated only by a higher rationalism, but . . . the almost instinctive work of men building wider and wider spheres of affiliation."[12]

Notwithstanding the powerful antipathy to government control, the need for some centralization of cultural efforts was real enough. The wartime experience had generated an explosion of interest in the potential of cultural relations, but it had also demonstrated a lack of system in organizing cultural exchanges. Most programs were conducted individually by universities or other private agencies without regard to any overall policy and with no thought to an efficient harmonizing of efforts. The formation of the Carnegie Endowment had been the first sign that the days of cultural laissez faire were ending. Now the organization of international cultural relations for peaceful purposes demanded a further integration of domestic cultural efforts. The demands of internationalism threatened to overtake the capacity of domestic organization to meet them.

Stepping into the breach between need and capacity was a rapidly maturing philanthropic community that provided both the financial resources and the impetus to centralization. After the endowment's organization in 1910, a host of new institutions came into being and gave a new policy dimension to corporate philanthropy. After Carnegie's death, the huge Carnegie Corporation, under the leadership of Frederick Paul Keppel, had the resources not only to supplement the endowment's annual programs in cultural relations, but also to support cultural interests of its own. The gigantic Rockefeller Foundation entered the scene in 1913 and, after meekly focusing on medical and scientific research for its first decade, it began in the 1920s to show a decided interest in cultural relations. Other Rockefeller offshoots like the In-

ternational Education Board, the General Education Board, and
the Laura Spelman Rockefeller Fund became similarly interested.
Lesser philanthropies with like concerns, most notably the John
Simon Guggenheim Foundation, also came into being in this period. All these organizations were based in New York City, while
their personnel and their programs became well known to one
another. This close knit philanthropic community would play a
decisive role in the organization of American cultural policy.[13]

The Rockefeller Foundation's program in international medi-
cine was the technical model for all forms of cultural cooperation.
Besides achieving measurable results in the conquest of disease,
the foundation's program in science exemplified the beneficence of
cultural interchange. The President's review for 1919 declared
that "more and more, nations are coming to recognize their interdependence in health as in industry, government, science, and culture," and that the fellowship program was part of a larger scheme
to promote "a constant exchange of knowledge and suggestion
among the many countries of the world." By making travel and
study in all parts of the world possible and by broadening the fellows' horizons and experiences, these programs were thought to
be "effective in breaking down national isolation." By 1933 the
Rockefeller Foundation adopted "the improvement of international understanding through cultural interchange" as one of its
principal policy goals. Simon Guggenheim's funding of Latin
American fellowships advocated a similar "commerce of the mind,
of spiritual values." The constant resort to the analogy with commerce was typical of a liberal mentality that looked at politics,
culture, and trade as a seamless web of mutually reinforcing fila-
ments.[14]

Philanthropic internationalism was a direct reflection of the beliefs of its most influential practitioners. From his childhood days,
John D. Rockefeller, Jr., had been inculcated in "a global kind of
thinking." This outlook was evident not only in the internationalist influence that he brought to bear upon the programs of the
Rockefeller Foundation, but also in his personal giving. With a
view to promoting intercultural fraternity, during the 1920s Rockefeller financed the construction of international houses at Columbia, Chicago, and Berkeley, and paid for the erection of an
American House at the Cité Universitaire of the University of

Paris. The foundation's president during the critical days of the
1930s, Raymond Fosdick, was no less cosmopolitan in perspective. His faith had been tested in the fight over the League of
Nations and by his brief tenure as an American under secretary
general, a commitment confirmed by his continued involvement
with internationalist organizations.[15]

The heads of the other major foundations were of a similar cast
of mind. Frederick Keppel had once been secretary of the Association for International Conciliation and editor of its journal. Although Keppel took a long view of modern intercultural activities
as being simply the continuation of age-old scholarly migrations,
he also recognized their current political utility: Wars did not begin spontaneously; rather, they resulted from frictions – and international understanding would reduce frictions. Henry Allen Moe
of the Guggenheim Foundation agreed, arguing that international
understanding could not be achieved except through cultural relations, and vice versa. "There is a circular process here into which
advanced students fit," Moe concluded, without bothering to further analyze the nature of the circularity. Keppel was more intro-
spective when he doubted that "this trend toward the international in foundation programs was the result of deliberate
decisions." It was, in truth, more a matter of weltanschauung than
of policy.[16]

The foundations in the 1920s were operating in an environment
in which the American vision of a privately organized international community received its first – and probably last – full-scale
trial. An upsurge of interest in cultural relations, characterized by
a proliferation of private domestic organizations with international
interests, was a significant part of this experiment. Some of this
enthusiasm was traceable directly back to the first heady days of
the Paris Peace Conference, when ideas for all forms of international cooperation were thick in the air. The American Council of
Learned Societies, for instance, grew out of a French proposal to
form an International Union of Academies, which was to be an
interallied group of humanistic societies. Two U.S. academics,
James T. Shotwell of Columbia University and Charles H.
Haskins of Harvard, both of whom were present in Paris for du-
ties at the peace conference, attended the initial meeting in Paris
in May 1919. Haskins quickly realized that membership in the

new international body "presupposed the existence in each country of a single body or group authoritatively representative of the humanistic studies."[17]

Because the U.S. had no such organization, a meeting was held in Boston in September 1919 under the auspices of the American Historical Association, and after adoption of a constitution, the ACLS formally went into operation the following year. Its purpose seemed disinterested enough at first look: "To bring together workers who are interested in one or another of the phases of cultural relations, to increase their realization of the essential unity of the subject, and to facilitate interchange of helpful facts and ideas." But it turned out that a republic of letters and a more worldly structure were not unrelated. In a statement on the plans and needs of the ACLS, John Franklin Jameson of the AHA argued that "the avoidance of war, and a score of other primary interests of humanity, are not to be well secured without a more solid and complete, as well as a more diffused knowledge." It was no accident that the guiding spirits behind the creation of the ACLS were scholars who had actively participated in the prosecution of the war and the organization of the peace, either through the National Board for Historical Service or through Woodrow Wilson's band of experts, The Inquiry.[18]

The relationship between international and domestic organization became quickly evident when the ACLS saw an opportunity to become "the general staff of the humanities" within the United States. It was, after all, difficult to have a foreign policy, even in the humanities, without having a coherent domestic policy. For a number of years, however, the ACLS languished for want of funds because of its competition with the Social Science Research Council for overall domestic leadership in the intellectual arena. The SSRC proved more attractive to the philanthropic community because it promised practical use for the tools of social science, especially reform uses, whereas the ACLS could suggest only vague benefits to be derived from its humanistic stewardship. But when the ACLS resumed it earlier internationalist emphasis in the late 1920s, it finally came into its own. Starting with its championing of Far Eastern studies, it began to promote concentration in regional areas by encouraging holistic studies of culture and civilization, past and present. The growth of these new specializations

was watered by a steady sprinkling of largess from the foundations, thereby allowing the ACLS to influence their development
through the judicious use of research grants. With its representation in the Union Académique Internationale and its internationally oriented study programs, the ACLS became the dominant
scholarly body in the field of cultural relations. To a considerable
degree, then, domestic organization occurred through the international back door.[19]

Of well-established organizations, one of the more important to
develop cultural policies was the American Library Association. In
the aftermath of the battle over the League of Nations, the secretary of the association declared: "America as a whole may not be
internationally minded. But the librarians of America are so
minded." The ALA formed permanent committees on international relations, showed an active interest in library developments
abroad, and took the lead in forming an International Federation
of Library Associations. The ALA's internationalism also had
evangelistic undercurrents. By the 1920s, American librarians had
come to view themselves as servants of democratic public opinion
who exercised vital cultural responsibilities apart from the mere
cataloging and storage of books. With their emphasis on service
and dynamic library techniques, American librarians had a missionary justification for their international interests. Especially in
Latin America, the ALA complained that "our library methods are
virtually unknown." The foundations, recognizing that the printed
word remained a primary vehicle of cross-cultural communication,
agreed in principle with the ALA's approach and continued to encourage the association's activities. During the 1920s the ALA developed a comprehensive set of cultural programs including visits,
fellowships, library training, and exchange of publications. Inevitably, its enthusiasm always outdistanced its resources.[20]

Given the development of a cohesive philanthropic community
in the postwar years and the proliferation of public interest in cultural relations, the initial plans of the Carnegie Endowment
proved to be too ambitious. The endowment had assumed too
great a burden in terms of policy, financing, and operations without making sufficient use of the nation's other resources. With the
postwar interest in European reconstruction and Far Eastern matters, a more comprehensive and integrated global approach was

needed. This would at least require an organization in the United States dedicated to the full-time coordination of cultural relations. As Butler came to realize: "The government of the United States has no such official organization and stands in no direct relationship to the schools, colleges, universities and research institutions of the country. Therefore it is almost necessary to organize a central body that can serve the interests of all these in respect to international relations and international interchanges." Such considerations led to the founding in 1919 of the Institute of International Education, the nation's first body devoted exclusively to the systematization of cultural relations.[21]

The institute was designed to act as a clearinghouse for a broad array of international activities. Its first director, Stephen Duggan, a professor of government and education at City College, was convinced by the war of the need to create a greater international-mindedness. Although the institute was eventually to concentrate on educational matters, it was, as Butler quickly appreciated, "not educational in the narrow sense at all." For its goal was not knowledge as such, but peace through international understanding. During the 1920s the institute, which began as a ward of the endowment, gradually attracted a broad base of philanthropic support and its board of trustees came to include major representatives of the nation's educational establishment. At the same time, mainly through Duggan's hard work, the institute struck permanent roots by virtue of its organization of the technical functions of educational relations, becoming the national nerve center for student exchanges.[22]

This private national structure was completed by the U.S. relationship to the Committee on Intellectual Cooperation of the League of Nations. Founded in 1922 and including among its membership such luminaries as Mme. Marie Sklodowska-Curie, Albert Einstein, and Henri Bergson, the committee had been formed as an afterthought to the league's more practical, specialized agencies. During its life it published theoretical conversations among some of the world's leading thinkers, campaigned for the elimination of chauvinism from European textbooks, and promoted studies that might have policy uses. A few had hoped to make the committee a bastion of internationalist policy experts. Sir Alfred Zimmern of Great Britain, for example, argued that the postwar world was doomed unless it called to its aid "those who hold the keys to the solution of its problems." Although Zimmern thought of the committee as the ideal nucleus for a world university, others simply considered it as a sort of superacademy. In any case, such disagreements were rendered inconsequential by a chronic shortage of operating funds. The committee took on institutional permanence only after the French promised an annual subsidy and furnished quarters for a permanent secretariat in Paris. As the initial step in forming a global intellectual network, the Parisian Institute encouraged the formation of national committees of intellectual cooperation.[23]

An American committee was formed in 1926 through the labors of Dr. Robert A. Millikan, the Nobel Prize–winning physicist from the California Institute of Technology. Other members included Elihu Root, Raymond Fosdick, Vernon Kellogg of the National Research Council, and Herbert Putnam, the librarian of Congress. They sat as individuals, but they were expected to involve their organizations in any research requests that might devolve upon the National Committee. The ACLS, the IIE, the American Council on Education, and many other internationally minded groups came together under the umbrella of this organization, which was described as "almost a model representation, for international purposes, of the various groupings and interests of American intellectual life." The absence of formal U.S. government backing disturbed no one, as it was widely assumed that "the nature of the subject necessarily calls for the collaboration of educational and scientific, rather than governmental agencies." Butler in particular was pleased with this arrangement, insisting that the United States was "steadily and effectively" represented in world intellectual councils. Indeed, the fact that this representation was private in nature, with its base in "the sphere of Liberty," made it "not less important, but rather more so, than had it originated in the sphere of Government." The financing of the committee came, as might be expected, from the Carnegie Corporation, the endowment, and from John D. Rockefeller, Jr.'s, bottomless pockets.[24]

Largely as a result of American pressures, the international committee in the 1930s ceased to function exclusively as a scholarly clearinghouse as more and more it sought to put scholarship, especially political science and the social sciences, to work in the solution of political problems. Aided by subsidies from American foundations, the Paris Institute sponsored a series of international studies conferences that hoped to develop answers for a number of "burning questions of the moment." Although a few individuals resisted this development, viewing it as a debasement of scholarship, Butler and his associates justified it as the necessary first step in the quest for "technical ways" of molding public opinion and bringing to pass the International Mind.[25]

Whereas Butler yearned somewhat romantically for "a change in the heart of man," his colleague James T. Shotwell described the committee's purposes in more modern terms. For Shotwell, civilization was the product of an ongoing contest between science and history, with science struggling heroically to hurdle the archaic political structures that history placed in its path. Convinced that the replacement of ancient prejudices with a common understanding was specifically a scientific function, he sought to bring the committee's attention to "dealing with the vital principle of culture itself, which in time might do something to change the external relationships of government into a real society of nations in which there would be a friendly appreciation of common cultural interests instead of a competitive economic or political outlook."[26]

Among the host of projects favored by the cultural enthusiasts, the infatuation with developing an international auxiliary language came closest to exposing their core beliefs. Beginning with Andrew Carnegie's quixotic attempt to simplify English spelling, beneath their numerous linguistic undertakings lay the conviction that the world's problems were the result of faulty communication. In Duggan's words, there existed, preternaturally, "a unity among men which transcends differences in their forms of government, but to know it and to understand it they must be brought together." According to Nicholas Murray Butler, they were combating an ancient biblical curse. "Our troubles began at the Tower of Babel," he insisted. It seemed to him that "when language was multiplied and men were dispersed, the problem of organizing the world had its beginning." If national tongues were guilty of perpetuating the narrow mentality of nationalism, then the breaching of linguistic barriers would mark a major advance in promoting an international outlook and restoring to man his natural, prepolitical understanding.[27]

However, everyone recognized that at Babel "more things than language were confounded," and linguistic tariff walls were only the first of numerous barriers that needed to be surmounted. Although global integration was being aided by the growth of international trade and by advances in technology and communications, this functional interdependence was accompanied, paradoxically, by a simultaneous strengthening of political nationalism. The reduction of armaments posed still another major difficulty. In both of these cases a reliance on political solutions was to be avoided, for politics was the cause of man's problems, disturbing his natural sense of community. It followed, then, that the sine qua non of global harmony was cultural rapprochement. Global prosperity would be attained only following the recognition that cooperative liberal economic policies were the key to success, and military disarmament would come about only if preceded by a moral rearmament. In this calculus, goodwill between nations contributed more to national security and welfare than would huge military outlays or selfish economic policies. Given this optimistic and universalistic view of human nature, the attainment of a global harmony of interests depended on the recreation of the pristine sense of community existing before Babel. In the quest for this mythic understanding, cultural relations would play the role of a secular glossolalia.[28]

Under the leadership of American corporate philanthropy, there evolved by the end of the 1920s a private institutional system for the conduct of cultural relations. This network was characterized by a comfortable correspondence between idealist ends and nonpolitical organizational means. From the liberal cultural perspective, achievement of world peace and prosperity depended not so much on the expansionist dynamics of capitalism as on the common properties of human intelligence. Consequently, the system emphasized the free movement of ideas and stressed the dangers to the commerce of intellect of a European-style centralizing nationalism. The emphasis on private, "voluntarist"[29] initiative was a direct result of the antigovernmental bias of the pioneers in cultural relations. This private national policy structure also struck a balance between domestic tradition and the complex demands of international involvement, making possible full participation in an increasingly coordinated and interdependent, yet informal, transnational system of intellectual cooperation.

All things considered, this system of cultural policy fitted nicely into the general U.S. "Open Door" approach to foreign affairs in the 1920s.[30] The liberal internationalist outlook, in cultural affairs and foreign policy as a whole, solved a basic riddle of American foreign policy by promoting American global interests without involving the nation in weltpolitik or resorting to an undesirable reliance on state power. But in the pessimistic climate of the 1930s, with a tendency toward cultural nationalism and the aggressive employment of cultural policy for political ends clearly evident among the major powers, the voluntarist approach was less satisfactory. Clearly, the informal system erected in the 1920s was not designed to function, much less survive, in a world of power diplomacy. But the problem was that a governmental cultural role based on political premises would have required the repudiation of the liberal creed upon which traditional American policies of cultural interchange were based. Indeed, a shift to nationalist techniques would poison the very ends the program was designed to encourage and would require the dismantling of the entire informal policy structure.

Were it not for a threatening international environment, there would have been little inclination to tamper with the system as it then stood. But the statist philosophies of the USSR, Germany, Italy, and Japan were reflected not only in their military and economic policies, and in their ruthless statecraft, but also in their adoption of cultural diplomacy as an explicit weapon in the arsenal of national power. For Secretary of State Cordell Hull, the political and economic collapse of the depression decade was "completed by the break-down of the commerce of mind and culture." The "spirit of super-nationalism," observed Stephen Duggan, was producing "a system of competing cultures that makes little allowance for anything of value in other countries." Obviously, this spreading rash of extremist nationalisms constituted "the very antipodes of the nineteenth century principle of individual freedom." Totalitarian cultural policies posed, if not an immediate threat, a grave philosophical challenge to the American faith in the vitality of liberal cultural processes.[31]

Probably at the urging of Laurence Duggan (Stephen Duggan's son, formerly an assistant director of the IIE who had gone on to become chief of the State Department's Division of American Republics), Assistant Secretary of State Sumner Welles became the first government official to define publicly the foreign policy importance of cultural relations. Reflecting the Roosevelt administration's regional preoccupations, Welles described them as "but another aspect of the policy of the 'good neighbor,' " which sought "political relations free of suspicion and misunderstanding, economic relations conducive to a healthy international trade, and cultural relations leading to a wider appreciation of the culture and civilization of other peoples." In a number of speeches delivered before educational groups in 1935, Welles stressed the fundamental unity of the various strands of transnational contact. "The three phases of our relations – political, economic and cultural," he explained, "are inextricably linked together, though not commonly so supposed." And in all three spheres, Welles concluded, "the breaking of barriers" constituted "the major problem in foreign relations." Welles's conception of the liberalizing role of cultural interchange provided a stark contrast to the egoistic Kulturpolitik of other nations.[32]

These initial exhortations, intended to stimulate greater private interest and actions in cultural exchanges, had little effect. Undaunted, the State Department next perceived an opportunity for publicizing cultural affairs in connection with the upcoming Inter-American Conference for the Maintenance of Peace to be held in Buenos Aires at the end of 1936. Previous inter-American conferences had passed numerous resolutions of intellectual solidarity, to little practical effect. The Pan American Union created a Division of Intellectual Cooperation in the 1920s, but it was little-used and ineffectual. Following the Montevideo conference in 1933, a number of National Committees on Inter-American Intellectual Cooperation were set up to coordinate cultural interchanges, also with little success. The U.S. committee, appointed in 1935, held only one meeting before lapsing into bureaucratic somnolence. Thus the State Department's decision to submit a proposal for annual government-subsidized exchanges was a major departure from a tradition of benign neglect.[33]

The individual selected by Cordell Hull to shepherd a student exchange convention through the conference committee was ordinarily accustomed to tending a more spiritual sort of flock. Dr. Samuel Guy Inman was a minister of the Disciples of Christ and an early and unflagging advocate of improved cultural ties with Latin America. The founder and editor of the magazine *Nueva Democracia* and one of the first to teach a college course in inter-American relations, he was also an energetic member of dozens of Pan American organizations of all types. Inman was a philosophical idealist. He believed, for instance, that the Good Neighbor Policy was a direct result of the cultural pressures for rapprochement: "This appreciation of the intellectual life of Latin America has developed a demand in the United States that our Government change its policy toward our southern neighbors." To take another example, although he recognized the French to be exemplars of realism in foreign affairs, he was convinced that their success derived not from their material strength, but from the "power of cultural attraction." In any case, cultural power was decisive. As in Aristotle's metaphysics, so in geopolitics: Form determined matter.[34]

Out of the Buenos Aires conference came a convention by the signatories for the annual exchange of two students and one professor. But Welles viewed this demarche as only a catalytic agent and he continued to look to the private sector for the development of substantial programs in cultural relations. In hitting the sawdust trail to publicize the convention, Inman drove this point home by arguing that it was "useless for governmental representatives to sign treaties if their people are not prepared, in intellect and sympathy, to support such agreements." It was necessary, he insisted, "for both government and private agencies to take the promotion of this spiritual *entente* seriously." But by the end of the year, Laurence Duggan concluded that there had been a "failure of most of our colleges and universities to assume their proper responsibilities with respect to educational interchange."[35]

Hull and Welles were agreed that some governmental mechanism would be required to fulfill the obligations under the Buenos Aires convention, but by the end of 1937, partly because of a delay in the Senate's ratification, no action had been taken. Hoping to prod the department into activity, Inman launched a letter-writing campaign in which he played up the threat of Axis cultural subversion in Latin America. Inman's scare tactics failed to rouse the department, however. Reports from the missions, although they acknowledged cultural activity by the Axis powers in Latin America, minimized its significance. In fact, to some Foreign Service officers the danger seemed to lie in another direction. Selden Chapin, for instance, argued that the concern over Axis cultural penetration in Latin America "perfectly fits the Communist book" and cautioned against the acceptance of "deliberate leftist exaggeration." Laurence Duggan's assessment, although less conspiratorial, also minimized such a threat. Writing to Inman early in 1938 in an attempt to still his fears, Duggan argued:

While . . . reporting on this subject is a new activity for our Foreign Service Officers, it points to the conclusion that possibly the press in the United States for various reasons is over-playing the danger of the activities of Italy and Germany. There are all the professional jingoists, who always like to play up a scare. Then there may be some American business interests which believe that they may get larger orders from some of those countries if they create within those countries the impression that they really are about to be devoured . . . Some of the comments we have received from our missions would indicate that the intensiveness and blatancy of the propaganda has had exactly the counter-effect. Instead of making converts it has persuaded people that they do not wish to live under governments of the type now existing in Italy and Germany . . . That propaganda is going on there is a fact; that it is efficacious is still somewhat open to question. The important thing seems, with respect to our proposed cultural activities, not to act on a competitive counter-proposal basis but rather to proceed to develop real cultural relations that cannot be accused of being propaganda . . .[36]

Two months later, the assistant secretary of state for administration, George Messersmith, was singing a different tune before a House appropriations subcommittee. "We had information from Brazil, from the Argentine, from Peru, in fact from most of the countries in South America," he testified, "that certain governments are pressing on them professors and students and technical advisers of various kinds whom they are sending and paying all their expenses, and the effect of it has been very real." This was nothing new, and the additional complaint that the U.S. cultural institutions had been doing "relatively little with regard to Latin America" was by now commonplace. But his characterization of foreign cultural programs as "very real activities of an emergency character" that were causing "serious damage to our interests and prestige" transferred the justification for a U.S. cultural program from idealistic rhetoric to the more forceful language of national interests. Echoing the previous appeals of some more power-oriented department officers, Messersmith argued that "aside from the emergency involved, we should have been doing things of this kind for some years."[37]

But Messersmith was arguing from a very narrow conception of national interest. He promised the subcommittee that the cultural program would be modest and would not swell bureaucratically, and once it came time for the department to take action in cultural policy, he urged that it only "make haste slowly" in devising a strategy and implementing a program. Nor did he even wish the State Department to assume dominant responsibility for a cultural program. The fact was that Messersmith's argument for the employment of national power in the pursuit of cultural objectives was so cautious and minimal that it was possible for him, and for other national interest advocates within the department as well, to mesh their viewpoints with a program based largely on the idealist and voluntarist precepts elaborated during the 1920s.[38]

Actually, the department had given only slight consideration to the foreign policy uses of cultural relations. The first extended analysis of the question was contained in a memo written by Richard Pattee of the Division of American Republics early in 1938. After summarizing the cultural propaganda efforts of other nations, Pattee recommended following the standard internationalist formula rather than adhering to European prescriptions. "Political relations without understanding are useless," he declared. "Political penetration carries with it the stigma of imposition; economic, the accusation of selfishness and force. Intellectual cooperation means interchange and the free play of ideas." Only in his conclusion did Pattee depart mildly from tradition. Although he credited private agencies with doing some excellent work in Latin America, he argued that understanding was "not achieved spontaneously, not through the haphazard and ineffective undertakings of isolated individuals. Governments may legitimately aspire to make known the best of their civilizations."[39]

By early 1938, the listless response to their appeals for expanded private cultural initiatives had convinced Welles and Duggan of the need for additional governmental measures. Thinking on the subject was still so confused at this time, however, that serious consideration was given to vesting responsibility for the coordination of cultural relations with the Office of Education. But Laurence Duggan finally came to reject this notion. Reasoning that it was time for the State Department to adopt a coordinating function, he began to sound out the philanthropic community for their approval of "a coordinated program in which the government and private organizations and individuals could cooperate without overlapping." Private organizations, he argued, "despite familiarity with the field of educational relations, have not and cannot think in terms of a coordinated program. Each person is carrying on his own ideas of work."[40]

At a meeting with representatives of the major private cultural organizations held on May 23, 1938, the department revealed its plans to create a new Division of Cultural Relations. It was immediately made clear that the government was contemplating no radical departures from tradition. On the contrary, Welles stressed his conviction that the State Department could do little more than fulfill the terms of the Buenos Aires convention; the brunt of the cultural burden would continue to be borne by the private sector. When asked by the House Committee on Appropriations about the proposed division's functions, George Messersmith explained that its work would be primarily "to assist the foundations and universities in this country."[41]

This modest approach had numerous arguments to support it. For one thing, the financing of cultural relations was still perceived to be a private responsibility. Part of State's relationship with the private sector, then, was one of dependence, and it could only hope that it would, as Welles urged, "cooperate with us in carrying the financial burden." Another factor, as noted by Laurence Duggan in a speech at the Army War College on January 5, 1938, was constitutional in nature. "The Federal Government does not control education in this country as it is controlled in other countries," he explained, "so that it is a question of persuading our colleges and universities to send professors or to give scholarships and fellowships." Just as important was the existence of a voluntarist tradition that dictated a primary role for private groups. After the Buenos Aires conference, Laurence Duggan explained in a radio interview that "in a democracy such as ours the primary responsibility rests upon the individual citizen and the government is merely the agency of its citizens." Finally, a cultural program had to pass muster with an increasingly conservative Congress, which was suspicious of the New Deal's penchant for creating new bureaucracies and extending the policy reach of the governmental apparatus. Certainly the voluntarist approach did not hurt the department's case.[42]

The first chief of the new division, established in July 1938, was Ben Cherrington, who for the previous twelve years had been the director of the Foundation for the Advancement of Social Science of the University of Denver. This foundation had its origins in a bequest from a wealthy Denver businessman, James H. Causey, who claimed to be "moved by a spirit of interest in Liberalism . . . in the hope of seeing Liberal causes advanced." The "improvement in international relations by improved understanding of national viewpoints" seemed to him to be a practical objective consistent with his moving spirit, and the new foundation soon chose to concentrate on the field of international education, defining the essence of international relations from a cultural framework. Through conferences, seminars, introductory courses in foreign relations, lectures, adult education, and a regular series of radio broadcasts, Cherrington enthusiastically sought to expand the horizons of his fellow Westerners, all in the belief that the final fruit of the foundation's efforts in reeducation "must find expression in action." His experience suited him admirably for the new position's main task of stirring up interest in cultural relations, and Cherrington approached his new job as if it were an extension of his work at the foundation.[43]

The new cultural program was immediately fitted into the regional framework of the Good Neighbor Policy. Invariably, however, descriptions of the importance of cultural relations were made in universalist rhetoric. The emphasis upon "an ever-increasing intercommunication between all of the American nations – an intercommunication of ideas, of goods, of human beings" was the same prescription being applied to the rest of the world. As Sumner Welles liked to point out, "Underlying all of the complex pattern of international relationships is the basic need for a real understanding among peoples. No specific problems can be permanently and satisfactorily solved unless there is knowledge and sympathetic understanding among all of us of the national lives, the needs, and the aspirations of the other." This theme, that mutual understanding formed the basis of peaceful international relations, would see endless repetition by the department in years to come.[44]

Similarly, in terms of planning, the cultural program was expected eventually to burst out of its regional straitjacket into more comfortable global apparel. The reason was not far to seek, for as Cherrington maintained, "Culture in its essence is cosmic." To nationalize it or regionalize it would only stultify its inherent universalism. In concentrating initially upon Latin America, Cherrington indicated that the department "was simply focusing our efforts in one area of the world where the door seems to be wider open." The Good Neighbor Policy – at least in its cultural aspects – was less a carefully articulated regional program or a realistic response to outside pressures than a paradigm for the global application of the principles of law and order, and the peaceful pursuit of liberal economic and cultural relationships.[45]

To the degree that there was a differentiated outlook with respect to Latin America, it was related more to questions of internal socioeconomic development than to world politics. Typically, the State Department viewed relations with its southern neighbors as a problem in the dynamics of cultural lag. Thus Welles could attribute the underlying causes of political instability in Latin America to the fact that "the Anglo-Saxon type have (sic) had six or seven hundred years of education and training in the science of government and human life," whereas the less fortunate American republics' short duration of political apprenticeship had made it "impossible for them to absorb the theory and the principles and the spirit that underlies a structure of free government." Charles Thomson, who was to become the assistant chief of the new division, felt that the United States had "a certain moral mandate for the countries in those areas, a cultural mandate."[46]

This desire to point cultural relations in the direction of modernization seemed to depend on the ability to work with or stimulate the development of modern intellectual elites. In the case of a few nations who had failed to develop such a stratum, the task would be considerably complicated. The State Department representative in Tangier, for example, declared that "so far as Morocco is concerned, the cultural level of the country has not yet risen to a point where any effective cultural exchanges with the United States would be possible." Although Latin America had advanced beyond this level, and although a number of nations had achieved considerable degrees of technological and cultural sophistication, cultural relations could still not be conducted according to any broad, populist conception. As Richard Pattee argued, "The striking role of the intellectual minority in the Hispanic American nations is undoubtedly the point of departure for any contact with public opinion in the American Republics. It is too little recognized that public opinion as such is nonexistent outside the limited circle of the intellectuals." In Latin America, at least, the elitist bias surviving from Nicholas Murray Butler's gentlemanly conception of cultural relations was reinforced by the realities of class structure.[47]

Elitist orientation notwithstanding, Cherrington planned to focus the division's activities on what he called "genuine cultural relations"; that is, the program would be "definitely educational in character" and it would emphasize "the essential reciprocity in cultural relations." According to his view the division should not be allowed to become "a diplomatic arm or a propaganda agency." Cherrington was convinced of "the futility, even the absurdity of the export of culture by any government," for propaganda carried with it the "implication of penetration, imposition, and unilateralism." There was a practical side to this reasoning about propaganda that calculated not only external appearances but also internal consequences. To adopt propaganda methods would require an unthinkable degree of centralization of policy and administration within the U.S. national government. Assistant Secretary of State Henry Grady appeared to be making this point when he asserted that "culture is a social phenomenon" as opposed to a political category. The separation of the two was axiomatic. "The idea of an 'official culture,' " Welles solemnly announced, "is alien to us."[48]

Thus the new division went to extraordinary lengths in pledging its fidelity to the principles of cultural freedom. Cherrington was determined to "make the good offices of government available to private enterprise," for he was convinced that the process of cultural exchange was "essentially the privilege and responsibility of the people acting through their own organizations and institutions." He ceaselessly reiterated the claim that the department had "no intention of encroaching upon activities which pertain logically to private initiative." In terms of policy, Cherrington and Hull insisted that "the responsibility for the formulation of policies of interchange, for the direction and control of those policies and programs, should be vested in private citizens and private agencies." The upshot of all these protestations was that the State Department consigned itself to "a secondary role" in cultural relations. It would be at the "beck and call" of private interests, helping only to make the necessary contacts with foreign governments, providing necessary information, and only incidentally administering a few activities properly within the sphere of federal control.[49]

Although alarmist attitudes regarding Axis cultural penetration of Latin America were increasing at this time, the cultural program went on as if there were no crisis. Although it soon came to be the conventional wisdom among cultural stalwarts that the Division of Cultural Relations owed its existence to a resentment at "the misrepresentation of American life that was going on in South America," Cherrington remained determined to "very carefully avoid having anything to do with current State Department political policies." He continued to insist on a compartmentalized policy of cultural exchange for its own sake, separated from political considerations. "It would seem very important," he remarked, "for us to stress the divorcement of our activities from the Department of State." As long as the threat to Latin America was not perceived to be very serious, there was no need for more drastic measures.[50]

These self-denying ordinances left the division with only two basic functions: to stimulate greater financial pledges from private sources and to bring a greater degree of coordination to cultural policy. For a number of reasons, the hoped-for philanthropic cornucopia failed to materialize. Many foundations were geographically constrained, either by limitations written into their charters, as in the case of the Carnegie Corporation, or by tradition, as with the Rockefeller Foundation's unceasing absorption with China. Also, foundations ordinarily liked to make grants for planning rather than for program uses, for they were hesitant to commit to operations funds that might be better used in more innovative ways. Then too, the larger philanthropies had already developed vested bureaucratic interests that, for fear of cuts in their budgets, opposed increased expenditures for cultural relations.[51]

Organizational matters proved to be more tractable. As a first step in institutionalizing private influence in policymaking, the division created a General Advisory Committee, whose members represented the most influential old-line cultural organizations. Although it was chaired by Cherrington, the committee, instead of acting as a "lightning rod" or a figurehead for the department, immediately became the center of policy debate and decision. Indeed, so remote a policy role did they consider the State Department to play in cultural affairs that it was deemed proper for the Division of Cultural Relations to express only "an informal opinion" on projects submitted for its consideration. Power was to reside where it had always rested – in private hands. It was not surprising, then, that the cultural agenda developed by the division early in 1939 followed closely the precedents set by privately initiated programs. So great was this influence, in fact, that one of the larger budgetary items called for the payment of travel expenses incurred in the process of encouraging the citizenry in its cultural responsibilities. Even then, harsh criticisms came from those within the department who thought the program to be "too ambitious."[52]

The only remaining step was to ensure that private cultural activities were effectively concerted under some overall guiding framework. To this end, a series of conferences was called by the division, to which it invited experts in the fields of education, art, publications, library matters, and music, in order to discuss more effective means of organizing cultural relations. Not surprisingly, the main theme of the meetings held in Washington in the autumn of 1939 was the private sector's dominant role in planning and implementation. "Yours is the ticket to write," said Assistant Secretary Adolf Berle. "You have come to plan, we to aid you to the best of our ability." Continuation committees were entrusted with the implementation of a host of resolutions, with many of these in turn becoming subcommittees of the General Advisory Committee. In most cases, the conferees recommended an expansion of private cultural initiatives. Everyone seemed elated by these meetings and their outcome. "Never before in the history of the

United States," crowed Waldo Leland of the ACLS, "had there
been such a broad consultation in matters of foreign policy." It
remained to be seen whether the enthusiasm that had been generated would be translated into substantive results, or if the principles of voluntarism, as had happened in Herbert Hoover's time,
provided only an illusion of action.[53]

The creation of the Division of Cultural Relations and its early
programs were a logical culmination of historical trends rather
than a new departure. Cordell Hull saw this clearly enough when
he explained that the general idea behind the early cultural program was "to complete the broad structure of intellectual cooperation by supplying one of the elements which has hitherto been
lacking: the cooperation of Government." It was the ultimate re-
finement of a system that had been patiently constructed by phi-
lanthropists and private organizations beginning with the creation
of the Carnegie Endowment. Care was taken throughout to ensure
that liberal scruples regarding the freedom of ideas were protected against possible political contamination. Ideas and their organizational concomitants were in harmony. Ironically, pressures
arising from World War II introduced discontinuities and disturbing new departures in the program just as its conceptual purity had
achieved a complete organizational victory.[54]

CHAPTER 2

Wartime departures from tradition

As pressures for a mobilization of cultural resources multiplied, the fledgling cultural program was conscripted into World War II and found itself face-to-face with some unforeseen policy problems. A struggle soon developed over the direction of Latin American policy when advocates of an expansive concept of national security began to challenge the State Department's traditionalist, nonpolitical view of cultural relations. At the same time, emergency conditions in the Near East and China intensified the strain of idealism always present in cultural policy. Although these developments proceeded from quite different assumptions, they had identical organizational consequences: In both cases cultural policy became linked to foreign policy proper. Whether in the pursuit of security or in the service of ideals, these developments foreclosed a return to more detached uses of cultural relations.

Cherrington and the officers of the Division of Cultural Relations were well aware that war would likely create nationalist pressures on the cultural program. Their hope was that a propaganda program, if necessary, could be handled by a separate emergency agency, leaving the cultural programs free to operate according to traditional rationales and methods. A memo by Cherrington, written in May of 1940, bluntly stated the need to adhere to liberal ideals in both domestic and overseas applications: "The program should go forward in harmony with the two basic principles on which the Department has been operating – that of partnership between the Government and private initiative, with the Government the junior partner, and the careful observance of the spirit of reciprocity in relationship to the other American republics."[1]

A crucial bureaucratic development was the creation on August 16, 1940, of the Office for the Coordination of Commercial and Cultural Relations between the American Republics, whose name was later shortened to the Office of the Coordinator of Inter-

American Affairs (CIAA), headed by the thirty-two-year-old Nelson Aldrich Rockefeller. At President Roosevelt's insistence, this new agency explicitly included cultural relations within the compass of its emergency functions. In justifying its inclusion, Rockefeller took the position that "intellectual imperialism, the imperialism of ideas, was at the moment just as serious a threat to the security and defense of the hemisphere as the possibility of a military invasion." Driving hard at the national security theme, Rockefeller emphasized that his plans constituted a "special, emergency program which in no way duplicates that of the Department of State." By combining the rhetoric of emergency and a willingness to spend government money, Rockefeller made the State Department's program appear stodgy and conservative by comparison.[2]

The activist orientation of this new agency was unmistakably charted in its early policy deliberations. At a meeting of the Policy Committee of *his* Cultural Relations Division, Rockefeller quickly indicated his dissatisfaction with "the concept loosely called 'good neighbor.'" Another approach was necessary, one more realistic and attuned to the nation's immediate security needs. To start with, the committee unanimously resolved to jettison the idea of reciprocal benefits in a cultural program. It agreed that "the greatest emphasis should be placed on interpreting the United States to Latin America rather than vice-versa." It also decided to promote projects of a short-term nature that would reach large numbers of people in an effective manner. Although the coordinator's programs bore a superficial resemblance to traditional cultural pursuits, the emphasis was on "expediency and speed." Permanent values were not overlooked, but immediate needs were given precedence.[3]

Besides its more self-interested perspective, the coordinator's program differed from the State Department's in that it was unashamedly regional in character. The fact was that the coordinator's program included not only anti-Axis sentiments, but anti-European undertones as well. Although it was frequently noted at this time that Western Hemisphere nations were acting in a sense as "trustees of the great European cultures," as often as not the coordinator would argue for the general displacement of European influence throughout the region. His approach was particularist and pragmatic, in contrast to the universalism and idealism so evident in the State Department's early cultural program. Nevertheless, because World War II was perceived at least in part as being a cultural struggle ("the present conflict is distinctly philosophical," noted Adolf Berle), a regional program of cultural self-defense was generally accepted by liberals as part of a wider, global struggle of ideas.[4]

The difference in orientation was partially disguised by the coordinator's personal background and philosophy. Reared in a family tradition of social responsibility, Nelson Rockefeller had formed intimate connections with the East Coast cultural and philanthropic communities. Naturally enough, many of the top positions in the new agency were held by members of an elite who brought to their task the well-worn voluntarist principles of their circle. Rockefeller's inheritance extended to principles of action as well. The primary difference between the CIAA and the Department of State, apart from its heavy emphasis on national defense, was the fact that the CIAA was liberally endowed with congressional appropriations. But Rockefeller had no intention of turning his emergency creation into a mammoth administrative bureaucracy, choosing instead the traditional philanthropic expedient of stimulating exertions in the private sector. The CIAA would be primarily a funding agency operating on the basis of contracts with private groups, and its operations were modeled directly after those of the private philanthropic foundations.[5]

Indeed, this influence appeared to be so pervasive that one close observer swore that Rockefeller suffered from a "foundation complex." This blend of governmental activism and philanthropic tradition resulted at times in some rather strange policies. A case in point was provided when "philanthropoids" Henry Allen Moe of the Guggenheim Foundation, Frederick Keppel of the Carnegie Corporation, and David H. Stephens of the Rockefeller Foundation formed a committee of three and were given a CIAA grant of $100,000 to distribute as they saw fit in the form of Inter-American Fellowships. The use of tax exemptions to stimulate private exertions was one thing, but in this case an enthusiasm for the appearance of private giving, rather than its substance, led to the dubious extreme of having the government supply the funds.[6]

Rockefeller's early relationship with the Department of State was troubled, as it was generally believed that his intention was, as his friend William Benton put it, to "revolutionize the State Department." Indeed, with a budget of $3,500,000, even Laurence Duggan had to admit that "the responsibility for introducing action in the cultural field rests with him." Apprehensions within the State Department were fueled because his ambitious programs threatened to eclipse entirely the Division of Cultural Relations. Waldo Leland of the State Department's Advisory Committee felt that Rockefeller was going too far, too quickly, and argued that "the determination of policy and major decisions involving policy must be a function of the Department of State." Political officers within the department, especially those in the Division of American Republics, were quick to agree with Leland.[7]

Sumner Welles forced a showdown early in 1941 by putting the issue of policy control squarely before the president. Roosevelt came down on the side of the State Department, ordering Rockefeller to keep it informed of all his projects and to obtain its approval before going forward. Unhappy with this rebuff, Rockefeller went so far as to propose that the State Department take over his entire cultural program. But Hull, in the belief that policy and administration were separate matters and that the CIAA was only a temporary agency, turned down this offer. Finally, a Joint Committee on Cultural Relations was established, consisting of one representative of each agency with Waldo Leland as chairman and representative of private interests. In the division of labor that was adopted, State played the decisive role in policy, the CIAA provided the money, and private organizations furnished the operating know-how. Thereafter relationships between the two agencies in cultural matters were generally amicable. In the process of defending its territory, however, the State Department had seized a policy responsibility that it continued, in principle, to eschew.[8]

The department's fear of entanglement in cultural policy was demonstrated by its reluctance to create the position of cultural attaché. George Messersmith, in particular, fended off a mounting number of such proposals. He argued that the introduction of U.S. cultural attachés to Latin America meant that the Latin nations would have to receive similar attachés from Italy and Germany who would actually be "no more than poorly concealed political agents." In addition, Messersmith claimed that cultural attachés were superfluous, because the Foreign Service as a whole was "representative of the best there is in our culture and tradition." Undoubtedly, in the back of his mind was the unhappy memory of the 1920s, when the Commerce and Agricultural Departments had stationed their own representatives overseas, beyond State Department control.[9]

By mid-1941, a heavy cultural work load and the need to control the coordinator's multiplying programs produced a grudging concession when cultural relations assistants or officers were permitted as part of the new Foreign Service Auxiliary. It was not until mid-1943, however, that the title "Cultural Relations Attaché" was approved so that attachés could officially be added to the diplomatic lists. The seemingly temporary status of these new officers, who were recruited mainly from the academic community, underscored the department's attachment to traditionally cautious ways and indicated the difficulty it had in viewing cultural relations as a legitimate diplomatic function.[10]

Nevertheless, the coordinator's frank emphasis on propaganda forced the State Department to reconsider its thinking. A changed attitude was most notable among the career Foreign Service officers. "All rules are off in the present game," argued one proposal to combat Nazi propaganda in Latin America. Another officer insisted that "anything which is done in the cultural fields is in itself propaganda," although he advocated maintaining the distinction between cultural relations and propaganda – presumably for propaganda purposes. The ambassador to Brazil, Jefferson Caffery, came to advocate a short-term cultural offensive totally subsidiary to the war effort. Civilian diplomats like Ambassador Claude Bowers in Chile were less aggressive, but nonetheless advocated an instrumental approach. "We must sell the idea that the United States is now the world's most important intellectual center," Bowers argued, "and that Chileans must in future look to it rather than to Europe for educational and cultural opportunities."[11]

But this was a minority position. Leading officials of the Division of American Republics like Philip Bonsal and Ellis Briggs, as well as Political Adviser Laurence Duggan, were skeptical of what seemed to be a force feeding of American culture. Duggan thought much of the coordinator's program to be simply "hoopla," possessing not even defense significance. Many in this group favored modest advances and were skeptical of an overly ambitious program. Inordinate expansion during the war would only lead to the inevitable postwar cutbacks by a retrenching Congress, thereby confirming the widespread suspicion among Latin Americans that the wartime program was actually an insincere expression of American attitudes. In addition, a mammoth U.S. program would be difficult to justify on a cooperative basis.[12]

The denizens of the Division of Cultural Relations, although pricked by the spur of necessity, agreed that radical departures in policy were undesirable. Charles Thomson, who succeeded Cherrington as chief of the division in 1940, warned that "it would be unfortunate if the emphasis of the present cultural relations program were too much disturbed, since concentrated propaganda would defeat the very purpose for which it was intended." Obviously there needed to be some changes, if only to shift the emphasis from humanistic to economic and psychological factors. Thomson solved the problem to his satisfaction by arguing that there was an important distinction to be drawn between "instructive" and "destructive" propaganda. The crucial difference was that a purveyor of bad propaganda did "not consider the objects of its pressure as equals whose opinions are to be respected, but as victims to be despised and overcome"; good propaganda, by contrast, "was simply an effort to urge other people to think as one thinks." Thomson admitted that the cultural program might, in some of its phases, "border closely on this second, or 'instructive' type of propaganda." But he insisted that both types needed to be distinguished from the permanent understanding fostered by genuine cultural relations. In either case, it was clear that the Division of Cultural Relations would have to assume a more active role than it had originally contemplated.[13]

The government's new assertiveness was matched by a corresponding deference on the part of private organizations. The funding of cultural programs by this time clearly had become a governmental function, and both the Carnegie Endowment and the Rockefeller Foundation now busied themselves in financing study visits and providing planning grants rather than in subsidizing cultural programs themselves. Nevertheless, to insiders the relationship between governmental and philanthropic responsibilities still seemed confused. At the suggestion of Philip Jessup of the Carnegie Endowment, in May 1941 the department and the CIAA met with the major philanthropic organizations at a two-day conference in Princeton, New Jersey, to discuss the need for a "suitable unified working organization." According to the report of a Foreign Service officer who was present, it was at this meeting that the foundations "indicated a desire for more leadership on the part of Government." Although the word "cooperation" was still used to describe the relationship, by mid-1941 the private sector was beginning to relinquish its former primacy in funding and policymaking.[14]

Certainly the State Department and the CIAA did their best to stimulate what became a near craze for Pan-Americanism by the fall of 1941. Hundreds of "institutes" or seminars on inter-American relations, financed by the foundations, the ACLS, and the CIAA, were held throughout the nation. Pan-Americanism was promoted in the schools by means of essay contests, speech competitions, and poster contests. Assorted groups, from bar associations to Catholic organizations to women's clubs to poetry societies, were encouraged to develop programs that would result in contact with kindred Latin American organizations. Stories and poems of Latin writers were placed in American magazines. Special Latin American workshops were held in many colleges during the summer session. Through the system of contracts issued by the coordinator's office, resources were tied to enthusiasm, bearing fruit in a bewildering congeries of cultural projects. Inter-American demonstration centers were funded; museums received subsidies to display Latin American art; and private organizations in major ports of entry were paid to organize welcoming facilities for distinguished Latin visitors. Now that money and encouragement were coming from the top down, the reliance upon private energies in the purely domestic sphere resulted in an explosion of activity.[15]

The nation's academic communities were also mobilized behind the hemispheric cultural concept. During the 1930s, the ACLS's Committee on Latin American Studies had sought to encourage Latin American research, with little success. But by 1940 the "harder" Social Science Research Council began to display an active interest, and a Joint Committee on Latin American Studies was formed that year. Early in 1942, the National Research Council joined the committee. An "Outline of Research in the Study of Contemporary Culture Patterns in Latin America," prepared by Preston E. James, candidly attempted "to focus the attention of North American social scientists on Latin American problems of pressing international concern, especially on those questions which are important in the formulation of American public policy." The committee became mainly an advisory body to the government. It passed on the scholarly merit of proposals in its field, with the constant aim of developing Latin American studies in the United States and promoting closer working relationships with Latin American scholars. The committee's status was enhanced by an increasing amount of foundation and government funding of research related to Latin America. Although as the war wound down the committee began to cherish visions of becoming a planning rather than an advisory body, to a large extent it had already conceded this function to the government. Indeed, as soon as the government lost interest in the committee's activities, its raison d'être disappeared and it once again went into decline.[16]

The tendency to integrate the informal cultural network within the framework of governmental policy was illustrated by the reaction of the old League Committee on Intellectual Cooperation to the Nazi takeover of the Paris Institute. The fear was, as Edith Ware of the U.S. National Committee expressed it, that the Germans "might use the existing machinery of the National Committees to orient the cultural life of Latin American countries with the Nazi-Fascist drive for world domination." The problem was not only to prevent a pro-Nazi intellectual coup, but also to divert the traditional pro-European orientation of the Latin intellectuals into an inter-American framework. Henry Allen Moe, with his revulsion of "the whole Paris gang" and its "spiritual and mental bankruptcy," betrayed the anti-European animus of some members of the U.S. committee. The choice was thus not pro-Nazi or anti-Nazi – it was pro-America versus pro-Europe. At the suggestion of the Argentine committee and with the active encouragement of the State Department, a meeting of the Western Hemisphere national committees was called in Havana early in 1942. As it turned out, the conference rang with denunciations of the Nazis although it failed to agree on specific programs of intellectual cooperation to replace those of the Paris Institute.[17]

The full impact of the changing governmental role in cultural relations could be seen most clearly in the overseas aspects of the program. At the domestic level, the contract system minimized the government's visibility and its now-dominant role in policy was further concealed by the enthusiasm with which goals were accepted by the public and by the reliance upon the private sector to carry them out. Overseas, however, the need to expand the program and the new short-term orientation toward immediate results placed inexorable pressures upon the informal system of policy and administration to give way to a greater degree of governmental control. The result was that the traditional conceptions of the legitimate role of governmental cultural activities – whether of the national interest or the liberal universalist variety, both of which emphasized reciprocity and the primacy of the private sector in policy and administration – were challenged in nearly every one of the United States' overseas cultural activities.[18]

Because of their necessarily long-term nature, the student exchange programs were perhaps least vulnerable to wartime distortions. The most visible effect was an increase of foreign students, mostly Latin Americans, studying in the United States. Much of this growth was of what Henry Allen Moe called "the mushroom type," sprouting up overnight in the lush atmosphere of increased government funding for scholarships and travel and maintenance grants. Because South American universities possessed little appeal to American students, the traffic flow became extremely one-sided, a situation further accentuated by the decision in October 1942 to suspend such grants to U.S. students for the duration of the war. It was no longer possible to pay even lip service to the ideal of reciprocity.[19]

National security justifications soon came to dominate all exchange program rationales. It was frankly hoped that Latin American students would, as a result of their stay, be imbued with a politically helpful pro-American orientation. The CIAA's policy in all areas became to send men north and materials south. Thus it subsidized the visits of Latin dignitaries who, ostensibly invited and feted by private American organizations, were expected to take back favorable views of the United States to their homelands. As policy matured, the emphasis changed from promoting visits of "distinguished leaders" to inviting those with direct access to public opinion in their countries. A sharp eye was kept out for the ideological purity of cultural grantees, with loyalty to democratic principles the primary criterion. The Chilean poet, Pablo Neruda, was denied a travel grant because of his Communist party membership, and Sumner Welles personally vetoed a grant to Jacques Maritain because of his Gaullist sympathies.[20]

The attitudes of American travel grantees were sometimes less than disinterested. A supercilious appraisal of the Latin nations by playwright-novelist Thornton Wilder ("In the long run the adherence of these republics must be gained by force. They will continue to make the charge of imperialism, but they are not ready for any other method.") received a sympathetic, if discreet reading in the State Department. But the comments of literary figure Waldo Frank ended in public fireworks. On a trip to Argentina that was secretly subsidized by the CIAA, Frank publicly accused the regime of Acting President Ramon Castillo, then governing under a "state of siege," of pro-Fascist sympathies. After being swiftly declared persona non grata, Frank was assaulted and beaten in his hotel room by a band of pro-Fascist thugs. Although the incident stirred up a hornet's nest, the State Department was not displeased, for Frank had managed to place Argentine fascists in a poor light while heartening that nation's prodemocratic forces.[21]

There also began to take place a trend toward the bureaucratic absorption of what were once private functions. Under wartime conditions, the ever-present activism of organizations like the American Library Association easily adjusted itself to the idea of governmental direction. Eager to be of assistance in the common effort, the ALA *Bulletin* saw "a unique opportunity for service and a continent ready to receive it." Given the ideological character of the war, the printed word appeared to be "as important as bombers, and ideas as potent as machine guns." With CIAA money readily available and a complaisant mood among private interests, the government quickly stepped in to expand, and later to supplant, the activities pioneered by private groups.[22]

The case of the Biblioteca Benjamin Franklin in Mexico City was typical of this process. It was originally intended to solicit private funds, perhaps with some foundation backing, for a Mexico City library. But not until the CIAA became interested in 1941 did money become available. At first, ALA officials involved in the library's administration argued that the embassy "should not be mixed up with the project, nor, for that matter, should the State Department be in it." The belief was that private control of such libraries would remove them "that much farther from any suspicion of serving as agencies of cultural imperialism." It was initially thought that the library could develop private sources of support, but this turned out to be a false hope. Continued dependence on government funding meant rising State Department influence. By late 1943, the State Department insisted on a veto power over appointments of library directors, and the library's functions came to be closely integrated with the cultural operations of the U.S. embassy.[23]

Questions of policy and administration were raised in even more acute form with respect to the development of pro-American cultural institutes throughout Latin America. The Instituto Cultural Argentino Norte Americano was created in the late 1920s, and by 1939 ten of these institutes had sprung up throughout the continent, often with the assistance of the local American colony and interested natives. They were all-purpose cultural organizations, combining libraries, English classes, lectures, exhibits, and assorted activities in the interest of extending cultural appreciation of foreign policy, but apart from an occasional foundation grant, they were left to their own devices. With the availability of CIAA funds and an emergency mentality, the State Department was now disposed to take another look at policy.[24]

A few department officials recommended that financial aid to these institutions should become "a long-range propaganda program undertaken by this Government . . . in order to compete successfully with other leading powers." Besides teaching English, the institutes could be used as "nuclei for pro-United States cultural 'propaganda' in general." But most departmental personnel agreed with Louis Halle that the sole legitimate function of the institutes was "disseminating the truth" about the United States. For that matter, it had already been decided in April 1941 to channel dubious propaganda responsibilities to the coordinator's operatives in Latin America, leaving the institutes to perform their time-tested activities under local control. People like Ellis Briggs also feared that the institutes would become local pork barrels and that a sudden infusion of funds would make postwar withdrawal pains all the more acute. But the mere fact of the institutes' existence made them convenient targets of policy, and the CIAA favored a large program of aid.[25]

As with the libraries, the original intention was to maintain the spontaneous and autonomous character of the institutes by providing them with assistance only until they became self-supporting. People like Waldo Leland feared direct and continuing aid because it put the United States "in the position of supporting the kind of institution which other governments regard as major instruments of propaganda." It was thought, as William Schurz later recalled, that the institutes would be "suspect to some degree." Pursuing this point, Charles Thomson argued before the Joint Committee on December 1, 1941, that "cultural activities seemed more genuine if there were no direct governmental tie-up."[26]

It was finally decided to subsidize the institutes, but the desire to avoid the appearance of propaganda precluded a mimicry of European instrumentalities. The result was a program of governmental support with the appearance of private funding and control. To avoid restrictive national legislation, funds for Brazilian and Argentinian institutes were funneled through the New York banks of allegedly "private" committees. But the main conduit was the American Council of Learned Societies. The CIAA and the State Department eventually came to favor direct governmental support of the institutes, but were stymied by the discovery that the CIAA appropriations bill prohibited the delegation of authority for grants-in-aid to another government agency. So the ACLS remained as "fiscal agent" throughout the war, hiring institute personnel and transmitting funds. For all of this administrative chicanery, it was commonly assumed in Latin American political circles that the institutes were supported by the U.S. government.[27]

The department perforce became deeply involved in the institutes' affairs. First it sought the appointment of American directors or executive secretaries, who would be more amenable to departmental suggestions. Then the local cultural attachés frequently came to play a major role in defining institute policy. Gradually, there developed an acceptance of the force of circumstance. To begin with, there was no gainsaying the fact that a dynamic institute could be "an important, if indirect, instrument of anti-Axis influence." "Whether we wish it or not," argued Thomson in response to a charge of excessive departmental meddling, "we have a stake in the effective operation of such an institute. If it is badly administered, it reflects on our national interest, especially by contrast with a similar organization of another nation. If it is well run and active, it reflects favorably on this country." The idea of the department as only a "clearinghouse" for institute activities would persist into the postwar period. But centralizing pressures would continue to mount throughout the war.[28]

The question of aid to American-sponsored schools in Latin America raised perhaps the most acrimony in discussions of cultural policy. In 1941 it was estimated that the total number of Axis-sponsored schools in Latin America was 862, of which 670 were German, 58 Italian, and 134 Japanese. The consequence of this widespread educational network, as a CIAA officer explained in a "realistic appraisal," was that German culture "is respected and anti-American indoctrination inevitably results. The whole system leads to political sympathy for Germany and an anti-American point of view." Some U.S. diplomats were quick to point out the "burning desire" of Latins for American schools. Added to such observations from the diplomatic corps was a series of importunities for aid from individuals and organizations sponsoring American schools in Latin America.[29]

By early 1942, many of the German schools had been closed, leaving a shortage of superior educational facilities in some areas. For the CIAA, this development represented an opportunity "to break the hold that Germany has had on the intellectual and cultural life of many communities in those countries." It was readily agreed that some emergency aid, excluding assistance to denominational and company-sponsored schools, was probably necessary. Once that was decided, however, some of the same thorny questions began to crop up: What would be the government's role and how was the program to be administered?[30]

As an interim solution, aid to the approximately two hundred U.S. schools in Latin America was funneled through a CIAA grant to the American Council on Education. Meanwhile, Andrew Corry of the coordinator's office was sent on a tour of South America to obtain data for recommendations regarding permanent policy. His report, submitted in September 1942, set off a debate that would continue through most of the war. Corry claimed that an active program of governmental assistance would achieve important political, economic, and cultural objectives. Citing Napoleon ("Of all political questions that of education is perhaps most important."), he recommended an extensive program of aid to existing schools and an aggressive program of aid to and encouragement of the development of new schools. The main goal of this policy was "to offset the Axis-oriented and other non-American foreign intellectual and educational institutions."[31]

Corry's ambitious proposals provoked the near-unanimous opposition of the Cultural Relations Division, its civilian allies, and the political officers of the State Department. For an internationalist like Waldo Leland, the coordinator's proposals violated all the traditional norms of cultural relations. Accustomed to the informal approach of the 1920s and 1930s, Leland thought Corry's plan was "so large and comprehensive that it seemed to take on the proportions of a propaganda program." In the process, it raised "the whole question of the change from private to public benefactions." The existence of short-range emergency justifications did not warrant violating "the profound conviction that democratic nations cannot utilize the same means as those employed by non-democratic powers." For Leland and others, the fundamental question was "whether or not a program of cultural relations can be used as an instrument of national policy."[32]

For officers of the Division of American Republics, the answer to this last question was "of course," so long as the program of cultural aid was discreet, modest, and realistic in its ambitions. They, too, firmly opposed the Corry report's recommendations, but from the narrower framework of national interest. Philip Bonsal, chief of the division, did not feel that long-range planning of a grandiose sort was justified because of emergency congressional largess. On political grounds, a bloated program was illogical and self-defeating. If the Axis powers lost the war, then Fascist ideology and cultural influence would surely disappear in any case. Economically and politically, it would be more to the U.S. interest to extend aid directly to the Latin governments, as most school systems were nationally run. Finally, national sensibilities might be wounded by such an ambitious program. From a pragmatic standpoint, pressing too hard could only prove counterproductive in the end.[33]

It was decided not to finance any new schools abroad and aid to nondenominational schools was limited to supplying some personnel and materials. In addition, the Department of State concluded that the main effort should go into aiding national school systems. After the department absorbed the coordinator's programs in mid-1943, these principles became enshrined in policy. The funding was handled through the American Council on Education, which established an Inter-American Schools Service to act as a service and liaison agency, with the ACE as fiscal agent. As for direct aid to Latin governments, the CIAA undertook pioneering programs of aid through its Inter-American Educational Foundation. Because of the sensitivity of officials to the politicization of education, the schools program suffered from few political and bureaucratic incursions. But the sharp disagreement on policy was a sign of the potent forces pushing the State Department toward a more active role in the formulation and execution of cultural policy.[34]

The war produced a schizophrenic Latin American program. On the one hand, there resulted a sharp clash of principles between the aggressive national security arguments of the coordinator and the traditionally informal approach to cultural relations favored by State Department internationalists and national interest advocates alike. This dualism was reflected in pronouncements of the influential House Committee on Appropriations, which at times criticized propagandist tendencies in the program whereas at others it lamented the lack of immediate, tangible results. The conceptual division was also encompassed in the bureaucratic struggle between the State Department and the coordinator. Even after a working relationship was created, basic differences were transferred to the particular details of policy over the entire range of wartime cultural activities.[35]

Many hoped that the war's end would bring a return to the chaste behavior that characterized the program's beginnings. The unlikelihood of such a restoration was demonstrated by the program's expansion to other regions of the globe, where the tendency was toward an intensification of the idealistic strain of cultural policy. In fact, the greater the distance traversed, the more idealistic did policy become. If expansion had resulted only in the reappearance of an indomitable missionary spirit, there might have been some cause for optimism on that score. But matters were not so simple. Rather than maintaining a separation between cultural and political affairs, idealistic overseas involvements brought them closer together, to the point that they were nearly indistinguishable. The net result was an ingenious, if at times disturbing, merger of public and private approaches to cultural relations that pointed not to the simplicities of the past, but to even greater complications.

Although worldwide operations had been envisioned at the time of the division's creation, it was not until U.S. entry into the war that arguments for expansion began to take on urgency. The division was partly concerned to get into action overseas in order to forestall the creation of bureaucratic competitors similar to the CIAA, but its central motivation was to take advantage of the opportunity presented by the global scope of American military involvement. A host of pseudo-strategic proposals, most of them unsuccessful, was served up for introducing the program to Spain, Australia and New Zealand, South Africa, and even to Canada, where an anticonscriptionist Québecois minority was disturbing neighborly solidarity. But all this was in the realm of speculation. Whenever it was intimated that an expanded program was simply the cultural arm of military strategy, hackles were raised. The division steadfastly refused to be dominated by realistic or geopolitical considerations.[36]

It was for this reason that the more hardheaded Division of European Affairs poured cold water on what were thought to be impractical cultural proposals. "The exchange of professors, students, and lecturers has gone on for years," wrote Theodore C. Achilles of Anglo-American cultural relations, "with limited and not always fortunate results, and it is *not* believed that this field should take up any appreciable time or funds." Despite, perhaps even because of, a long history of cultural contacts, there remained a sticky residue of anti-British sentiment among the American public. Although Ambassador John M. Winant was already making great strides in introducing an Alan Nevins textbook into the British elementary and secondary schools, Achilles and his division preferred to rest their faith in the power of the press, radio, and movies. This skeptical attitude led to the entire Commonwealth being treated to a media approach by the Office of War Information. Only in the case of the Near East and China did the Division of Cultural Relations receive a congenial welcome from the geographic divisions.[37]

By April 1942, officers of the Division of Near Eastern Affairs (NE) had become "aware of decreasing 'cultural relations' between those countries and the United States," and they were concerned to put a halt to this trend. NE was also sensitive to bureaucratic competition, preferring to see cultural activities remain under departmental control rather than leaving them to the OWI. But the need to take into account a heavy British and French cultural influence deriving from their widespread colonial interests in the region slowed planning for an American program. It was necessary to tread gingerly lest these powers receive the impression that the United States was attempting to supplant their influence. Also requiring consideration was a British offer in 1942 of joint cultural ventures in the Near East. After giving it serious thought, the Americans declined. British prestige was low because, as Ralph Turner argued, Britain had "a century of bad, if not evil, repute to live down in those areas, as well as current weakness." Reasons of pride also dictated nonacceptance. Stuart Grummon felt the United States ought "to drive [its] own program rather than run alongside the British as a sort of good-natured carriage boy."[38]

The major point to be kept in mind was that in the Near East America's cultural influence always had exceeded its physical power. As Colonel H. B. Hoskins of the Office of Strategic Services (OSS) emphasized to the General Advisory Committee, the Near East and China were "the only two areas in the world in which American intellectual influence is considerably greater than that of any other country." Of central importance were a number of schools, most notably Robert College in Istanbul and American University in Beirut, which had taken root "only by slow and steady growth over a period of many years." Because of their largely secular status and their private funding, these institutions were presumed to be "free from the imperialistic bias ascribed to German, French, and British cultural activity." As a result of severe inflation and unsettled wartime conditions, these schools found themselves hard pressed financially. Their influence and their plight made them ideal instruments of Near Eastern cultural policy.[39]

The rationale of the Near Eastern cultural program was a mixture of idealism and antiimperialism. Aid to American schools would provide a significant contribution to modernization and the raising of living standards. Although Gordon Merriam of NE insisted that the United States had "no political interests or antagonisms in that area," there was in fact a quasi-political justification for American cultural involvement: It would provide a fillip to American prestige. As Ralph Turner argued, "The general dislike of the imperialism of Germany, France and England [among these peoples] should be prevented from being extended to Americans." By drawing an explicit contrast between European imperialism and disinterested American policy, the United States was priming itself, if not for a political competition, then for a cultural contest on informal terms. This in itself was a significant departure from previous U.S. policy.[40]

The identical voluntarist scruples regarding means that had acted to limit and disguise governmental involvement in the Western Hemisphere were also present in Near East policy. President Bayard Dodge of the American University of Beirut, although he was willing to solicit and accept a federal subsidy, deeply feared bureaucratic intrusions on his institution's independence. The structural consequences of aid also needed to be considered. As Dr. George Shuster, president of Hunter College, pointed out to the General Advisory Committee, government money "must of necessity change to a certain degree the character of a receiving institution." Once that happened, it was generally "impossible to return to the *status quo.*" Governmental aid was also harmful to the objectives of the cultural program, as it might make the recipient schools appear less than disinterested. According to Stephen Duggan, an "official subsidy might cause the existing prestige to suffer." Thus Gordon Merriam suggested that a program of aid, "while it should not be advertised, should not, on the other hand, be concealed." What all this added up to, however, as William A. Eddy of the OSS later put it, was a "policy of keeping the government behind the scenes."[41]

The President's Emergency Fund provided the rather modest sum of less than $450,000 for fiscal 1944. Only one cultural attaché was appointed, Donald E. Webster to Ankara, rather than the ten originally planned. A series of small grants-in-aid to the Near East College Association and the Near East Foundation provided for library improvements, scholarships, professorships, and projects in engineering, health education, and agricultural extension. Modest grants were also made to the Phelps-Stokes Fund for support of the Booker T. Washington Agricultural and Industrial Institute in Liberia. In addition, funds were provided for such projects as the compilation of the Redhouse Turkish-English Dictionary, and for the publication, through a grant to the American Board of Christian Foreign Missions, of a history of the United States in Arabic.[42]

Although the General Advisory Committee tried to stick by the venerable principles of two-way cultural exchange, the combination of premodern cultures, the history of colonial domination, and wartime circumstances served to inflate American aspirations. Idealism was transformed into a missionary impulse. Unable to resist temptation, Ralph Turner observed that "the Moslem peoples have certain individualistic and democratic elements (in spite of fatalism) which we can develop." In Ankara, Donald E. Webster was even more prone to this sort of expansive idealism. "I have come to feel more strongly," he wrote after becoming established as cultural attaché, "that we have a responsibility there which may be termed 'secular-missionary.'" Webster foresaw a comprehensive, if beneficent, American influence: "We want to have this small but strategically located country not only friendly to us but also able to think things through in patterns similar to our own in politics, economics, social welfare, and the many other phases of our culture." Even Gordon Merriam, who shared a good number of Webster's ideals, thought this a bit much. "This may be going too far," he noted. "The Turks are not Americans and never will become Americans, but it will be a fine thing if we can help them to be good Turks."[43]

But such strictures were made only halfheartedly, as illustrated by the handling of the Afghanistan problem. Early in 1943, the Afghan Ministry of Foreign Affairs requested American teachers for Habibia College in Kabul and a few engineers for employment with the Ministry of Public Works. In a conversation with Van Engert, the U.S. minister, a government official indicated that the

Afghans were "quite willing to entrust to us most of the technical development of the country as well as the education of its youth." This would represent a break with the nation's previous dependence upon German technical and cultural expertise. Engert argued that the United States' "exceptional standing" with the Afghans was due to their "belief in [the] disinterestedness of our motives." The department noted that this seemed to be "a rare opportunity not only of access to a new nation in the making but of helping it and guiding it in connection with the intimate problems of mental and moral development which the pressure of modern forces has created." The presence of American teachers would help "to make American idealism and justice and vision a positive and constructive force in the whole of Central Asia."[44]

Of course, it helped that the American engineers and teachers would displace a number of Japanese currently holding these positions. If the United States could not furnish the teachers, Paul Alling hinted that the Afghans would "turn elsewhere," to nations ideologically and politically opposed to the United States. Thus there were "political considerations" that made cultural cooperation with Afghanistan "of far more importance than would be indicated by the size and relative obscurity of the country in question." The OSS offered to finance the scheme, but funds were found within the department to supplement the salaries of a number of American teachers hired by the Afghans. The incident was a nice example of the blending of ideals with a challenge to the imperialist political structure of the area.[45]

Afghanistan was only one instance of a general tendency for Near Eastern nations to look for a more active American cultural role. As a dispatch from Beirut put it, the future of American cultural institutions in the area was "particularly bright." Despite this rise in prestige, John A. Wilson of the University of Chicago's Oriental Institute and Colonel William Eddy of the OSS, both of whom were active in the early planning of the Near East cultural program, complained early in 1944 that "there was no clear or basic set of ideas." It remained unclear whether the department's Near Eastern activities were merely of an emergency character or whether they were to be the incubator of a permanent program. Basic policy rationales were also muddled. All told, there was serious cause for concern because at that point in time it appeared "doubtful" that the Bureau of the Budget would approve another year of funding.[46]

The confusion was fundamental. On the one hand, it was argued that cultural activities were "intimately connected with considerations of security and national defense," Congress being told that "the maintenance of political stability" in the Near East required a continuing program of cultural cooperation. But although the public justifications were made in strategic terms, the program's policies sprang from idealist motives. The result was that a convincing argument, one way or the other, for continuing the program, failed to be made. In part this failure derived from an absence of crisis in the region. Because the Near Eastern countries had remained neutral in the war, and because an American military interest was only indirectly apparent, policy suffered from ambiguity. But China was different – it provided a test of cultural idealism under fire. There the wartime crisis and the strong tradition of U.S. involvement in Chinese affairs produced a cultural policy that left little room for ambiguity.[47]

The China program was the lineal descendant of numerous private cultural and educational efforts undertaken by Americans beginning in the mid-nineteenth century. An original missionary purpose had long since given way to secular enthusiasms in which the object of American efforts, according to Raymond Fosdick, was "to make over a medieval society in terms of modern knowledge." Modernization was only half of the equation, though, for Americans always made certain to promote the equally desirable (and, to their eyes, necessary) goal of China's democratization, preferably on the American model. The primary vehicle of China's initiation into modern democratic life was education, and by the 1930s a remarkably broad combination of religious, philanthropic, and secular efforts had helped to make American educational influence in China second to none.[48]

The outbreak of the Sino-Japanese War in July 1937 disrupted the extensive system of private contacts built up over the years. It was not until 1941, after U.S. relations with Japan had seriously deteriorated, that suggestions were first made to have the government step in to take over where private initiative had left off. Because of China's status as a beleaguered ally, the Roosevelt administration listened sympathetically to such proposals. Lauchlin

Currie, FDR's adviser on lend-lease aid to China, quickly grasped the connection between material and intellectual forms of support; in particular, technical experts could make a valuable "contribution to the strengthening of Chinese economic and industrial resources." Similarly, aid to Chinese students in the United States could help to develop a competent cadre of technicians, which would in turn strengthen China's capacity to resist Japanese agression. With help from the President's Emergency Fund, the Division of Cultural Relations established a China Section which, by early 1942, planned the dispatch of a dozen technical advisers to China and embarked on a program of assistance for the nearly one thousand Chinese students stranded in America by the war.[49]

The idea of cultural lend-lease, which quickly became the program's dominant policy concept, departed from tradition in that it stressed only the technological side of the Sino-American relationship. Although it aimed also at "maintaining the morale of the intellectual classes in China," the governing intention was to promote projects "of the most immediate benefit to China." This meant that, for the sake of the war effort, the idealistic strain in American policy would be deliberately muted. As far as the embassy in Chungking was concerned, this was all to the good. "Having in mind Chinese sensibilities," it advised, "it is desirable to avoid any suggestion of 'cultural' missions to China . . . the least said publicly in that direction at the present time the better." This was a recommendation with which the Department fully agreed.[50]

This pragmatic approach to cultural policy fit in with a growing Kuomintang emphasis on Chinese cultural nationalism. In *China's Destiny*, a theoretical tract published in 1943, Chiang Kai-shek demanded that "education throughout the country focus on the concept of statehood, and place the ideology of nationalism before everything else." A crucial element in this scheme was the attempt to combine modern technical education with established cultural traditions. Thus a Central Cultural Movement Committee formed in October 1943, in conjunction with an officially sponsored revival of Confucianism, began to publicize the traditional Chinese virtue of obedience. Chiang preferred to solidify his rule by combining a powerful bureaucracy with blind loyalty, rather than to rely on the American formula of democratic control and decentralized political administration. Logically, his policies pointed to the observance of the oft-quoted anti-Western, antiliberal maxim: "Chinese culture as the substance, Western science for use." The State Department's emphasis on technical assistance, to the degree that it avoided thorny ideological questions, formed a perfect complement to the Kuomintang's domestic policies.[51]

A series of incidents quickly demonstrated the tenacity with which the Kuomintang pursued its emphasis on cultural isolation. An inquiry by the State Department in 1943 regarding the possibility of providing aid to Chinese intellectuals and academics, who were known to be enduring harsh physical privations, was rejected by the government with the assertion that such assistance would destroy the dignity of the recipients. In addition, the modest program for sending Chinese professors for visits to the United States was complicated by the Kuomintang's insistence that the scholars receive indoctrination in nationalist principles before being allowed to depart the country. As for the more than one thousand Chinese students who were to be sent to the United States for technical studies, the Chinese made certain to select only those who had successfully completed a program of careful ideological screening. By early 1944 the Kuomintang's hand had become so oppressive that a group of Harvard professors protested its policies, and even pro-Chiang *Time* was moved to criticize the "dictatorship over China's thinkers."[52]

In the face of such fierce chauvinism, Americans connected with the cultural program gradually came to regard U.S. policy as wrongheaded. The earliest and most eloquent critic was John King Fairbank, a Harvard professor of Chinese history who, in connection with his information-gathering activities in Chungking for the OSS Research and Analysis Branch, had become a de facto cultural attaché for the U.S. embassy. In 1943, Fairbank came to disagree strenuously with the cultural program's technical emphasis, arguing that it could better serve as an instrument of "aid in the struggle for 'democracy' or social betterment in China." By tacitly condoning the Kuomintang's intellectual repression, the United States was contributing to China's "intellectual starvation." Because the Kuomintang's policies were also depressing the morale of Chinese intellectuals, the effect was ultimately injurious to the war effort.[53]

Fairbank believed that "ideas are as important as technics," and he insisted that the Kuomintang, especially the so-called C-C clique headed by Minister of Education Chen Li-Fu, was bent on promoting "intellectual stultification." According to Fairbank, Chen and his cronies held "pernicious and antiquated views in regard to the process of intellectual adjustment to the modern world which China must sooner or later make." He also thought that the revival of Confucianism was disastrous, being "both a source of and a vehicle for atavism, chauvinism, and xenophobia." He urged that American policy be reoriented in the direction of the liberal arts and that cultural contacts be managed on a nongovernmental basis, "in order to avoid the intervention of the nationalistic Minister of Education." In his dealings with Chinese intellectuals and with representatives of American cultural bodies, Fairbank wasted no opportunities to plead for cultural contacts unencumbered by nationalistic or technical baggage.[54]

The State Department took no official notice of these complaints until mid-1944, when it became apparent to many policymakers that Chiang's actions were simply wasting energies better put to use in prosecuting the war against Japan. The cultural program now began to emphasize the need for intellectual reform in order to bring about a "strong, democratic China," for it seemed clear that China could not become strong unless it were first democratic. Without a measure of democratization to generate popular support and to provide innovative energies, all the technical aid in the world would be of little avail. Thus, J. Hall Paxton of the Chungking embassy suggested that the United States "ought to give the Chinese the benefit of the best minds available on problems more fundamental than how to make bits and lathes." Even Lauchlin Currie came to conclude that the United States "must further the program of cultural relations by aiding those people who share our views." Nearly everyone now came to favor a reorientation of cultural relations in a humanistic direction in order to provide China's intellectual elite with what seemed to be an indispensable contact with liberal ideas. Cultural policy was returning to its idealistic roots.[55]

All this was not so easily accomplished, however. To be sure, there were formidable physical difficulties in making contact with liberal Chinese, but these paled before problems of technique and principle. Cultural relations were still supposed to be noncoercive and nonpolitical. Yet a program aimed at intellectual liberalization and the introduction of democratic principles was bound to meet with determined opposition from the Chinese government. At the same time, diplomatic pressure to this end would be a violation of liberal canons regarding the free and reciprocal movement of ideas, as well as a repudiation of the voluntarist tradition. The solution that came most readily to mind was to emphasize private people-to-people cultural contacts. If the Chinese protested, they could be accused of violating the principles of intellectual free-dom, whereas the U.S. government's interest in promoting China's liberalization could be handled by traditionally acceptable private means. But a dilemma remained, nonetheless: Private in-terests were incapable of assuming responsibilities that, for rea-sons of principle, were forbidden to a more amply endowed gov-ernment. Thus the only way to satisfy both principle and performance was by providing covert government backing for os-tensibly private cultural ventures.

A number of abortive "private" initiatives were soon launched in the new humanist direction. University of Chicago anthropolo-gist Robert Redfield was persuaded to undertake a survey of the state of Chinese social science. This project, although nominally sponsored by the Social Science Research Council, had the secret financial backing of the Rockefeller Foundation and was enthusi-astically, if discreetly, endorsed by the State Department. Because of medical problems, however, Redfield was unable to make the journey. The American Library Association, with Fairbank's active encouragement and State Department cooperation, secured an in-vitation to China for Columbia University librarian Carl White, who hoped by his presence there to "help bolster the position of the Chinese liberal." Despite his enthusiasm, transportation diffi-culties prevented his getting to China by the war's end.[56]

The need to preserve the appearance of informal cultural con-tact resulted in a covert OSS interest in cultural policy. Early in 1943, Columbia University's School of Journalism was invited by the Chinese Ministry of Information to establish a graduate school of journalism in Chungking. Dean Carl Ackerman quickly ar-ranged for a "private donor," actually the OSS, to finance this op-eration. As it turned out, both sides were deceived. The Kuomin-tang attached the school to a political institute designed to churn out loyal party bureaucrats, while the Americans, for their part, saw the experiment as an ideal means of introducing the censorship-prone Chinese to American journalistic ethics and the principle of freedom of the press. With such widely differing expectations, it was not surprising that the venture turned out poorly. Nevertheless, the OSS maintained its secret interest in Chinese cultural affairs. Early in 1945 it sent Bernard Knollenberg, the librarian of Yale University, on a China mission, and also dispatched a jurist "to assist in the formulation of Chinese legal concepts."[57]

None of this had much impact on the China tangle, but it spoke volumes about American attitudes toward foreign affairs. The transition from technical to humanistic policy marked a return to traditional U.S. perceptions of Sino-American relations as being primarily cultural in character. The expectation of seeing a "strong, democratic China" was based on the belief that the absorption of American liberal ideas and values would give to the Chinese an intellectual and political base for successful modernization. The political tactic of treating China as an equal, implicit in the technical approach, was scrapped because of what seemed to be Chiang's backward-looking and counterproductive fixation with traditional Confucian values.

The fact of growing governmental involvement in cultural policy, not only in China but in other regions as well, did not mean that cultural policy was becoming politicized – although there were those who called for such an approach to Latin America. Actually, more nearly the reverse took place as foreign policy issues began to be framed in idealistic cultural terms. If that were indeed the case, a greater State Department involvement in cultural policy was not only desirable, but necessary. Viewed from the exhilarating heights of planning for the postwar world, this development was more to be welcomed than feared.[58]

CHAPTER 3

Planning the liberal ecumene

The evolution of cultural policy in Latin America and China produced some discomfiting liaisons with politics. Nevertheless, planners had every intention of banishing politics – accommodation based on the use of power – from a postwar system of cultural cooperation. In bringing to pass the liberal ecumene, the dilemma was how to reconcile the existence of American power (and the power of America's allies) with liberal scruples that constantly derogated its use. If power would not be made to disappear completely, its safest lodgment appeared to be in a system of multilateral cooperation. This widespread enthusiasm for multilateralism was not caused by any inherent technical virtues of the system as such; rather, the multilateral framework was to be the outward sign of an inner transformation that would radically redefine the meaning of politics.

The role of cultural relations in bringing to pass the liberal utopia came up for debate quite early in the war. In his 1942 book, *America's Strategy in World Politics,* Nicholas John Spykman rejected as fantasy the idea of cultural rapprochement. "The assumption that people who are fundamentally different will necessarily begin to like each other as they become better acquainted is erroneous," he snorted, "and disproved in daily life." Even more ridiculous was the idea that, in a world dominated by power, states cooperated because of friendly feelings for one another. "Sympathy does not determine policy," Spykman insisted, "policy tends to determine sympathy." For Spykman, intellectual cooperation was a worthwhile end in itself, but it had little value as an instrument of politics. Samuel Flagg Bemis, in his influential work, *The Latin American Policy of the United States,* released the following year, also emphasized the primacy of interests in shaping policy, although he too was quick to acknowledge that cultural exchanges were intrinsically desirable.[1]

Somewhat surprisingly, the Division of Cultural Relations took offense at these criticisms, despite the fact that they were consistent with its oft-proclaimed description of cultural affairs as a long-range pursuit independent of workaday political concerns. Stung by Spykman's remarks, Charles Thomson denied that the cultural program was in quest of some "romantic goodwill." Rather, it was designed to make peoples understand one another, and understanding was "a sound and sensible relationship." Cultural relations produced accurate knowledge, and accurate knowledge in turn could contribute to friendship. "Ignorance certainly will not," Thomson concluded. What he appeared to be saying was that even disagreement should be predicated on "mutual understanding." By erasing ideology and misconception, only the hard substratum of interests would remain to be dealt with – presumably politically. Thus in fact, if not in intention, Thomson succeeded in reaffirming Spykman's arguments.[2]

There was more to the cultural approach, however, than conceiving of it as a sort of intellectual maid service to political relations. Although cultural advocates had long agreed with the theoretical separation of cultural relations and foreign policy, at the same time most were unwilling to concede the permanent supremacy of power interests in international affairs. For people like Samuel Guy Inman, the distinguishing virtue of the cultural approach was its disgust for power politics and the pronunciamentos of "high brow realists." "It is precisely because of the failure of diplomacy during five thousand years, to produce anything but war," Inman argued, "that we now propose to try friendly understanding among people." Politics was the source of the problem; cultural relations, the preferred solution. This was the point of view that Thomson and others within the department soon came to adopt.[3]

The distinctions that the Division of Cultural Relations had originally tried to maintain between a form of nominalism and realism now began to break down, leading to an expanded conception of cultural cooperation. What Thomson actually believed was nearly the reverse of what he had said in his confused critique of Spykman. "So long as political and economic problems arise out of differences in social attitudes, in intellectual outlooks, and in the possession of knowledge, they are cultural problems," he now maintained. That is, political relations were actually a subset of cultural relations. From this perspective, political and economic affairs would themselves become part of the cultural approach. In a radical transformation of the traditional meaning of foreign policy, they too would rely upon understanding rather than on power conflicts for their resolution. Thus cultural understanding was necessary to "undergird the structure of political and economic association." The war was changing what was once a belief in the long-term efficacy of cultural relations into a chiliastic faith in its imminent success.[4]

Another group of critics questioned not the programs's assumptions, but its instrumentalities. Foremost among them were members of Congress who reproved the program's elitism. If cultural relations were characterized by direct people-to-people contacts, was it proper to restrict its benefits to the upper reaches of society? The art program, for instance, with its appeal to upper-middle-class sensibilities, impressed some legislators as being both inefficient and "undemocratic." "How are you going to get our viewpoint to the mass down there? You can't tell me that you can sell that to the masses," was the skeptical judgment of one congressman on the department's exhibit of modern art in Latin America. The art program's elitism was only part of a more reprehensible conception of culture as "high culture." If cultural relations were to constitute the base of a cooperative international order, to many it seemed that the pyramid ought to be turned right side up. In addition, the division had to contend with proposals from those, like Vice President Henry Wallace, who would make of cultural relations something akin to a technological populism.[5]

There was strong resistance within the division to such ideas. For one thing, agencies like the CIAA were better suited to promoting technical and economic cooperation. Besides, Latin Americans were already quite familiar with and critical of the American fetish of technological achievement. Despite the congressional blasts, members of the Advisory Committee continued to insist that the ninety percent could best be reached through their leaders. Officers like Richard Pattee questioned whether it was even possible to reach the masses directly. "We are faced with the very difficult problem of ascertaining whether there is such a thing as an articulate, coherent mass of rural population in a given country," he pointed out. Moreover, any attempt to deal directly with mass problems, say in Latin America, could easily provoke internal social and economic unrest and unquestionably alienate whatever government was in power. Finally, Pattee insisted that when Wallace and Congress were speaking of the masses, they were actually referring to a stratum "quite definitely in the middle class"; in the case of Congress at least, they were arguing on the basis of mirror images of their constituencies. If the masses had to be reached, perhaps the mass media were more appropriate for this purpose than a cultural program.[6]

These arguments over the relative importance of power, democracy, and technology indicated that more thinking needed to be done about the postwar role of cultural relations. Department officials had already begun to make detailed plans in the political and economic spheres, with many convinced of the need to break out of a disastrous pendulumlike historical movement. It was commonly agreed that prior to the war, only two ideas for keeping international peace had attained general acceptance. One was the idea of universal empire, exemplified by Rome and the Napoleonic system; the other, balance of power, which, according to Adolf Berle, had succeeded in giving "uneasy peace in Europe for short periods of time." Each of these systems was based on power and egotism. Isolationism, nationalism, power politics, empire – they all relied ultimately on the use of force to secure their objectives. What the situation demanded was, as Berle described it, "a harmonizing of nationalism and internationalism which should by itself be a system of peace and civilization." A conception of international interest had to be introduced.[7]

When the topic of postwar planning first came up at a meeting of the General Advisory Committee in September 1941, two views were immediately apparent. Ben Cherrington, who assumed the victory of "the spirit of universalism and the desire to cooperate" in the postwar years, broached the idea of an international organization devoted to cultural interchange. Cherrington revealed his extreme liberal orientation when he asked rhetorically: "Does the arrangement existing in the United States in which cultural relations are essentially the responsibility of the cultural organizations of the nation with the government acting as a service agency suggest a pattern for the world?" To ask the question was to answer it. Cherrington looked forward to a vast, decentralized global network of private cultural institutions interacting beyond the reach of national influence or imperial designs. It was the liberal vision at its purest.[8]

At the same session, the professorial Harley Notter of the Division of Special Research presented an alternative perspective. In a sweeping world-historical estimate of the future of the cultural program, Notter emphasized the fact that, historically, cultural influence "corresponded with the rise and tide of national power." In the New World, there had arisen national economic and military strength that exerted "a cultural influence of profound vitality and range." It was America's destiny to complete the global liberal revolution begun by Great Britain. "As England a century ago began to export its manufacturing secrets of industrial processes, tools, and methods to the incidental benefit of other nations," he rhapsodized, "we now must export the cultural equivalents deliberately for the advancement of peoples." Even so, the task would require a nonimperial approach, with a stress on mutual cooperation and a sense of humility. "It is a mature task we must do," Notter stressed, "at a time when we ourselves are not fully mature." Here was the voice of an expanded national interest speaking, one that attracted a good deal of attention and favorable comment within the department.[9]

Making allowances for wartime inflation, these two perspectives were essentially visionary restatements of quite traditional attitudes. Despite their evocation of a postwar world in which American influence would be of mammoth proportions, both curiously avoided coming to grips with the question of power; to be more accurate, their neglect of the question was their means of dealing with it. Cherrington would internationalize it, denature it, and Notter placed an altruistic stamp on the nature of American power that historically did not appear on the credentials of other nations. Nevertheless, at the time, the two views seemed to be poles apart. James T. Shotwell and Waldo Leland, as well as Cherrington, sharply disagreed with Notter's analysis, claiming that its implications were so far reaching that they would "radically change" the direction of the cultural program, turning it into "an instrument in the hand of the government of the United States for the achievement of social and economic (and by extension political) objectives in other countries."[10]

Charles Thomson adopted a position somewhere between Cherrington and Notter. Thomson argued that the Atlantic Charter placed upon the department the definite obligation to use cultural relations "as one of the basic instrumentalities for modifying international relations and attitudes, and for maintaining a better stabilized world order." Although the strictly national focus of the existing cultural program had proved "sound and practicable," Thomson argued that cultural relations of the future would require that "our aim be multilateral." This would be the best structure in support of "a great effort toward an underlying cultural unification of mankind." At the same time, it was conceivable – nay, even desirable – that "certain characteristics of one country's culture may take on 'regional' or universal importance, thus pointing the way to an easier achievement of national cultural aspirations." Such changes should not occur through coercion. Numerous political officers who studied the memo agreed, cautioning against the use of cultural methods "for the purpose of spreading of American ideas." In Thomson's synthesis, universalism, American influence, and the ideal of noncoercion received nearly equal emphasis. It was this formulation that would eventually become accepted policy.[11]

One of the few points on which everyone agreed was that relatively little was known about cultural relations and its connection with foreign affairs. Thus a basic prerequisite to the formulation of far-reaching policies was an extensive program of research. After consulting with foundation executives and the rest of the cultural relations establishment, the Division of Cultural Relations finally hired Professor Ralph Turner of Yale, a historian, to head up its new research program. Turner came highly recommended by Waldo Leland. "There are few men in his field who approach him in power of intellect," Leland stated. Turner was the author of, among other works, *The Great Cultural Traditions: The Foundations of Civilization,* a two-volume opus whose underlying thesis was that reorientations of cultural tradition resulted from conditions that caused fundamental changes in the way of life of the masses. Turner was a believer in the plasticity of culture, and he conceived of it as a human creation capable of change through the application of rationality and science. The research program, as envisaged by Turner, would include studies of the cultural programs of other nations, a study of existing organs and bodies engaged in international cultural activity, and an outline of a concrete, long-term plan for the U.S. program. The first two projects were farmed out to private bodies, while Turner concentrated on postwar planning.[12]

Turner immediately stirred up controversy with his view that cultural relations "should support concretely the foreign policy of the United States." It was axiomatic that any program would have to derive from domestic imperatives. Moreover, Turner reasoned, if cultural programs were to serve the national interest, "they must be developed in terms of the forces which, having their origin in American democracy, carry forward the development of the national life in both its internal and external aspects." Their goal should be to develop "an international situation under which American democracy can be secure and can develop." The vital factor in his analysis, therefore, was to determine what he called "the critical meaning of American democracy" and its effect as a factor in the organization of an international order. Troubled by this initial exposition presented at a meeting of the Advisory Committee, Cherrington immediately noted that a "fundamental issue" was involved. "Is cultural relations a matter of nationalism or is it to be an instrument in the international concept?" he asked anxiously.[13]

The showdown came over a series of lengthy planning memoranda produced by Turner in the autumn of 1942.[14] Overall, they were an attempt to apply what he called a "scientific concept of culture" to the cultural program. "The essence of science is control," he argued, and ideally cultural relations should be "planned social intercourse" or "controlled interchange." These controlled cultural programs could be successful only if they were based on a detailed knowledge of foreign cultures and if closely coordinated with diplomatic, political, and economic action. Because the current world war appeared to be a struggle for political and social unification on a global scale, as well as an episode in the continuing drama of modernization, it was important as a matter of policy to turn this process in a democratic direction.

Turner warned that modernization would continue in any case, "regardless of political policies and events," perhaps veering toward undesirable trajectories. The heart of the problem was the need to influence the most important element in the modernization process, the growing number of persons with a scientific and modern outlook – "carriers," Turner called them. As modern social structures emerged, the control of government and policy had to be placed "in those groups most sympathetic with and capable of democratic action." "By giving social groups favorable to democracy either an improved means of economic action or an expanded body of learning," Turner argued, "cultural relations . . . can be directed to promote democracy and oppose regimentation."

This was not all. Turner saw no necessary contradiction between the employment of power and the liberal democratic creed. In response to liberal criticisms, he maintained that the existence of power was "a primary political fact" and that American power was an instrument for good, not evil, that had to be used if the intertwined destinies of America and the rest of mankind were to be successfully realized. "By creating the world situation required by their national interest," Turner concluded, "the American people promote the liberation of all common men." America's national interest justified "both the exercise of power and the use of cultural relations programs in support of a world-wide advance toward a democratic culture." Here was a synthesis that transcended the old categories of national interest and liberal internationalism. Turner combined the heightened wartime expressions of these two traditional approaches, and at the same time he grasped the nettle of power – too avidly, in the minds of many. In the process, Turner also related intellectual exchange to broader cultural dynamics.

The outlines of a postwar program were sketched only lightly. Turner argued that the cultural program's objective in China should be "to develop 'carriers' for modern cultural materials . . . and to try to bring about a reorientation of the Chinese cultural tradition in democratic terms," a policy toward which the department was already beginning to grope. The rest of the undeveloped, unindustrialized world should be treated in similar fashion, albeit with less urgency. As for Europe, he recommended that America "work with the Soviet Government upon the highly critical problems of the post-war European reconstruction."As there were "no conflicts of national interest arising from strategic or economic considerations" between the two nations, Turner argued that "differences in political methods and religious outlook" were of little security significance. This was certainly a crucial unresolved point in his reasoning. If American foreign policy proceeded from the bowels of American democracy, might not "realistic" security considerations seem secondary when faced with antithetical ideals and methods? But discussion of Turner's program never got this far.

The meaning of these rather turgid memoranda was not immediately clear to everyone. Most departmental personnel selected isolated strains from the documents with which to belabor their own pet themes. Louis J. Halle of the Division of the American Republics praised Turner for showing the uncommon ability of going straight to "the philosophical and anthropological roots of policy." Turner had revealed "a thorough grasp of the fundamental objectives to which we, in common with all the democracies, are now dedicated." Another officer, thinking that Turner was advocating a program of cultural propaganda, found his arguments to be "pretty well in accordance with the contemporary theories of cultural manifestations even on the lower propaganda levels." This writer did criticize what appeared to be an excessive reliance upon elites, though. The Near Eastern Division ritually stressed a nonpolitical approach, suggesting "utmost tact and caution." Turner's breathtaking notion of cultural diplomacy was addressed only obliquely, if it was understood at all. From the tenor of most of the comments, the number of "the American Century" for much of the State Department was still nineteen.[15]

Harley Notter, whose views in some respects seemed to parallel Turner's, turned out to be his sharpest critic. Notter did grant that the conception of a cultural program unrelated to foreign policy was "preposterous." Yet he thought the defects in Turner's arguments were "fundamental." For one thing, Turner's reasoning about the effects of the cultural program upon alien cultures seemed "far more deterministic and calculated than was justifiable." The destruction of primitive cultures was "historically too serious to be set in motion without great care." Secondly, Turner had assumed the cultural hegemony of the United States. Without a "necessary reciprocal spirit," Notter felt, the program would lead the world at large to believe that the United States had "national cultural imperialist ambitions." Power based on unilateralism was passé; rather, a system based on Great Power understanding would be more desirable. If the United States did embark on an independent course, it would forfeit its moral and political arguments against other nations doing likewise. Power was a fact, but it had to be dissolved in a cooperative framework. Obviously, Notter had by this time come to advocate a sort of cultural condominium.[16]

Turner's proposals also drew some devastating cross fire from influential department officers. Philip Bonsal described them as "inconsistent with the type of world and the type of progress which we are all looking forward to." From the traditional perspective of the national interest approach, sound foreign policy made cultural exchanges possible, but Bonsal seriously doubted whether deeply rooted cultural changes could be guided by governmental action. Turner was being too presumptuous in his ambitions. Sumner Welles, although an internationalist in his sympathies, also had serious reservations about these ideas. Welles was not convinced that what he called "a true cultural relations program" should be used as an implement of foreign policy. Nor for that matter was he reassured by Turner's stress on elitism, by his emphasis on American cultural superiority, and by his failure to mention some form of international cultural organization.[17]

Discussion within the General Advisory Committee on February 23, 1943, sounded the death knell for Turner's theses, but not without some final alarms and confusions. Dr. Guy Stanton Ford of the American Historical Association rose to the defense of his professional colleague by pointing out that Turner and his memoranda "were in themselves a full exemplification of the American approach and the 'American way of life.'" Turner had simply "set forth in words the actual philosophy which had governed American action in the past." According to Ford, Turner's program constituted "not a foreign policy, but the national policy of this country . . . one that has grown up from our whole history, our attitudes, our outlook on the world, our record of triumphs and all that is instinctive in the American people." In other words, there was an organic relationship between the past and the direction of

American foreign policy. Attempting to follow up on this point, Alger Hiss explained that foreign policy "in a broader sense was the manifestation of the 'personality' of a nation and was not to be confused with foreign policy in a limited sense involving temporary and changing objectives." By this logic, foreign policy could not be false to a nation's inner being.

Most of those present, however, rejected this line of thought. What if foreign policy somehow reverted to the pursuit of predatory power interests? This was what worried people like Shotwell, Leland, Duggan, and Cherrington. Leland feared that the objective of foreign policy might change and drag the cultural program through some depraved back alleys. "Once cultural relations become the servant of policy," he warned, "there would be nothing to prevent their continuing in that capacity under a deteriorating policy." If compromised in this fashion, such activities then "ceased to be cultural relations and became propaganda." Duggan agreed that this course would "invalidate" the efforts of private cultural activities. Besides, this group was not convinced that Turner had captured the essence of "national policy," for that was what the earlier voluntarist policy system was all about.[18]

These members of the Advisory Committee did all they could to line up their organizations against Turner's recommendations. At Leland's instigation, an ACLS resolution called for a program "established on a long-term basis of free and voluntary exchanges between peoples, . . . determined only by cultural and intellectual considerations." Similarly, the U.S. National Committee on Intellectual Cooperation, dominated by Leland and Shotwell, came out against Turner. A memorandum by Dr. Isaac Kandel of Teachers College met Turner's arguments head-on. "The thesis that the foreign policy of the United States should be directed to modernizing and democratizing the peoples of the world does smack of imperialism," he claimed. Turner's proposals would also seriously distend the national structure of cultural cooperation that had evolved to date. "Cultural relations and intellectual cooperation cannot, indeed, thrive under a bureaucracy," Kandel noted, "and yet the tenor of Mr. Turner's report is open to the interpretation that an enlargement of staff is contemplated." It was not long afterward that the Turner memoranda, of which there were only a limited number of copies, were called in and consigned to bureaucratic oblivion. There was too much of Icarus in Turner's makeup for comfort, and not enough of Daedalus among members of the Advisory Committee.[19]

Actually, there was little argument over the reality of American power and its exceptionalism. It was widely agreed that the center of world culture was shifting to the United States as the result of the war. As Charles Thomson observed, the United States had changed indisputably from debtor to creditor in the cultural as well as the economic sphere. This fact of life necessarily demanded American leadership. As the American Library Association put it, the United States should "now and for a long time assume a share of world leadership in cultural fields as well as in economics, politics, and military affairs." Similarly, there was little doubt over the desirability of spreading American cultural ideals abroad. The American Council on Education was particularly explicit on this point: "The United States, with all her weaknesses and imperfections, embodies more clearly than any other nation . . . the civilized ideas and concepts which must underlie the new order if it is to be constructive." Given the widespread currency of these perceptions, others besides Turner fumbled for a synthesis of power and idealism. Henry Luce came up with "the American Century"; Max Lerner yearned for "a militant democracy, a democratic dynamism"; and, in a phrase that deserved to be forgotten, Esther Brunauer of the American Association of University Women called for "a democratic power politics."[20]

The problem with Turner's program was that it was framed in a national context at a time when the dominant trend of opinion, within the department and without, preferred internationalist solutions. The opinion was rife, as Stephen Duggan early observed, that the war would have to bring some form of "limitation of the sovereignty of the nation state." According to one enthusiastic librarian at an ALA convention, the nation needed "to rend the veil of parochialism, to pierce the illusion of nationalism." Nationalism was an artificial construct for him because culture was "really a universal thing when you get down to it." The examples of cultural interpenetration that he used were not very profound – his audience was intrigued to discover that the popular song "I'm Forever Blowing Bubbles" was lifted from Chopin, and that the pedigree of "Yes, We Have No Bananas" could be traced to Handel's "Hallelujah Chorus" – but the point was readily made. It was common-place observation among educators and others in the cultural community that the globe was interdependent and was undergoing, in Raymond Fosdick's opaque expression, a "process of cellular conjugation" that would determine the shape of the postwar era. The sheer scope of this interdependence seemed to demand internationalist solutions.[21]

If the department stumbled in its initial attempts to formulate a viable postwar agenda, other groups were quite prepared to run the race in its stead. Proof of the vitality of internationalist thought was found in a ground swell of activity in the private sector, where organizations were no less active in the cultural than in the political field. In particular, educational groups took the lead in promoting and forging an internationalist synthesis of power, intellect, and mass education in a postwar program of cultural relations. The Educational Policies Commission of the National Education Association was especially active in the cause. With its chairman William G. Carr, and influential members such as Ben Cherrington, Grayson Kefauver of Stanford University, and Kenneth Holland of the CIAA, the commission became a leading force in the drive for an international umbrella organization that would combine educational and cultural activities. The commission's basic document, *Education and the People's Peace*, released in the spring of 1943 to widespread acclaim, called for a permanent United Nations body modeled after the International Labor Organization. It would have something for everybody: Scholars, librarians, artists, and teachers could all participate under its aegis in various forms of cultural interchange. In addition, the agency would be a clearinghouse for educational data and a watchdog over the education of the world's masses. As it promoted programs of literacy and mass education, it would also see to it that education was not perverted for nationalist purposes. All this was to be achieved without any cession of national control of education, for membership would be composed of sovereign states. In brief, this position incorporated the paradoxical American view of education as an instrument of socialization which, somehow, escaped being defined as a manipulative instrument.[22]

In its own way, this activism presented solutions to the questions long plaguing the Division of Cultural Relations. The activists proceeded from the assumption that the basic issues of World War II were intellectual and moral, and required appropriate treatment. Postwar problems were viewed not only from the perspective of political mechanics, but in the light of a need for reconstruction of attitudes toward political problems. There needed to be a wider perspective than the old saws about the value of cultural exchange for its own sake. As Walter Kotschnig put it in his influential work, *Slaves Need No Leaders,* it was not education or cultural relations that needed to be furthered, "but security, peace and human welfare." The focus of the old League Committee on Intellectual Cooperation had been too narrow. "Their minds dwelt on a plane beyond the reach of ordinary men," Kotschnig complained. "To be practical, down to earth, meant for [the League Committee] the coordination of research and the protection of intellectual rights."[23]

The argument here was that only an organization that gave combined attention to cultural and educational activities could hope to be effective. Education derived its purposes and its direction from its cultural setting and, in turn, served as the medium for the transmission of intellectual and cultural values. It was evident to Kotschnig and to others like Malcolm Davis of the Carnegie Endowment that any new cultural organization would need stronger links to popular sentiment by means of "broader consistent education on international matters and methods." "An intellectual organization will have to face educational demands," Davis concluded. This view represented a great expansion of ambitions, insofar as all intercultural relations would be made part of a global educational process.[24]

Under the rubric of education, there was room for a broad range of opinion. Some, like Philip Jessup, saw in an international organization the possibility for the union of knowledge and power. Jessup advocated an independent bureau of experts "with full legal power to continuously consider matters social, economic, and political which threaten to affect detrimentally the peace, welfare and justice of the peoples of the world." Others, feeling that the conclusions of common sense carried too much weight in international relations whereas the scientific opinions of social science enjoyed no such respect, saw potentialities for the more direct application of knowledge. "We must take what we know of psychology, sociology, science, economics, biology, government and other fields of knowledge and combine them into new and daring patterns," said one enthusiast. At the same time, crusaders like James Marshall of the New York City Board of Education saw in an international educational body the potential for a functional international cooperation based on friendly individual interactions. Others simply desired uninhibited, widespread intellectual cooperation. The central point on which all agreed, however, was the need to make cultural cooperation contribute directly to the maintenance of peace and security. In contrast to the "idealism" of the 1920s, the movement actually thought it could wield irresistible political influence.[25]

It was late in 1942 that the State Department began to receive inquiries from private groups about the possibility of creating an international office of education. Ben Cherrington, in his capacity as chairman of the Committee on International Relations of the NEA, informed the department that "the systematic use of education as a means of promoting peace and democracy will have to be organized, however loosely, on an international basis and become a significant part of international relations and international law." In his writings, Grayson Kefauver was promoting the concept that enduring peace was possible only on the basis of "a widespread understanding of the interrelationship and interdependence of the different nations and the different cultures." In a modern world characterized by technological and cultural interdependence, political machinery would certainly prove ineffective unless it were "supported by widespread social understanding among the peoples of the participating nations." The problem, in Kefauver's mind, was to "search for a functional unity in the midst of cultural diversity." These ideas gained increasing acceptance among national educational and cultural leaders.[26]

Largely at Kefauver's initiative, in March 1943 the Liaison Committee on International Education was established. This was an umbrella organization concerned with promoting an international educational organization and postwar educational reconstruction. Its constituent members included the NEA, the ACLS, the ALA, the American Council on Education, the Institute of International Education, the Carnegie Endowment, the U.S. National Committee on Intellectual Cooperation, and other groups – in short, the cultural relations establishment. The Liaison Committee also took the lead in creating an International Education Assembly. In this fashion, groups like the Council for Education in World Citizenship in Great Britain which were actively pushing for international educational organizations were effectively linked to their American counterparts. In December 1943, the American Association for an International Office of Education, headed by James Marshall and Harlow Shapely of the Harvard College Observatory, was formed for the purpose of mobilizing public opinion among noneducational segments of the American public. Overall, the growth of pressure groups was so rapid and luxuriant that by early 1944 Assistant Secretary of State G. Howland Shaw was "thoroughly confused as to their various interests, slants, interlocking relationships, standings, etc."[27]

The State Department was forced to approach the question obliquely, via the detour of postwar educational reconstruction. In November 1942, the British Council had called together the ministers of education of the various exiled governments then in London. Through its regular sessions this group came to be known as the Conference of Allied Ministers of Education (CAME). Chaired by R. A. B. Butler of the British Board of Education and using the council as its secretariat, the conference formed subcommittees for the consideration of a wide range of European educational problems stemming from the war. Foremost among its concerns was the need to repair the massive physical devastation, but the need for cultural cooperation also came in for a good deal of discussion. Bilateral cultural conventions were approved and an attempt (doomed from the start) was made to produce a history of Europe from a universal perspective. Implicit in the discussions was the desirability of establishing a permanent agency to continue the cooperative programs begun in wartime. Butler in particular made no secret of his plans for transforming the conference "step by step, into a United Nations Agency in the educational and cultural fields."[28]

Shortly after the defeat of Turner's ambitious proposals early in 1943, the Division of Cultural Relations began to ponder postwar educational problems, especially the knotty question of "re-education" in postwar Europe. A meeting in Welles's office in April established the need to draw up a specific blueprint for educational and cultural reconstruction. "Reconstruction" was never strictly defined, but from the beginning it possessed spiritual as well as physical connotations. Nonetheless, department officials were not pleased to see the headline, "U.S. Now Planning To Educate Europe, Official Reveals," plastered over the front page of the *New York Times* in April. It turned out that Commissioner of Education John Studebaker had advocated, at a seminar on international educational reconstruction held at New York University, "education for democracy throughout the world." Clearly, spiritual reconstruction could become a controversial matter. The thinking was that it might be better approached from a physical standpoint first. In June, the General Advisory Committee approved the idea of a collective UN effort in educational reconstruction, looking toward the eventual formation of a permanent UN education entity as an essential part of any world organization. The committee hoped that this international organ would take over the United States' "habitual and unpopular role of missionary to the world."[29]

Shortly afterward, the department began to consider the possibility of sending a representative to the Conference of Allied Ministers in London. According to the report of the London embassy, there was a general feeling that a satisfactory program could not be pushed through without help from the United States. In previous discussions with British representatives, the department had learned that the British were eager to enlist Great Power, especially American, participation in the conference. Although Richard Butler looked forward to the establishment of some form of universal organization, he was convinced that its ultimate success would depend on the collaboration of the Big Four: the U.S., the USSR, China, and Great Britain. A truly cooperative program was inconceivable without their participation. In addition, American financial participation would undoubtedly be crucial to the success of any postwar organization. At the end of May, both the Soviet and American embassies in London dispatched observers to the conference sessions.[30]

To some Americans, this traditional Great Power approach had little appeal. A number of unofficial American observers were depressed by "a continental parochialism in the atmosphere" of the conference, a politics-as-usual approach that seemed devoid of any idealism. Turner would later be critical of the conference's emphasis on bilateral cultural agreements and was skeptical of its potential for future educational and cultural cooperation as it was then organized. Then, too, the hand of the British lay heavily over the proceedings, and some Americans suspected that the British, by means of export subsidies to their publishers and a book drive undertaken for the conference, were planning to replace German cultural influence on the Continent with their own. From Turner's perspective, the field could not be left to British imperial techniques. He regarded it as an American obligation, "politically and culturally," to provide leadership for Europe in place of that previously exercised by the Germans. The multilateral approach with American participation was necessary if the conference were not to degenerate into a traditional European political bartering session.[31]

Upon arriving in London in November 1943, Turner learned that opinion was favorable to transforming the conference into a more permanent body. He immediately prepared a lengthy memo for the department summarizing its achievements and setting forth his belief that American entry into the conference could be made "the occasion for its transformation into a United Nations agency and the shaping of an inclusive international program in the educational and cultural fields." However much military, political, and economic measures might deal with postwar problems, Turner felt that educational and cultural programs were the most direct means of developing "an emotional and intellectual orientation favorable to democracy and cooperative international order." The embassy fully backed Turner's recommendations, especially because the conference leaders were already talking of establishing a permanent "bureau" to address the postwar problems they had been discussing. The time appeared ripe for a move before the British, who already dominated the conference, froze it into a permanent organization.[32]

At this point, officers in the Division of International Security and Organization (ISO), who were charged with planning the general postwar organization, "applied the brake" to what they considered to be a "premature commitment" on the part of the United States. From their perspective, the formation of an international security organization took precedence over all else; ancillary structures could be fitted in later, once security arrangements had been completed. According to Esther Brunauer, who by this time had joined the department, "It would be unfortunate to create centers of power which it might be difficult to integrate in the postwar organization when it is established." Any future cultural organization would have to await prior agreement of the Big Four with respect to security organization. The only forms of international organization that would be permitted pending completion of the general framework were emergency structures dedicated to tackling temporary problems, such as the United Nations Relief and Rehabilitation Administration (UNRRA).[33]

In a way, this enforced halt was fortunate, for the department had not adequately prepared the way at home. Paradoxically, those who had been most critical of the department's inactivity were the same people who now worried about too active a departmental policy. For example, Stephen Duggan wrote to Charles Thomson that many educators had expressed to him the fear that Washington "might attempt to control our new educational activities in foreign countries for other than educational purposes" while excluding private organizations from policy influence. Also, the impression that the department was prepared to meddle in educational affairs abroad, especially strong in Congress, had to be scotched. A final inhibiting factor was that Congress was probably not disposed to act on such a proposal at this time.[34]

One important step in reassuring domestic interests was the hiring of Grayson Kefauver as a special adviser on educational matters. Another move, taken at the suggestion of Leland and Duggan, was to call an informal meeting of educational and cultural leaders at the State Department on January 7, 1944, at which both the department and interested parties outlined their views. This meeting approved a statement of policy that ruled out any intention of "imposing educational personnel, programs, or systems upon enemy or liberated countries." The meeting also endorsed the idea of a UN conference on educational and cultural relations and stressed the continued necessity of consultation between the State Department and private organizations. The result of these developments was a decision to work by indirection: to focus on the interim step of educational reconstruction before erecting a general postwar cultural agency.[35]

On March 20, 1944, the department announced the appointment of a U.S. delegation to be sent to London. The group was headed by Congressman J. William Fulbright, and included Archibald MacLeish, John Studebaker, Dean C. Mildred Thompson of Vassar College, Kefauver, and Turner. By April 9, a draft constitution for the new international body had been completed by the conference, and it was decided to present the text for study and comment to the governments of all the members of the United Nations. Although the proposed body was technically limited to reconstruction, people like Kefauver saw it as a "flexible developing organization" that, toward the end of its life, could be transformed into a permanent body. It provided for an Emergency Rehabilitation Fund to be administered by an emergency-fund committee dominated by the largest contributors. The program was to concentrate on the immediate necessities of providing physical aid and the training of educational personnel. All this, of course, would require congressional authorization.[36]

As the summer went on, nothing further happened and private groups began to complain that permanent organization was being imperiled by inactivity. Late in June the International Education Assembly came out with a strong plea for the establishment of an international education office. James Marshall spoke for his organization and for others when he accused the State Department of having followed a mistaken policy. "It was a tactical mistake to take only a half-bite of the cherry by limiting your present objective to rehabilitation," he wrote to Shaw. His colleague Harlow Shapely pointed out that there was a danger in overemphasizing temporary problems of reconstruction to the point of permanently neglecting a lasting postwar organization. The Educational Policies Commission once again wrote to Hull in August, this time urging him to include education on the agenda of the Big Four meetings at Dumbarton Oaks. The State Department was beginning to worry about the attitude of its constituency. "Unless something is done about this matter, we are going to have an awful lot of explaining to do," remarked one department official.[37]

The source of the delay was the Soviet Union. The Russians had to be consulted and the department was awaiting their answer. Enclosing the draft constitution in a dispatch to Moscow, the department noted that Soviet cooperation was "especially desirable for laying the foundation of a lasting peace." The preliminary soundings had not been encouraging. When asked for his impression of the conference in December 1943, the Soviet observer thought it was "too much subject to British influence" and was organized on "too exclusive a basis." On the other hand, he thought that a principle of representation following the precedents set by UNRRA and the Food Conference would give "undue and perhaps dangerous influence to small states." Another concern was the degree of control that such an organization would exercise over internal educational matters. Obviously the Soviets would tolerate no infringement of their prerogatives of sovereignty. Throughout the interview, the USSR observer "displayed a somewhat deprecatory attitude toward the Conference and intimated that the USSR would prefer to conduct its cultural relations bilaterally."[38]

On the other hand, as Kefauver had noticed at London, the Soviets displayed an "active interest" in the general security organization, "drawing a sharp differentiation between the Conference of Allied Ministers of Education and the type of organization represented by the proposed United Nations Organization." The response from Moscow – or the lack of it – was less than encouraging. The harassed ambassador, W. Averell Harriman, who by this time had accumulated a large backlog of unfinished business with the Soviet bureaucracy, indicated that because of the Russian habit of giving priority attention to military matters, it was "unlikely" that the Soviets would soon express their views on the subject. Harriman suggested that the United States go on to further talks with the British without waiting for the Soviet reply. The department, however, refused to accept these few negative signals from the Russians as an indication of permanent disinterest or opposition, preferring simply to believe that they had not yet formulated a position. Officially, the department clung to the view that it could not foretell the Soviet response, or the kind of cultural organization the Soviet government was interested in.[39]

Neither was the domestic scene propitious for action. Because of the Dumbarton Oaks meetings then in session, the State Department was inclined to wait for the completion of general plans for postwar organization before taking up educational and cultural matters. Then there was Congress to consider. A bill for a permanent cultural relations program was before the House and the department was of the opinion that it should be cleared away before proceeding to educational reconstruction. Assistant Secretary Dean Acheson, in charge of congressional relations for the department, was "very bearish on the chances for favorable action on the Hill in the near future." It turned out that the oblique approach was actually a dead end, for it soon became clear that Congress was extremely chary of appropriating relief funds of any sort through multilateral agencies. The model organization of this sort, UNRRA, was already under heavy attack for inefficiency and for alleged political misuse of supplies, and Congress felt that an educational agency, with its greater sensitivity, might be even more prone to such misadventures.[40]

The combination of Soviet and congressional disinterest in educational reconstruction, coupled with the success of the Dumbarton Oaks conversations, suggested to Kefauver the need for a radical change of plans. The Dumbarton Oaks agreements, in providing for specialized agencies, now made possible the development of a permanent UN agency in the cultural field. Kefauver suggested in late November that the United States shift from a temporary to a permanent agency and that the international rehabilitation fund be scrapped. The Soviets and the other Great Powers, of course, would still need to be consulted beforehand. As for reconstruction, Kefauver suggested other possibilities, such as Export-Import Bank credits or special congressional authorizations. But something had to be done. The ministers of education were "perplexed and a little stunned" that six months had passed without word from either the Americans or the British. Most of all, the opportunity for multilateral cultural cooperation was at hand and had to be seized. "Such cultural relations would have an important bearing on our political and economic relationships," Kefauver reminded his superiors.[41]

At this point, the department shifted back to advocating educational reconstruction in the larger, philosophical sense. A permanent organization now seemed "a more realistic approach to the problem." If domestic politics had dictated hitching reconstruction to cultural matters, they now indicated that they be uncoupled. As for relief, the new assistant secretary of state for public and cultural affairs, Archibald MacLeish, was now inclined to support an effort mounted by private U.S. agencies. MacLeish was reluctant to change aid over to a bilateral format because then, as he noted unhappily, the "conditions imposed will be conditions imposed by us." He had little choice but to keep the congressmen happy, however, and by May 1945 he was blithely telling a House committee that "we thought it was much better to deal with each country on a bilateral basis as we have done in so many other matters." The idea of a cooperative reconstruction program was dropped as a sacrifice to larger multilateral aims.[42]

Another consideration that led away from an organization focusing strictly on reconstruction was the increasing concern of academic groups – those previously dominant in the national cultural program – of being frozen out by a purely educational agency. As early as May 1944, Waldo Leland was warning Thomson that cultural relations in the realm of ideas and the arts were "of tremendous importance and should not be forgotten amidst more technical considerations." In the meantime, scientists were also beginning to ponder the future of their international relationships. The initial inclination of the National Research Council had been to base worldwide scientific cooperation solidly on the "Big Three," that is, the Russian Academy of Sciences, the Royal Society of Great Britain, and the U.S. National Academy of Sciences. By late 1944, however, its Division of Foreign Relations had begun to think of the problem in terms of relating scientific organization to a larger UN agency for intellectual relations. This concern paralleled the campaign of the influential British scientist Joseph Needham for some form of international scientific structure. These intellectual lobbies tended to divert concern from material reconstruction to more permanent questions.[43]

At a meeting of the Secretary's Staff Committee on February 2, 1945, MacLeish finally presented a proposal for a permanent cultural-educational organization within the UN framework. This time Leo Pasvolsky of ISO opposed the suggestion, on the same grounds his division had initially offered. "Until the general organization is established," he argued, "we cannot go ahead on the educational organization without the Russians, but afterwards we can." There it was again, in contradiction to everything that had been said to date about the importance of cultural cooperation. Politics took precedence. In a meeting with an impatient James

Marshall held about this time, Under Secretary of State Joseph Grew made essentially the same point. Grew stressed the importance of "not crossing any wires" before the holding of an eventual United Nations Conference and the establishment of a world organization. In the interim, plans could be presented to Congress and to the allied ministers of education preliminary to the holding of a conference at a later date. Everything depended, however, on the outcome of the United Nations Conference to be held in San Francisco in May 1945.[44]

By and large, the U.S. delegation at San Francisco was preoccupied with the political aspects of the charter. But people like William G. Carr and Cherrington, both of whom were present, lobbied for the inclusion of educational and cultural provisions within the charter of the Economic and Social Council. What difficulties there were stemmed largely from opposition within the American delegation to the idea of a specialized agency with power over educational matters. A number of congressmen within the delegation were under the impression that such an organization would sanction "propaganda abroad or subversive propaganda within the United States under international auspices." Others felt that educational provisions would prove to be a liability in the Senate debate over ratification of the charter. However, the passage of House and Senate resolutions on May 22 and 24 affirming the idea of international educational organizations soon quieted these fears. It remained only to hold out for a specialized international agency that would enjoy a good deal of autonomy from the UN and its political storms. Thus a proposal by Mexico for a Cultural Relations Council was opposed by the United States because it would give the UN authority over educational and cultural matters unacceptable to the United States. The appropriate articles were duly included in the charter. To the last, there was the determination to separate cultural matters from politics.[45]

The dilemma of American power seemed well on the way to resolution. Discussions in the Advisory Committee in early 1944 had disclosed the belief, as MacLeish pointed out, that bilateral cultural agreements were devices "used for hidden propaganda purposes." By March 1945, a conclave of the cultural program's major officials approved a policy recommendation that gave "full support to the development of multilateral conventions by the In-

ternational Organization for Education and Cultural Cooperation." It was realized that this policy was "at variance with the
policies of Great Britain and France" – they neglected to add the
Soviet Union – but it was thought to be in harmony with overall
U.S. policy. "By adopting the universalist approach," the memo
concluded, "it is hoped to strengthen both the proposed International Organization on Education and Cultural Cooperation and to
extend American cultural influences on a broad front." At the
same time, a comprehensive organization would lay to rest the
earlier wartime criticisms regarding the democratic and technological failings of the cultural programs.[46]

Belying these steadfastly idealist sentiments was the apparently
unwelcome fact that the creation of the cultural organization had
to await political agreement among the Great Powers. The horizon of unseemly political interference in cultural affairs extended
beyond the organization's creation, for it was commonly expected
that the Great Powers would exercise paramount influence in its
concerns even following its establishment. On the face of it, these
political facts of life seemed a direct contradiction of the conception of cultural understanding as the foundation of the new world
order. How, then, was it possible to avoid the interpretation that
power politics had not actually dominated this series of events?
Were American policy statements little more than rhetorical fig
leaves for another Holy Alliance?

In the face of much evidence to the contrary, it was assumed
that the successful conclusion of security arrangements among the
Great Powers was rooted, not in power concerns, but in a prior
desire to cooperate – and this made all the difference. From this
perspective, the UN was not a political structure as much as it was
the organizational articulation of an antecedent desire to work together. As the political scientist Robert MacIver explained it,
there existed only two alternatives for world order: internationalism or a power alliance. As he and most other cultural advocates
viewed the prospect of another Holy Alliance as an unbridled ca-
lamity, it was clear that the peculiar brand of "power politics" that
they sanctioned was based on the belief that the Great Powers
were united by a will to a common understanding, not by a temporary concurrence of interests. Had it seemed otherwise, the cultural enthusiasts would have revolted.[47]

Some of the reasons behind World War II's puzzling optimism become clearer when looked at in this light. Roosevelt's determination to establish a personal understanding with Stalin, evident in his radio statement following the meeting at Teheran that the two would get along "very well indeed," reflected in part the belief that personal rapport could help to establish a mutuality of interests. (Even the normally hard-bitten "Uncle Joe" seemed momentarily to succumb to this atmosphere at Yalta.) The refusal to settle political accounts during the war was not simply a means of delaying inevitable disagreements, but also the logical consequence of a belief that a common "understanding" developed among allies in the course of fraternal struggle could come to supersede political differences. The creation of bodies like the United Nations Organization, the Council of Foreign Ministers, and the Allied Control Council in Germany also owed something to this perspective, for in a sense they provided the necessary institutional arenas for the practical working out of a prior desire to cooperate. To an extraordinary degree, international relations were thought to hinge on the perpetuation of mutually favorable attitudes and perceptions. At least this was a widespread sense of the meaning of the word "cooperation" as it was then used. Unfortunately, this meaning was not universally accepted.

CHAPTER 4

The failure of internationalism

A bedrock principle underlying the cultural approach was the conviction that peoples ought to communicate directly with peoples. Although some governmental involvement seemed necessary, the voluntarist tradition dictated that the "task of institutionalizing a set of ideals," as one writer characterized it, should properly remain the preserve of the private sector. The multilateral format was only one expression of this desire to create a world system of cultural cooperation on an informal pattern. The encouragement of wholly private initiatives and the establishment of satisfactory bilateral cultural relations, especially with the Soviet Union, provided still other outlets for nonpolitical cooperation. Following the war, all the channels in the informal frequency band were tried, but with disappointing results. Ironically, they all pointed to the necessity of adopting precisely those nationalist forms of cultural intercourse that the informal approach was supposed to obviate.[1]

The State Department, for its part, urged private interests to spin a vast web of cultural contacts. One such attempt was made, tentatively, in the area of the performing arts. Prior to the war, the concert business in the United States and the management of performing artists had been largely in European, especially German, hands. With the cultural blackout caused by the war, entrepreneurs like Arthur Judson turned the occasion into an opportunity to increase the bookings of American artists, especially in Latin America. Judson's subordinate at Columbia Concerts, André Mertens, prior to visiting Latin America in 1944, characterized his trip as "a real cultural mission," emphasizing the fact that his organization felt "a moral obligation not to try to make money out of it for a while." Through his efforts, Latin Americans were able to hear Helen Traubel, Lauritz Melchior, and Yehudi Menuhin. What held for Latin America could also be true for Europe following the war. " 'Global Music' is not too strong a term to describe the eventualizing of the world plan," Mertens rhapsodized, for with the establishment of a European tour, long dammed-up American talent would find an outlet. Such initiatives fitted in perfectly with the State Department's postwar plans, for the private sector could organize the commercial aspects of cultural interchange and promote policy ideals at the same time.[2]

The problem was that Judson's plans might prove too successful. Although his disclaimers of cultural chauvinism were probably true, other aspects of his effort were less appealing. For one thing, Mertens's past connections were not such as to inspire confidence. Prior to his American career, he had been active in the German music cartel, with responsibility for sewing up the Latin American market. Mertens's references to his German connections and to some of his more unsavory business techniques employed in the service of kultur left a bad taste in the mouths of those to whom he confided his past. Furthermore, Judson, described by the department as the "Music czar (uncrowned) of the concert business" in the United States, made no secret of his ambition to organize a worldwide music cartel. The unleashing of private commercial interests always carried a danger, as Charles Seeger of the Pan American Union observed, that "through a number of tie-ups with industrial technology, commerce, and finance, music could serve as a medium for the building of a policy of economic imperialism for the United States." That would not do at all. The State Department gradually disengaged itself from its flirtation with the empire-building plans of Columbia Concerts.[3]

If some cultural interests were too expansive, others were too parochial. Some musical forces within the United States, especially the American Federation of Musicians and *its* czar, James Petrillo, cared little for cultural arguments. Petrillo was opposed to the grandiose schemes of orchestral management – "wolves and crooks" they were called – because of their excess take as middlemen. Worried about foreign competition, the AFM consistently stood as a bar to the entrance of foreign musicians into the United States, and the prospect of reciprocal business for American musicians touring abroad excited the AFM not at all. "AFM doesn't give a goddam whether United States bands play in foreign countries or not," one of Petrillo's executives snarled to a State Department interviewer. In addition, performing-rights organizations such as ASCAP had a trace of xenophobia in their outlook. "We must give less and less attention to the culture of Europe," one of its pamphlets said in 1944. "This culture has begot strange ideologies, and it is becoming more and more important to us that the impact of these cultures upon our citizenship does not breed here what it has bred there." ASCAP favored a policy of hemispheric isolation, and in fact the hemispheric system of performing rights that had developed organically over the years amounted to what one startled State Department official realized was a cultural equivalent of the Monroe Doctrine. A truculent parochialism, reinforced by deeply vested interests, also was not quite what the department had in mind.[4]

Even when the objectives of the private sector were more in harmony with liberal ideals, the results were not necessarily cheering. The attempt to promote the international flow of literature on a commercial basis stands as a good example. From the time of the establishment of the Division of Cultural Relations, one of the division's interests had been to stimulate the American publishing industry to greater interest in foreign markets. The first tangible step in this process was the journey of five publishing executives to Latin America in June and July 1943 as department travel grantees. Their report confirmed what everyone already knew: American books lagged far behind the European in prestige. As a remedy, they suggested the formation, with government assistance, of a private nonprofit export corporation to promote and coordinate book sales abroad. A meeting of the Foreign Trade Committee of the Book Publishers Bureau the following March ended on a note of urgency. "United States books should become favorably known before German and French books come back to regain the market once wholly theirs," the publishers concluded.[5]

The hazards of redefining the American postwar position in the international book trade were highlighted by a brief controversy with the British in 1944, following the "discovery" that the British were making plans to formally support their postwar book exports. The incident began when George Brett of the Macmillan Company learned that the British Publishers Bureau was setting up a Foreign Trade Committee. For Brett, this move indicated that Britain was "endeavoring to corner the Continental market for book distribution in the postwar world." There were other ominous signs. The British were restricting the marketing rights of books originally published in England and insisted on the British Empire rights to books resold for publication in Great Britain. These and other practices were "very annoying" to Brett. They seemed to point to the conclusion that the British were "in fact endeavoring to eliminate U.S. competition in world markets and confine the American publishers to the sale in the U.S. only insofar as a book in the English language is concerned."[6]

The British were in fact trying to protect their postwar markets from what they perceived to be the danger of American intrusion. A privately issued 1943 report of the British Publishers Association maintained that "the welfare of the British and American letters (and hence the welfare of Anglo-American culture) required the continuing existence of two primary publishing world centres." It followed that the British needed "a protected market comparable in extent to that of the American system." Talk of free markets and the Open Door was all well and good, but the Americans seemed to be "entirely unaware that the questions they were raising bore in any way upon the structure and stability of the British Empire." In a letter to Malcolm Johnson of Doubleday, Doran, Inc., Walter G. Harrap amplified these themes. "We are merely defending what we built," he asserted, and British publishers were unwilling to cede their markets "without a struggle." Because of the smaller size of the British home market, Dominion and Continental sales were absolutely essential in maintaining maximum operating efficiency and competitive prices.[7]

Nonetheless, American publishers reacted as if they were being faced with a bibliophile's version of the Navigation Acts. Asked to investigate the matter, the American embassy in London confirmed that the British were indeed following the maxim, "Trade follows the book." It also pointed out that the book trade had political importance deriving from its cultural and propagandist effects. American exports amounted to 5.5 million volumes per year or 2.5 percent of total annual book sales, whereas British publishers exported 48 million volumes per year, or roughly 30–35 percent of their gross annual output. But on the whole, the embassy downplayed the British export effort. The British Council had an annual budget of only 3.5 million pounds, whereas the

National Book Council, blown up in American minds to be a huge threat, actually operated on a small scale. The British Publishers Association itself operated on an annual budget of only 3,000 pounds. The scope and nature of British operations did not seem to warrant making it an intergovernmental issue.[8]

Still, American publishers were convinced of the need to revise their export mechanisms. In addition to expanded business, Brett felt that "the United States must play its proper role in this world-wide spread of the English language." A memo by Harry Warfel of the department backed up this enthusiasm. "The book is not now forcefully employed as an ambassador of good will or as an instrument to the introduction of United States technology, science, manufacturing, medicines, etcetera," he argued. He pointed out that "Germany, France and Italy controlled higher education, scientific research and technology in the other American republics, as well as in Russia and Japan, by uniting publications and educational activities." Apparently, the Germans had operated on the theory that if there were "any knowledge of value, it should appear in German," and with the help of such support, German had become the lingua franca of scholarship. This influence would have to be eradicated and supplanted, and American publishers were equipped with both idealistic and pragmatic rationales for desiring to do so.[9]

Their willingness to cooperate provided a perfect opportunity to merge cultural objectives with the Open Door tenets of commercial policy. The department felt that it had to take an interest in what was being done by private business in the cultural sphere. For one thing, reports from the missions argued that the United States was "missing the bus in this vital matter." For another, there seemed little danger of political repercussions. "We have a long way to go before any 'commercial-cultural imperialism' could be charged," argued Richard Heindel. Besides, there appeared to be little choice in the matter. "Competition with foreign cartels will destroy us, we are alone in the world," warned the Office of War Information's Llewelyn White, who was consulted in the book project. "The only way to have a progressive book industry is to give Government support and to put the active control of the program in the hands of industry." Reservations were expressed about the degree of government support, though. Active encouragement was fine indeed, but the government balked at the prospect of becoming a financial partner. Finally, the privately financed United States International Book Association (USIBA) was incorporated in New York in January 1945 as a nonprofit corporation.[10]

This organization cartelized the American book industry for overseas business only. It was to act as the sales agent abroad for U.S. publishers, and was to be supported by dues and commissions from its sales. Its organization came about despite the well-known fact that the U.S. book industry was "notoriously individualistic." USIBA's purpose was to assist the government's cultural relations program by promoting the sale of American books abroad, thus blending idealism with commercialism. "If this program is handled right on the right cultural level," argued Eugene Reynal, "we will build not only a vast new business for the future but new friends for our country and new horizons for ourselves." Yet it was a peculiarly conceived cartel. In March 1945, E. M. Crane of D. Van Nostrand Company argued that the creation of USIBA was "a move toward greater freedom in the international book trade than otherwise." Unlike most cartels, its objective was not to organize and divide the world market, but to break it up and to allow scope for American enterprise. Rhetorically, at least, it was a cartel to end cartels.[11]

USIBA lasted only two years before being dissolved early in 1947. One reason for its failure was that Europeans had little money to spend on anyone's books and USIBA was not equipped to deal with this problem – it could aim only for its share of scarcity. Despite some publishers' pleas, the U.S. government was unable to provide credits to foreign governments for book purchases or to use the machinery of the Export-Import Bank for this purpose. But the primary reason was internal, for the same individualism that had created the need for USIBA now led to its breakup. Edward Crane put the blame on a small "isolationistic" group of publishers for withdrawing their support. The sorry fact was that any cooperative venture required the cooperation of all. Soon afterward, George Brett mourned the failed attempt at "a wholesome worldwide distribution of books containing the ideologies of democracy."[12]

Initially, the department entertained hopes that the industry could launch a renewed export effort. "If the book trade can be made to pull together on these problems," one officer reasoned, "a great load of responsibility can be shifted from State to private industry." Although most departmental economic experts continued to think that the problem was one the trade should work out for itself, the publishers were increasingly insistent that money for book purchases be earmarked through various governmental aid programs. The whole problem of lagging exports was intimately connected with the problem of blocked currencies, about which private business interests could do little. But by late 1947, State Department officials like Assistant Secretary William Benton were beginning to despair of private difficulties sorting themselves out. The other alternative was to wait "until the Department is given the directive and the funds to do the job." It was a position that would gain increasing prominence within the government.[13]

The obverse of a purely private effort in cultural relations was a multilateral enterprise such as that envisioned by the proposed United Nations cultural organization. The basic premise behind this "promising plant in the herbarium of world government," as one official described it, was that world peace required the growth of a global sense of community. As the Frenchman Henri Bonnet put it in an eloquent appeal: "For once, let us show the way, let us supersede politics and define our ideals in such a way that politics will have to work for them." The problem of community was usually described in terms of reorienting men's thought processes. In a radio broadcast, Archibald MacLeish expressed this outlook perfectly when he stated that "our frontier today is in the minds of men whose job is to create a climate of opinion which will make war impossible." War was conceived partly as a state of mind, a view that can be traced at least as far back as Hobbes. The idea was put awkwardly, but accurately, by a State Department officer groping for the proper formulation. "The problem today," Charles Child asserted, "is to think ourselves into 'One World.'"[14]

The failure of the Soviet Union to agree to participate in the London conference planned for November 1945 caused a good deal of concern. The State Department fervently wanted the Soviets to join, feeling that Soviet "cultural isolation" could be, as Grayson Kefauver argued, "a cause of division among nations and a threat to peace." But Moscow chargé d'affaires George Kennan predicted that the Soviets would not join an organization the "aims of which might run contrary to control of thought and strict censorship prevailing in [the] Soviet Union," and he recommended that the conference be held without them, if need be. Elbridge Durbrow at the Russian desk agreed. The time had come, he maintained, when "with or without the Soviet Union, the other powers ought to proceed with the establishment of such international organizations as they consider necessary." Anxieties were calmed somewhat by reports from London that the Soviets were deferring consideration of the issue until the UN organization had established its Economic and Social Council. This continued to be the State Department's hope through the first months of 1946.[15]

When the conference finally met, there was a remarkable degree of unanimity in drafting the principles of the new organization. A major innovation was the decision to include scientific cooperation as part of its agenda, thus giving rise to the cognomen United Nations Educational, Scientific and Cultural Organization (UNESCO). Departing from the League's tradition of private intellectual cooperation, the new entity was to be composed of governments and not of individuals, as befitting a UN body. Furthermore, UNESCO was to promote peace and security directly, as opposed to the League Committee's goal of stimulating professional-intellectual contacts. As a balm to wounded French sensibilities, Paris was made the permanent headquarters. In addition, French insistence upon recognizing intellectual eminence found expression in the agreement to create private participating bodies or national commissions that would be related to the new organization. After the conclusion of the conference, a Preparatory Commission headed by League Committee veteran Sir Alfred Zimmern was charged with preparations for organizing a permanent secretariat and drafting a preliminary program for UNESCO.[16]

The concept of popular participation in UNESCO had a natural appeal to most Americans. Groups like the Independent Citizens Committee on the Arts, Sciences and Professions, and educators like Ben Cherrington and James Marshall were intent on "creating a widespread, democratic participation of the American people in the international organization." They hoped to turn "a charter of nations into a charter of peoples." Basically, they favored a return to the conference system of 1939, and their views on the public–private relationship also harkened back to those days. Others, such as the influential political scientist Robert MacIver, hoped that the representatives to UNESCO would "not be appointed as spokesmen for their governments but as the free representatives of the cultural life of their respective countries." These groups considered the call for national commissions to be an extension of the principle of voluntary association to the multilateral sphere under governmental auspices.[17]

After a series of consultations with private groups early in 1946, the department adopted the National Commission concept. Although it was agreed at one of the meetings that the locus of sovereignty was not at issue, ensuing difficulties produced a contrary impression. Agreement was cloaked in filmy language, such as the statement that the commission was "a means by which official personality becomes private personality." Once the decision had been made, arguments broke out afresh over the size of the commission. The State Department favored a small, directly appointed group, whereas James Marshall called for a large, representative body that would not become "an adjunct or colony of the State Department." Marshall steadfastly opposed the creation of what he called "a bureaucratic barrier between UNESCO and the organizations and the people." Marshall won a victory with Congress, which decided upon a cumbersome National Commission of one hundred members and which recognized the principle of representation. But the ambiguity remained. Although admitting that the commission would have to be "broadly representative," the State Department continued to maintain a penchant for a politically less troublesome system of virtual representation.[18]

Those who argued against identification with the State Department were generally the most vociferous in support of UNESCO programs that aimed directly at peace and security, whereas those favoring an enlarged governmental role were usually the exponents of purely intellectual activities for UNESCO. The first group felt that the department would politicize its cultural efforts, whereas the second felt that there was nothing to politicize as cultural relations were basically professional intellectual relations. In the forefront of those calling for a narrower political role for UN-ESCO were leaders in the specialized academic tradition such as Waldo Leland, scientists, and pragmatists like Luther Evans of the Library of Congress. Leland's position, as he argued it to Congress, was that "all possible emphasis must be put on the fact that UNESCO is dealing with educational, scientific, and cultural matters, *at the intellectual level,* and not with political or economic matters." There was, after all, "a danger of talking about UNESCO as though it were the Security Council." This view advocated what the sociologist Edward Shils called the "reconstruction of the International Republic of Learning." Luther Evans felt it was the function of the diplomats to prevent war, that "there was nothing education, science and culture or mass communications could do to solve this short-run problem" – and many agreed with his view.[19]

Others were much more ambitious. The big question for William G. Carr and the National Education Association was: "How can the nations best direct their respective educational systems to the inculcation of knowledge, attitudes and skills which 'contribute to peace and security'?" In its simplest form, the problem took the form of asking, as did one earnest delegate to the National Commission's first meeting, "What is it we want to write into the hearts of the people?" As UNESCO was an instrument of peace, the argument went, it ought to be actively used. The sense of activism could also be expressed in a more negative way, such as Stephen Duggan's suggestion that UNESCO should act as a watchdog and report "any educational or other cultural development in any country likely to disturb the peace of the world." The activist view of social science was seen in Robert MacIver's call for "the laying of the scientific foundations for the interpretation of people to people."[20]

Whatever the differences among program philosophies, there was unity on one underlying principle – the freedom of ideas. Harking back to the experiences of the 1930s, even Waldo Leland flatly stated that "without complete intellectual freedom collaboration in intellectual tasks is impossible." Freedom of ideas also meant freedom of communication, a concept central to all of UNESCO's proposed activities. Not only censorship, but tariff restrictions against books, differences in copyright laws, and exchange restrictions of all kinds existed as obstacles to uninhibited communication. "Can the United States indefinitely admit the right of foreign governments to cut off all contact between their people and the rest of the world?" Benton wondered. The answer was no. In a speech delivered before the National Commission, he argued that the assembled group was "at the beginning of a long process of breaking down the walls of national sovereignty and of persuading the peoples of the world to study each other and to cooperate with each other."[21]

All of these ideals notwithstanding, nationalism and politics were unwelcome intruders at the first General Conference held in Paris in November 1946. The most contentious issue was the selection of a director-general for the new organization, a prestigious post in the intellectual world. Very early Benton recognized that the United States could force the election of an American if it so desired. Through the first half of 1946, a rather desultory process of winnowing candidates took place in the State Department. Then, about the middle of August, it became apparent that Julian Huxley, the noted biologist who had taken over the direction of the Preparatory Commission after Zimmern had fallen ill, had become an avowed candidate and was in fact accumulating support rapidly. Suddenly it seemed necessary to produce an American candidate of comparable intellectual distinction, and in short order.[22]

Unexpectedly, the matter was taken out of the State Department's hands by President Truman, who decided that former Attorney General Francis Biddle, a lawyer, should be given the position. Truman was paying off a political debt and he simply assumed that UNESCO was as amenable to the workings of patronage as any other institution. For his part, Biddle agreed to become a candidate only if it were clear that there was no significant opposition to his selection, and he refused to openly campaign for the job. This opened up a can of worms for the State Department. For at the same time that it discovered a nearly unanimous distaste for Huxley among American intellectuals, it was stuck with Biddle, an eminently uninspiring candidate.[23]

Opposition to Huxley within the United States was intense, and all sorts of withering fire was directed at him. He was supposed to be a weak administrator; as an extremely acerbic individual, he tended to alienate people; he was a popularizer rather than a working scientist; he was also left-wing in his political sympathies. His greatest defect to American eyes, though, was that he was an atheist. But neither was Francis Biddle any prize. Members of the delegation who went to Paris expecting an open election were disgusted with the department for its failure to consult with them on the decision, and disappointed with its quality as well, for Biddle was entirely innocent of intellectual or literary pretensions. But the British would not be dissuaded from presenting Huxley's name in nomination before the executive board or from giving him their moral support. On the other hand, Biddle disdained to campaign, and the department was prevented from nominating a stronger candidate by the president's decision.[24]

The result was a half-hearted promotion by the State Department of Biddle's candidacy, which foundered as soon as it was launched. By the end of November, Benton had convinced himself and Secretary of State James Byrnes that there was "no important reason why we should insist on an American" as director-general. But to withdraw Biddle would be to elect Huxley. So the Americans stalled and hoped the executive board might providentially find an alternative candidate. A compromise worked out between Leon Blum of France and Benton whereby Huxley would have been demoted to chairman of the executive board was rejected by the British. They finally agreed to a plan wherein Huxley consented to serve a truncated term of two years rather than the six stipulated in the charter. As part of the bargain, it was also agreed to appoint an American deputy director-general, Walter Laves, as a counterweight to Huxley and to give the executive board expanded powers at the expense of the director-general. After all these Byzantine moves, Huxley was overwhelmingly elected.[25]

An event that consumed less total energy but that burned with greater intensity was the brief flare-up of East–West sensibilities at the conference. Consternation broke out when Wladislaw Ribnikar, the Yugoslav delegate, attacked the thesis that "wars are made in the minds of men" as directly contrary to the truths of historical materialism. Ribnikar warned that exclusive insistence upon this philosophy would hinder, rather than promote, cultural cooperation between nations. Ominously, Ribnikar reminded the delegates that cultural cooperation was inconceivable without the collaboration of the Soviet Union. To the American embassy in Moscow, alert to any ideological explanations for Soviet behavior, Ribnikar's polemic was "a highly significant statement." Ambassador Walter Bedell Smith even thought it might be some sort of mistake, for he believed that no Soviet representative "would have dared so incautiously to snatch aside the veil from real Soviet objectives." He concluded that "it must have been a gratuitous somersault by an anxious but as yet improperly trained seal." Great Power suspicions were closing in on UNESCO.[26]

The mingling of politics and intellect, ideological or otherwise, came as a shock to most of the Americans present. In his report to Secretary Byrnes, Benton frankly stated that "this has been a political conference," while also expressing his amazement at the fractiousness of intellectuals in general. He was seconded by Arthur H. Compton, who thought that UNESCO might become "a major arena for international political struggle." Europeans certainly did not hesitate to view cultural matters from a political perspective, as the Huxley incident demonstrated. To some it appeared that the European nations were using cultural politics in an attempt to compensate for their diminished prestige in other areas. The French at least made no bones about it, frankly admitting that this was "one area where they could maintain their position as one of the great powers." The brief tiff with the Yugoslavs was yet another surprising portent. Benton concluded from all this that UNESCO would become "a hotbed of politics." "Men will struggle to control it," he predicted, "for ideas are weapons." He recommended that in the future Americans needed to be "more politically aware and informed."[27]

These episodes provided grist for Benton's rapidly maturing belief that UNESCO policy should properly be integrated with the rest of the State Department's operations. To date, his calls had gone unheeded and the UNESCO Relations Staff remained a bureaucratic backwater. Benton was especially irritated to discover that men of military background, such as Walter Bedell Smith and Dwight D. Eisenhower, seemed to show a greater appreciation of the importance of cultural relations than did many of the "trained" political officers. But he continued to press his case. "It is important for the department and its political officers to recognize the great present and potential importance of informational and cultural activities at the international level," he told Byrnes following the conference. UNESCO activities could not afford to be ignored by the department. Benton was convinced that "the only job of selling so far as UNESCO is now concerned, is to sell it to the State Department itself."[28]

Early in 1947, the department showed a flurry of interest in UNESCO. Its attention became riveted on potential sub rosa Communist infiltration of the organization rather than on political worries as such. A number of appointments made by Huxley appeared to have been made for the purpose of promoting left-wing viewpoints within the secretariat. Ambassador Jefferson Caffery in Paris was clearly troubled. "Should Moscow succeed in gaining control or even influencing the vast machinery proposed in UNESCO," he speculated, "the Comintern would enjoy a perfect cover for all sorts of operations, including the highly important economic and scientific espionage." The problem was worrisome to some members of the National Commission as well. President George Shuster of Hunter College thought that the exposure of Communist infiltration would shock Americans, and that something needed to be done. "We cannot wait until some sort of inquiry threatens the life of the organization as a whole," he concluded.[29]

The issue was precipitated within the department by a memorandum of Feburary 7, 1947, from General Hoyt Vandenberg, the director of the Central Intelligence Group, to President Truman, which pointed up the danger arising from the appointment of known Communist sympathizers to sensitive UNESCO positions. The conclusion was that UNESCO had "*considerable* potential for trouble." Under Secretary Dean Acheson quickly called a department meeting to consider the matter. Shortly thereafter, the political officers sent a joint memo to Benton in which they stated their conviction that there existed a grave danger of UNESCO being turned into an ideological tool and in which they recommended tightened departmental control over its activities. Ironically, Benton was now placed on the defensive within the department for failing to implement policies that he had been solitarily advocating all along. In any case, the Moscow embassy was soon relieved to learn that the department was taking a "firm position with respect to efforts now underway to effect penetration and eventual ideological control of UNESCO."[30]

Yet it was easier to acknowledge the problem than to do something about it. The Paris embassy spoke to Walter Laves, who suggested the appointment of a personnel officer, preferably American, sympathetic to the department's point of view. But this was only a long-range solution. The department also discussed the matter frankly with the British and urged them to go along with the United States in deliberately delaying recruitment decisions at meetings of the executive board. Meanwhile, the department was attempting to develop security-cleared candidates of its own for consideration. Pressure was also brought to bear informally upon Huxley, with Benton arguing that "ideologies as such are out of place in UNESCO." The department was not objecting to the appointment of Communists from member states, but of Communist sympathizers from Western states. Although Benton was conscious of the undesirability of national governments intruding into the affairs of the secretariats of international organizations, he believed that in this case "national interest" made it imperative for the United States "to exercise whatever influence we can short of direct interference in Secretariat affairs."[31]

These initiatives were only partially successful because the problems of UNESCO ran deeper, down to the very foundations of its internationalist architecture. The department was extremely limited in its ability to take political action because UNESCO was not politically designed. Thus it could not even legally control the activities of its representative on the executive board, a body that dealt with such critical issues as admission of new member states, relations with nongovernmental organizations, choice of top personnel, and coordination of UNESCO policy with the UN. It was theoretically possible for a member to disagree with his government's stance on any issue, although it was soon obvious that most members were following their governments' "lines" very closely, even if in an unofficial capacity. The first U.S. representative, Archibald MacLeish, was not happy about being asked to represent official U.S. government positions, and he did so only grudgingly. When he resigned early in 1947, the department noted that "he carried out the letter but not the spirit of the informal arrangements." The situation was so anomalous that MacLeish's successor, Dean Richard McKeon of the University of Chicago, had to be briefed "informally" by the department regarding the sensitivity of his position and asked to cooperate.[32]

By April, the department was convinced that executive board representation should be at the governmental level. Arguments to the National Commission proposing a constitutional amendment stressed "the always possible conflict between national interests and the views of members of the Executive Board acting as individuals." The National Commission appointed a subcommittee to investigate the problem, and a draft report issued in August delivered a split decision. One faction sided with the department, whereas another disagreed with the need to amend UNESCO's constitution. "Such action by the United States Government would have an unfortunate effect on public opinion within the United States where great importance is attached to UNESCO and the conception of UNESCO as an agency through which 'peoples can speak to peoples,'" its opponents argued, "particularly in view of the state of ideological warfare in which the world now finds itself." The move might be interpreted by other nations as a cynical abandonment by the United States of the ideals on which UNESCO was founded. The issue was finally put before the next meeting of the General Conference held in Mexico City in December 1947. After a few months, the temporary committee appointed to study the American resolution advocated no change in the existing system of representation. The United States would have to assure the assertion of its positions on the executive board by means of informal understandings with its representative.[33]

If this were not enough, the State Department found itself being circumvented by UNESCO in decisions that it felt properly called for its prior approval. Huxley and the secretariat had enthusiastically begun to make liaison arrangements with all sorts of dubious global professional organizations. All this was done without consulting the department. One example of the secretariat's obliviousness to national sensibilities was its invitation to the playwright Lillian Hellman to attend a meeting of theater experts in Paris in July. Hellman, although not a Communist herself, had a long history of association with Communist activities. Upon learning of the invitation, the department worried that her attendance might "embarrass the Government and bring unfavorable reaction in the public press and elsewhere." It did. Congressman Karl Mundt soon demanded to know "what the Department intended to do to make certain that spokesmen for this country abroad are representative Americans in the same sense that spokesmen for Russia, for example, are representative of the USSR when they speak in international deliberations" Mundt's inquiry was not to be taken lightly, as he was the principal sponsor of the legislation for a permenent cultural relations program then before the House.[34]

The department immediately cabled to Paris requesting that Huxley withdraw Hellman's invitation, implicitly threatening reduced participation in UNESCO unless a system of prior consultation were introduced. The cable arrived too late to change the decision, but in the following week, the department came up with a new policy regarding the appointment of U.S. nationals to serve in international organizations, one that argued that there were compelling reasons to see that "the American point of view was represented by truly representative Americans." It took the position that any international organization should at least consult with the department before making appointments or issuing invitations. This was desirable "for general political reasons and because this government is generally in a better position than an international body or any international official to ascertain who are the best and most truly representative experts within its own country." The problem with Miss Hellman was that she was not an official U.S. representative, and the solution seemed to lie in formalizing representation as much as possible. As it turned out, Miss Hellman did not cause any controversy while in Paris. But by September, UNESCO was providing immediate notification to all governments concerning its appointments of experts.[35]

Not only was the department straining to define national authority abroad, it was also having similar problems in its own backyard. From the beginning, the relationship between the National Commission and the department had been "somewhat edgy and uncertain." The basis for this uneasiness lay in the widespread belief in unhindered popular communication. Milton Eisenhower, the first chairman of the National Commission, expressed this sentiment when he told its members that "you and I do not look upon ourselves as members of the State Department or as instruments of an exclusively national policy." Some members like James Marshall actively denigrated the "cult of expertness" in foreign affairs, and questioned whether peace could be achieved by technicians, no matter how high-minded. Marshall insisted that "men, rather than states . . . are the ultimate foundations of good will," and that voluntary bodies were "the backbone of any organized popular participation in international affairs." Prior to the Mexico City conference, Eisenhower issued a press release claiming that "*private citizens* participating in National Commission work in the United States have determined the policy of our country in this highly important international conference." In some respects, the National Commission had done its job too well.[36]

In no other nation in the world did a National Commission conceive of its role in so sweeping a fashion. In fact, most UNESCO members had no National Commissions at all, and the ones that did exist were politically docile bodies. But in the United States, given the tradition of private policy influence, the locus of policy control was still in question in the minds of many. A number of commission members thought that the UNESCO Relations Staff should either be separated from the Department of State or be semiautonomous within the department. Even though on a number of occasions Benton had referred dramatically to the commission as "a veritable NRA of pressure groups," both he and the department were more responsive to a popular anti-Communist ground swell that coincided with the department's maturing political perception of UNESCO. As a result, the department came increasingly to insist on its primacy in matters of policy.[37]

This situation produced short tempers. Upon hearing of the National Commission's balkiness at its annual conference held in Chicago in September 1947, especially in connection with the issue of separation from the State Department, Loy Henderson of the Office of Near Eastern and African Affairs dashed off a scorching memo:

The State Department represents the people of the United States in its relations with foreign groups. For a group of citizens to bypass the Department and attempt to represent the people of the United States to the people of other nations is actually usurping a function of the Government and is setting up an institution with no responsibilities to Government, although supported by Government, which might follow policies frustrative of foreign policies of Government. If they wish to indicate their voice as free citizens of a democracy, they may do so, but such a voice should not be subsidized by Government funds and should not be heard in a United Nations organization in which other participants are governmental organizations.

Henderson insisted that the policies of the commission "must run parallel with the foreign policies of the Government," and there was no doubt in his mind as to who made policy. His viewpoint was backed by an opinion from the department's legal adviser that downgraded the National Commission's role to an "advisory capacity." This was the voice of the Logan Act speaking; but more importantly, it was an outright repudiation of the premises upon which the cultural program had been founded.[38]

Realistically, the department was in no position to demand obeisance from the National Commission. For the time being, the department could only, as a member of the UNESCO Relations Staff discreetly put it, "continue in education of the members of the National Commission about the attitudes of the Department – with the aim of forestalling any separatist tendencies in the Commission and of improving the Department's public relations throughout the country." Benton's assessment of the Chicago meeting was a little more optimistic, as he had become accustomed to working with a mulish National Commission. According to his version of events, "the fear that the Commission might be made a Department 'stooge'" seemed to be abating. But then, Benton judged the commission by its adult potential rather than by its adolescent delinquencies. He urged the department to accept it "as an opportunity in private and public relations for the department as a whole, and not merely as part of a headache involved in the handling of UNESCO, as some have tended to regard it." These "solutions," however, could just as well have been considered evasions of the problem.[39]

The difficulty was that each side had now come to think in terms of "two worlds" – the department, in terms of East and West; the National Commission, or at least its die-hard liberals, in terms of the world of power and the world of education – and the two sets of images were not congruent. The State Department now took the position that universality would have to reflect American national values, and not the reverse. Benton's deputy, Howland Sargeant, freely argued that "in the atmosphere of cooperation offered by UNESCO, the world can be persuaded of the advantages of tolerance and free opinion, the American way of life." And Benton, who had earlier noted with surprise the tendency for other nations to use UNESCO as an instrument of national policy, had by this time lost his innocence. "We shall not hesitate to use it ourselves for this purpose as long as our policy is world peace," he vowed. Given the increasing frequency of such assumptions, Benton's personal assistant, John Howe, predicted that soon UNESCO would be under pressure to become "the intellectual spearhead of the non-Communist world." Indeed, the tip was already being sharpened by people like Ann O'Hare McCormick, who wondered "how to reach the people of Russia over the opposition of their own government."[40]

The Second General Conference of UNESCO, which met in Mexico City in December 1947, typified the irritations under which American policy was laboring. Educators like Reuben Gustavson and James Marshall claimed that the delegation meetings suffered from the department's presence, were "too political," and tended to make UNESCO "a small sounding board of the U.N." But in Benton's estimation, political questions were "the most important problems with which the delegation had to deal." Thus the delegates were made to swallow their castor oil in the form of a full briefing on the dangers of Communist influences within UNESCO. And quickly enough, the Americans became embroiled in a debate with the Poles over accusations of U.S. cultural imperialism. Then too, the continuing attempt to shape a program for UNESCO witnessed some unseemly scientific wallowing in the political mud. Small wonder, then, that Benton could lament the absence of the "evangelical spirit" that had typified the London conference. Somehow, it had all given way to "arguments about the budget, conflicts between the educators and the scientists, and most depressing of all, to the dialectical exchange with the Poles." The pure hopes of 1945 had been overtaken by less edifying realities.[41]

The major problem, of course, was the Soviet Union. UNESCO had deposited many of its hopes in the Bank of Great Power Cooperation, only to find its assets had been frozen. The difficulties experienced in UNESCO derived in part from the inability of the United States to establish a satisfactory relationship with the USSR on a bilateral basis. Even the universalist Ben Cherrington had been clear on the overarching importance of this point: "The central objective in the United States foreign policy should be to discover how to cooperate effectively with Russia," he had argued in mid-1945. No one, of whatever persuasion, would have disagreed with his estimate. The question was how to bring it about. As it turned out, the informal approach also failed on this level of contact.[42]

Wartime auguries of future cultural cooperation between the two nations were mixed, but, on the whole, promising. Prior to the establishment of diplomatic relations in 1933, informal cultural contacts had been the primary mode of contact between America and Russia. Attached to these excursions, however, had always been the disagreeable aroma of questionable ideological purpose or the unedifying quest for profit. But now that the atmosphere of wartime unity seemed to presage genuine cultural cooperation, both the public and the private sectors made haste to prepare themselves for the new day. There were at the time, as Henry Allen Moe later recalled, "pressures from the general atmosphere" urging friendly cultural contact with the Soviets. The foundations, as usual, were in the forefront of the movement with their increasingly generous support of Eastern European and Slavic studies, and enrollments in Russian language courses were booming in colleges across the nation. The prospects for extensive cultural exchanges seemed very promising when Stephen Duggan revealed in 1943 that he had been approached by a Soviet official who requested his cooperation in arranging for student exchanges with Soviet universities following the war.[43]

The view from Moscow, however, was not so auspicious. Following the Moscow conference in October 1943, Ambassador Harriman presented a series of modest proposals for wartime cultural collaboration between the two allies. After fruitless attempts to coax a response from the Soviets, George Kennan finally complained to Harriman that there was "relatively little interest on the Soviet side in what we are trying to do." Kennan was arguing on the basis of a background memo written by John Paton Davies, sardonically titled "Why Russian Culture Stinks!," which enumerated all the instances in which the Soviets had been unresponsive. Housing for the information program, the breakdown of movie arrangements, lack of contact with Soviet editors, the failure of the Soviet news agency TASS to distribute or use American materials – absolutely no satisfaction was given. The Soviet cultural agency, VOKS, was described as "cheerful, verbally cooperative, and completely inefficient." For Kennan, however, the matter involved considerations more vital than bureaucratic efficiency. "It is a question of the spirit, not of the detailed execution," he maintained. The fact that the Soviets were instituting bilateral cultural contacts with the Finns, Bulgarians, and Italians was a disturbing indicator of a perhaps deliberate neglect on their part. Tired of endless wrangling with the Soviet bureaucracy, Harriman soon turned a deaf ear to all State Department entreaties to arrange cultural missions on the grounds that nothing could be done until the conclusion of the war.[44]

Stateside, there seemed little cause for alarm, as many people considered truculence to be historically ingrained in the Russian psyche. As Secretary Hull maintained, "So they have a different psychology – that is all . . . it takes a little time for them to adjust themselves to the internationalist harness, so to speak." In any case, the pressures that had been contained during the war soon escaped in bursts of enthusiasm for cultural contacts. A prominent librarian informed MacLeish that the nation's curators were "getting restless" over the question of adding Russian books to their libraries. By June, the Library of Congress had called a conference on Russian acquisitions to discuss plans for building up the Russian resources of the nation's major libraries. Stephen Duggan eagerly called for the beginnings of large student transfers. Others soon began to clamor for such disparate projects as sending the Red Army Chorus to the United States, dispatching the Boston Symphony Orchestra on a tour of the USSR, or, mystifyingly, sending a U.S. football team on a goodwill visit. More impractically yet, MacLeish, in his new capacity as assistant secretary of state for public and cultural affairs, suggested to Harriman that a cultural attaché be appointed for the Moscow embassy. MacLeish thought that Lillian Hellman, who had recently spent some time in Russia at the special invitation of the Soviets, would make an ideal choice. The fact that the Soviets had invited nearly fifty American scientists to the 220th anniversary celebration of the Russian Academy of Sciences in May offered an encouraging sign for such initiatives.[45]

George Kennan remained skeptical. Feeling that groups at home were deluding themselves, he warned in a dispatch of May 23, 1945, that "insuperable obstacles" confronted "even the most rudimentary cultural interchange." "As long as a rigid police control effectively shields all but a tiny group of Russians from contact with foreign influence," he predicted, "cultural exchanges between the Soviet Union and other countries will be held to a minimum." Kennan thought it "dangerous to permit the impression to grow in American intellectual circles that a large increase in cultural contacts is technically possible and is favored by the Soviet Government." A conversation between Andrei Gromyko and Elbridge Durbrow held in July seemed to confirm Kennan's forebodings. Gromyko tartly ended discussion on the topic with the remark that "the objective was excellent but the time was hardly ripe." In other words, the political climate was not temperate enough to support cultural initiatives.[46]

But the cultural community bubbled over with an irrepressible optimism, especially following the return of Harlow Shapely and others from what was trumpeted as a vastly successful conclave of scientists in Moscow during the first week in June. And indeed, such an attitude still dominated the thinking of the cultural personnel within the department itself. Harold Lasswell's recommendation that the United States and the Soviets adopt a mutual policy of "condemning cultural armaments races and psychological warfare" was not lost on Benton. The department smiled on a proposal tendered by Harlow Shapely in October on behalf of the National Academy of Sciences and the American Philosophical Society to invite a large delegation of Soviet scientists and scholars to the United States. From the viewpoint of James B. Conant of Harvard, scientific interchange appeared to be one of the few open channels of communication between the two nations. "On all other fronts there is bound to be so much suspicion and misunderstanding as to make communication difficult," he reasoned. Other interests mounted persuasive arguments as well. Thus in October 1945, Kennan found himself staring at yet another departmental request to sound out the Soviets on a comprehensive program of cultural exchanges.[47]

By early 1946, a gap had opened between the perceptions of Russian experts within the department and fervent exponents of cultural interchange. The embassy and the Division of Eastern European Affairs were disgusted not only by Soviet intransigence, but also by what appeared to be an unseemly scrambling for favors from the Soviets by private American interests. They came to prefer a more formal, national approach to the chaos of indiscriminate importunities. The embassy recommended that a single coordinating agency be set up in Washington to handle cultural topics and that all requests be handled through the embassy. In addition, Soviet experts thought that all exchanges should be handled on a strict quid pro quo basis. A conference held in the department on February 27, 1946, sought to reach a consensus on exchange policy. It was agreed that private bodies could continue to solicit scholarship visitors from the USSR, so long as it was clear that the exchanges were to be "a two-way affair." Even this was a bit too much to concede in the thinking of the Moscow embassy, for it seemed pointless to pursue an objective that had been politically occluded.[48]

One rationalization used by people like Stephen Duggan to account for Soviet noncooperation was that the extent of physical destruction within the USSR was so great and the chaotic economic situation so desperate that exchanges would be embarrassing to the Soviets. "The Russian Government simply does not want the West to know how bad it is," he insisted. Even the embassy had temporarily adopted this view. Moreover, many people still clung to the belief that misunderstanding was in fact caused by the absence of cultural contacts. Both theories were discredited in 1946 by the discovery that the Soviets were welcoming students from Eastern Europe for study in the USSR. In addition, the arrival in Moscow of twenty-five North Korean cultural leaders during August was publicized with much fanfare in the Soviet press. Adding insult to injury, TASS responded to a letter from Senator Daniel Brewster, who had criticized Soviet cultural isolation, by reciting a long list of "distinguished" Americans who had visited the USSR, pointedly mentioning Henry Wallace and Lillian Hellman, among others. Elbridge Durbrow, Kennan's replacement in Moscow, cited these events as confirmation of his previous suspicion that "Soviet unwillingness to accept American students at [the] present time is motivated by political considerations."[49]

Nevertheless, the cultural community continued to press for exchanges. The Rockefeller Foundation invited a group of Soviet scientists to attend the Princeton bicentennial celebrations at its expense; Cornell University invited four Russian students and one professor; and the American Library Association unilaterally shipped books to the Lenin Library, hoping to receive a kindred response. Despite inquiries from the embassy, nothing happened. Cornell continued to press the Russian embassy in Washington even after the Moscow embassy had given up. By November, Ambassador Smith had had his fill. "OK," he scrawled on a dispatch, "I think that we went too to [sic] much effort on this matter. I do not believe that it is consistant [sic] with the dignity of the U.S. or its institutions to beg and beg for our courtesies to be accepted." This sense of wounded national pride, in addition to playing havoc with the ambassador's spelling, further soured the embassy on the merits of the informal approach, or of any cultural approach for that matter.[50]

The American cultural community was not so easily daunted, however. At their insistence, further initiatives were launched in 1947, when the embassy was asked to invite fifty Soviet scholars to the United States for conferences with their American counterparts, with the understanding that the visit would be reciprocated, of course. In addition, Laurence Duggan, who had recently replaced his father as the director of the Institute of International Education, insisted that the department proffer scholarships which had been guaranteed by more than a dozen American academic institutions over the past year. An obstacle that instantly arose was the possibility that the visitors might have to register as foreign agents under the terms of the Foreign Agents Registration Act of 1938, although the Attorney General indicated that so long as they were engaged in "bona fide" scholastic pursuits they would not be harassed. The embassy predicted that this condition would serve as "a convenient out for the Soviets." And in fact Andrei Vishinsky did cite this statute in declining the invitations, claiming that it obstructed cultural contacts between the two countries.[51]

The last gasp came when the ACLS sent Professor Ernest J. Simmons of Columbia University's Russian Institute as its emissary to Eastern Europe and the Soviet Union to promote cultural relations and to survey the prospects for Slavic studies overseas. Simmons came armed with a number of specific proposals for cultural cooperation. In contrast to the State Department's emphasis on reciprocity and a formalized national approach, Simmons's proposals demanded no quid pro quo of the Soviets. In addition, he sought "to keep the mission, as far as was possible, where it properly belonged – on a non-governmental basis." But two weeks of dickering elicited only a Kafkaesque meeting with an official of the Lenin Library, followed by an equally unproductive interview at the Foreign Ministry. Simmons was totally disillusioned. "Culture in the Soviet Union is political," he later wrote, "and there is a direct correlation between all cultural manifestations and Soviet domestic and international policies." Following this episode, the department decided to leave U.S.–Soviet exchange projects "severely alone." Suggestions for renewed efforts were dismissed with the comment that they would simply "waste valuable time."[52]

Clearly, these episodes established a pattern of failure for the informal approach to cultural relations. Domestically, private groups were unable to cope successfully with the international environment; in a multilateral context, the unexpected emergence of cultural politics vitiated the idealist premises upon which UNESCO had been founded; and finally, the failure of successive initiatives with the Soviet Union established the futility of dealing with the Russians on an informal bilateral basis. Each of these events pointed to the State Department as the logical focus of policy, a role that the department now seemed more than willing to assume. The informal policy system needed to be replaced by more formal, bureaucratic structures.

From another perspective, given the scope of American postwar involvements, the fact that the new era was to be one of power politics rather than the hoped-for harmonic understanding seemed to leave no choice except for the United States to participate on that basis. The question was, Could such a transformation be achieved when both the traditional operating philosophy of the cultural program and its inherited institutional structure denied the premises of realpolitik? Could the United States, within its established traditions, adopt a policy contrary to those traditions without at the same time repudiating its past? The answer was yes, but it would take a little doing.

CHAPTER 5

The politics of institutionalization

For a nation to function effectively in a world of power relations it must possess a competitive conception of the international system, an administrative mechanism for deploying national resources, and domestic backing for its policies. The U.S. cultural program encountered serious obstacles in all three areas. To start with, its intellectual and institutional traditions were uncongenial, even antithetical, to the requirements of realpolitik. Then too, World War II left it unsuited for use as a political instrument because all postwar plans were made on the basis of informal, liberal, internationalist assumptions. The only "positive" development had been a steady centralization and bureaucratization of cultural policy, but this change only evoked among private interests a primordial fear of governmental encroachments. Given this legacy, a substantial realignment of perceptions, administrative forms, and political support was necessary before a workable substitute for the informal approach could be institutionalized.

One unanticipated consequence of the war was the concentration of power in State Department hands. On the surface, the influence of private cultural agencies remained formidable, causing department officers to grouse occasionally about their lack of policymaking authority. But much of this complaining was, as William Schurz admitted, "hocus pocus" that gave private groups "the appearance of a large measure of independence." The fact was that by 1944 the department had shed its earlier fear of being directly associated with overseas cultural activities and was determined to take a more active interest in their administration. To Waldo Leland and the ACLS, who were weary of administering a congeries of governmental programs and who yearned for a more decorous scholarly existence, this new assertiveness was not altogether unwelcome. Indeed, Leland was firmly "opposed to the ACLS acting as a cover agency for the government beyond the period of national emergency."[1]

113

This reluctance to play the role of governmental "stooges" did not mean that members of the General Advisory Committee were willing to jettison the voluntarist system. Leland bluntly informed Charles Thomson that "the Federal Government has by no means a *tabula rasa* upon which to write its programs." People like Stephen Duggan, Carl Milam, and George Zook of the American Council on Education insisted on the continuing importance of relying on private organizations to carry on cultural work without department interference. "Governmental support must be accepted but circumscribed," warned Duggan. But such criticisms were made from a growing sense of weakness, for many "private" cultural functions now depended on continuing government support for their existence. As Leland was well aware, the cultural program was "in a period of transition" from private to public support, a change that precluded any return to prewar patterns.[2]

For its part, the department could sympathize with such arguments while insisting that private participation in the cultural program and private administration were "not necessarily synonymous." One area in which it chose to augment its influence was in its dealings with the cultural institutes: The policy of concealment and the fiction.of their autonomy had become "cumbersome and embarrassing." As Charles Thomson's successor, Bryn J. Hovde, explained: "The Division now tends to avow, rather than to conceal, their connection with American embassies." The changed attitude was also apparent in the book and library programs. Gradually the State Department began to take over the ALA's responsibility for selecting titles for distribution in Latin America, and by late 1945 it was insisting that gifts be acknowledged as coming from the U.S. government rather than from the ALA. The "point of contact," an important consideration to some minds, was no longer people-to-people. The administration of the Biblioteca Benjamin Franklin in Mexico City witnessed a similar trajectory. By late 1946 it was decided, for budgeting and policy reasons, to run the library as part of the diplomatic establishment, bruising some sensibilities in the process.[3]

The Institute of International Education, by now a financial ward of the government, barely survived a bureaucratic tug-of-war between the Department of State and the Office of Education. On the assumption that an expected flood of student exchanges would require "expanded services by a central agency, " the Interdepartmental Committee on Scientific and Cultural Cooperation suggested the Department of Education as a new administrative focus. Alarmed by this "unwarranted extension" of federal authority, Stephen Duggan launched a letter-writing campaign that secured a reaffirmation of the institute's central role in exchange programs. But the victory was Pyrrhic, for the same report that guaranteed the IIE's continuance also spoke of student exchanges as a means of "implementing foreign policy." More disturbingly, it based its recommendations not on the belief that private administration assured the people-to-people character of cultural relations, but on the administrative criterion of "maximum efficiency." Bureaucratic rationality now superseded the continuity of tradition or liberal principle as a policy rationale. Ironically, the eclipse of voluntarism was hastened by the policies of the large foundations, which now used the government's enlarged role as a justification for discontinuing their grants to private cultural groups.[4]

The logic of bureaucratic centralization inexorably pulled the cultural programs into the foreign policy mainstream. In January 1944, the Division of Cultural Relations was renamed the Division of Science, Education and Art and lumped together with a number of other divisions into a new Office of Public Information (OPI). John Dickey, the director of the OPI, knew little about the cultural program and was disinclined to give his attention to cultural affairs. Members of the General Advisory Committee were appalled by this reshuffle, fearing that the program's linkage with "information" functions brought it into uncomfortable association with propaganda. Ben Cherrington immediately began to inform legislators and policymakers that genuine cultural interests "might be exploited for ulterior purposes." Faced with an angry constituency that demanded a restoration of the program's liberal orientation, the division was again rechristened the Division of Cultural Cooperation. But nothing else changed. If anything, the cultural program's relationship to the information function would grow even more tangled.[5]

The two were drawn still closer together in December 1944 with the appointment of Archibald MacLeish to the newly created post of assistant secretary for public and cultural affairs. MacLeish was a liberal's liberal, a loyal New Dealer, and a fervent internationalist – a curriculum vitae that nearly capsized his nomination in the conservative Senate Committee on Foreign Relations. He was also a believer in the potency of cultural relations. "If the people of the world know the facts about each other," he told the committee, "peace will be maintained." Given this conviction, he argued that "the cultural relations of the government are its most important foreign relations." But MacLeish's outlook did not conform to the standard prospectus long peddled by the cultural advocates. Although he persistently supported an enlarged international role for men of arts and letters, he viewed specialist or "highbrow" exchanges as essentially exclusivist and nondemocratic in character.[6]

MacLeish's populist instincts led him to place his faith in the new technological media, especially radio communications. ("The world is wired for sound," he once crowed in enthusiasm.) With the aid of new technologies, peoples could be placed in direct contact with one another on a daily basis, with the result that popular attitudes could become "major influences in foreign relations." MacLeish intended to treat domestic public information activities and foreign publicity as different sides of the same problem, both contributing to public understanding. Picking up some of this enthusiasm, Bryn Hovde speculated that the impact of modern mass media in effect provided "the equivalence of hot house methods."[7]

The mass media approach to cultural relations seemed to solve several difficulties simultaneously: It was faster, it seemed more effective, and it was certainly more democratic than traditional approaches to cultural interchange. In addition, it meshed perfectly with the American predilection for technological solutions to political problems, and it held untold possibilities for mass education and the ability to put to use the burgeoning social sciences of communications. The one possible drawback to this media approach – its susceptibility to unilateral, nationalist uses – seemed trifling to MacLeish. "Any such program would either now or later become reciprocal, since there is a universal law of culture as well as of physics that action produces reaction," he insisted. Thus when it came time to formulate a program for UNESCO, MacLeish was in the forefront of the zealous American movement promoting the mass communications approach. "Books and libraries and education are always ours," he reasoned. "Mass communications are therefore the big thing on which to concentrate."[8]

MacLeish's brief experience as head of the Office of Facts and Figures predisposed him to give a high rating to the cultural potential of the wartime information services. The war had already blurred the distinction between information and cultural activities, a development reinforced by the Office of War Information's adoption of programs of an increasingly cultural nature. As the war drew to a close, the OWI began to think in terms of long-range activities. Like any good bureaucracy, it sought to perpetuate its functions, even if the needs calling it into existence had disappeared. Beginning with a library that opened in London in May 1943, the OWI soon established a far-flung system of overseas libraries. It also dabbled in exchange programs of its own, being especially active in bringing foreign journalists to the United States. Indeed, according to Edward Barrett, there was hardly a method of human intercourse that the OWI had not attempted. Many of its long-range activities were undertaken with the hope that the State Department would incorporate them into a permanent peacetime program.[9]

If the OWI needed the State Department, the reverse was equally true. The department was eager to begin worldwide operations for its cultural program – hitherto only Latin American activities were authorized on a statutory basis, whereas the programs in the Near East and China had been financed from the President's Emergency Fund – and the OWI network appeared to provide an infrastructure capable of instantaneous expansion. Early in 1945, a joint State–OWI Planning Committee on Cultural Relations and Information was set up to discuss the marriage of the two enterprises and to haggle over the dowry. After a few meetings, agreement was reached on a postwar merger. Until enabling legislation for a worldwide program was passed, it seemed desirable for OWI to carry out programs that the Department of State would later establish permanently. Consequently, the OWI began to appoint both public affairs officers and cultural officers to its outposts and to concentrate increasingly on activities of a cultural nature. Following the recommendations of a special study commissioned by the OWI, on August 31, 1945, President Truman signed an executive order amalgamating the postwar remnants of the OWI, the information services of the CIAA, and the Office of Public Information into a new Interim Information Service.[10]

Although the two functions were drawn together bureaucratically in a marriage of convenience, the union was not a happy one. The cultural personnel were instantly outnumbered by mass media experts whose enthusiasm for "selling America" seemed to substitute crass Madison Avenue techniques for the principled traditions of cultural relations. "Through the OWI we undertook this responsibility of salesmanship to win a war," said one enthusiast. "We must continue it through the State Department to maintain a peace." The effect of this sudden inundation upon the psyches of the old-line cultural personnel was shattering; for a group of people who hailed largely from academic backgrounds, having to defer to journalists and admen in the formation of cultural policy was a serious blow to already battered sensibilities. "The intangible elements of esprit de corps and morale, which are so vital to successful administration, have been given very little consideration in all these changes, with the result that both are at an all-time low," a rueful William Schurz wrote to his suffering colleagues.[11]

Under the stewardship of William Benton, who succeeded Mac-Leish to the position of assistant secretary in September 1945, the status of cultural operations would decline further, although, paradoxically, cultural activities could find no more enthusiastic backer than Benton. Benton's background touched on many of the elements that were fused into the postwar cultural program. His family history could point to missionary forebears in the nineteenth century who had actively propagated both the gospel and American-style education in what is present-day Syria, to the point of establishing a school identified by the family surname. Starting in advertising as a partner in what became the successful firm of Benton and Bowles, Benton moved on to the ownership of the *Encyclopaedia Britannica*, founded the Muzak Corporation, and became vice-president of the University of Chicago, where one of his greatest interests centered on the potential of educational broadcasting. As a personal friend of Nelson Rockefeller, he was appointed in the autumn of 1940 to the policy committee that was instrumental in charting the course of the CIAA's new cultural program, and as a prominent collector of modern art he had the dubious distinction of being perhaps the first to suggest governmentally subsidized tours of collections of modern American painting. Altogether, his career seemed to suit him ideally to the task of merging the disparate elements of the postwar program into a coherent whole. He realized that jealousy existed among the different personnel so suddenly thrown together, but he resolved "to scramble all three into an omelet as rapidly as possible." He went into his job breaking eggs rather than walking on them.[12]

Superficially, Benton's ideas seemed to parallel those of his predecessor MacLeish. He too was an ardent promoter of mass communications as opposed to the "slower" cultural media. The two approaches did not appear as opposites to him, but rather as complementary means along a continuum for achieving the objective of mutual understanding. The cultural approach, with its "slow" media (exchanges of persons, books, art, and so forth) focused on influencing elites and envisioned beneficent results in long-range cultural readjustments. The informational approach, using the comparatively "fast" media of radio, film, and print journalism, was technologically oriented, populist in its partiality for undifferentiated mass audiences, and attuned to achieving immediate results in the form of altered opinion or attitudes. When viewed as part of a continuum, the various media tended to shade one into the other without sharp qualitative changes. To Benton's mind, there was no question of one method being inherently more "shallow" or "superficial" than the other, for both were concerned with improving mutual understanding. It was with all these instrumentalities in mind that Benton proclaimed his belief that "the promotion of cultural relations between peoples, in their broad and all-inclusive sense, is at the heart of political relations."[13]

Yet the similarities between MacLeish and Benton masked a serious disagreement about ends. Basically, it was the difference between the liberal internationalist outlook and the nationalist approach that separated them. It was with the calipers of national interest that Benton measured the efficacy of the cultural programs, whereas MacLeish looked at the new informational techniques as innovative means for attaining traditional cultural objectives. In one sense, MacLeish, with his enthusiasm for radio and his millenarian sense of immediacy, was unrepresentative of his type. For although each approach could theoretically employ the entire media spectrum, the fact was that their advocates tended to sort themselves out according to media preference: National interest types preferred information programs, whereas liberal internationalists clannishly clung to traditional modes of cultural intercourse. Given these predispositions, the Office of War Information and the information services of the CIAA were simply the bureaucratic and media personifications of the national interest outlook.[14]

Benton saw his organization's task as "the projection of America to the world." He was in complete agreement with his friend C. D. Jackson of *Time*, who argued that "unfortunately, the word 'cultural' has become attached to State Department thinking in connection with The Projection of America." Both the cultural and informational programs were viewed as chores in international salesmanship, as sort of an educational Muzak or pleasant background noise against which to conduct foreign relations. If an information program were undoubtedly most effective in the short run, over the long haul student exchanges were "the soundest and finest kind of 'selling.'" Benton never tired of extolling the influence of the Boxer Indemnity students in Chinese politics and their role in advancing the cause of liberalism in China, and he also paused frequently to ladle out encomiums to the fine work of acculturation performed by American educational institutions in the Near East. He especially enjoyed repeating the impressions of a former minister to Iraq, whose conversations with Iraquis educated at the American University of Beirut had made him feel "just as if I were talking to a friend from California."[15]

Caught between the demands of bureaucratic rationalization and the nationalist enthusiasm of the information advocates, the cultural program quite abruptly became an integral part of foreign policy. When President Truman declared, without necessarily being sure why, that an information program was essential to the nation, organizational logic alone dictated the same for cultural relations. Certainly, most departmental personnel overseas heartily endorsed the addition of this new foreign policy instrumentality as a means of countering rival national programs. Touring officials invariably came back with recommendations for more efficient, coordinated, and expanded cultural efforts. Despite lingering apprehensions from the cultural old-timers and a few field officers about mixing culture with information, everyone soon enough adjusted themselves to the new dispensation. Thus a great divide was traversed without fanfare or even the realization that it had been crossed.[16]

As much as Benton and the department trumpeted the merits of the new information program (the "so-called cultural program," as Benton somewhat awkwardly took to describing it), their arguments failed to convince a skeptical Congress. Attempts to pass legislation for a worldwide cultural program began in 1944, when bills were introduced on two occasions by Congressman Sol Bloom (D-N.Y.), the ineffectual chairman of the House Foreign Affairs Committee. It was apparent from previous appropriations struggles that the program was unpopular with some of the more conservative congressmen. Their criticisms derived from doubts as to the program's efficiency, and, more fundamentally, its effectualness. Many of the items in the program – the art exhibits in particular were a favorite target – appeared to be "of little or no value." "I cannot get any enthusiasm about this cultural relations program," complained one congressman. The word "culture" left a politically sour taste in the mouths of many conservatives, and the appointment of the liberal MacLeish to the post of assistant secretary for public and cultural affairs did little to remove it. Given these sentiments against the program, Representative Bloom was quoted as saying that "all the educators want it passed but nobody else does." The bills never made it out of committee.[17]

Not only did the department have to contend with the residual skepticism concerning cultural affairs, but also with a long-nurtured resentment against the supposed liberal transgressions of the OWI. Of all the wartime agencies, the OWI was perhaps the least popular among legislators increasingly fed up with the New Deal and its liberal-bureaucratic tendencies. To its enemies, the postwar information program seemed simply to be a warmed-over serving of New Deal leftovers. When the latest bill, H.R. 4982, came up for consideration before the House Rules Committee in February 1946, Chairman Eugene Cox (D-Ga.) characterized the State Department as being "chock full of Reds" and "the lousiest outfit in town," and accused it of seeking to "revitalize the OWI" through the proposed legislation. Congressman Clarence Brown (R-Ohio) joined in the assault with the remark that "the people of this country are getting a little fed up with this cultural relations stuff." Privately, Cox informed Benton that ten of twelve members of the Rules Committee were against anything the State Department favored because of its "Communist infiltration and pro-Russian policy." Moreover, Cox explained that the fact that the Foreign Affairs Committee had unanimously reported out the bill meant nothing, legislatively. He told Benton that "it was a worthless committee consisting of worthless impotent Congressmen; it was a kind of ghetto of the House of Representatives." It took all of Benton's considerable charm to prevent Cox from bottling up the bill in committee. When it was finally brought up for a vote before the full House in July, it passed by a comfortable margin.[18]

The contretemps in the Rules Committee was only a foretaste of sharper jolts to come. So long as the global program did not have statutory authority, it was dependent upon annual interim appropriations. Beginning with the 1947 appropriations bill, the House Appropriations Committee deleted funding for the information program on the grounds that such activity, which constituted "a radical departure in the methods of conducting our foreign relations," should first receive formal legislative approval. Only through the intercession of the Senate, where Benton had ingratiated himself with the powerful Arthur Vandenberg, were the cuts partially restored in conference committee. Despite the fact that Benton had presented what he considered to be minimal budgets, his funds were cut even further and the program outside the western hemisphere was severely curtailed. Added to these setbacks were the beginnings of a significant opposition among the wire services and the paper press to any program of governmental news dissemination, printed or broadcast, on the grounds that it would be taken for propaganda and impinge on the integrity of the American press. Finally, in the rush of business to adjourn the 79th Congress in the autumn of 1946, the permanent enabling legislation was never put to a vote in the Senate, although there was a good chance of its passage at that point. The department would have to go through the legislative mill all over again, but this time with a Republican Congress elected on the belief that the public had "had enough" of New Deal innovations.[19]

In their thinking about cultural relations, many congressmen considered the issue largely in domestic terms and in the narrow national interest categories congenial to the 1930s. The important issues for them were the number of Communist New Dealers in the State Department and the problem of bureaucratic usurpation of private functions. Benton had already used the necessity of trimming down the wartime bureaucracies as an occasion for indiscriminately ridding the department of suspected Communist sympathizers. Nevertheless, members of the House in particular continued to insist that the department had not been thoroughly disinfected. Also, the comparative novelty of some of the issues involved did not seem to justify the creation of yet another bureaucracy. As a report of the House Appropriations Committee argued: "Our forebears planted on this soil the seed of liberty and freedom which, if properly nurtured, should outgrow our boundaries and reach out into the rest of the world, not through a centralized disseminating agency, but through the force of its own dynamics." Why was a national program necessary, the committee wanted to know, when UNESCO had already been established and was presumably prepared to undertake mass media and cultural functions? The primary considerations here were domestic imperatives rather than international needs. The main question was whether, not how, to proceed.[20]

A good example of the persistence of this "fundamentalist" pattern of thought lies in the ill-fated art brouhaha of early 1947. A wartime erosion of private influence both in the selection and in the administration of art exhibits had left the department with a free hand in these areas by the war's end. Its interest in promoting art had originated in the belief that painting was an excellent medium of cultural internationalism, but was later modified by the more egoistic "informationalist" desire to display American art in its most recent florescence. The result was an exhibit of forty-nine modernist paintings called "Advancing American Art," purchased with leftover OWI and CIAA appropriations, which began to tour Europe and Latin America at the end of 1946. Although it received nearly unanimous plaudits abroad, both from foreign publics and the American diplomatic missions, once discovered early in 1947 by the Hearst Press and some of the more conservative members of Congress, the exhibit became the object of a frightful caterwauling. All sorts of allegations began to fly about: The artists were Communists and leftist New Dealers, the paintings were unrepresentative of popular democratic tastes, modern art was subversive of traditional civilized values, and so on. As long as the controversy was in full voice, it threatened to swamp the entire information and cultural program. Not until the exhibits were recalled, the art program eliminated, and the individual responsible for the purchase of the paintings dismissed did the hubbub quiet down and were indignant congressmen somewhat appeased.[21]

The important point about this incident was not its practical effect upon the demise of a relatively insignificant aspect of the overall cultural program; rather, it stood as a symbol of the continuing vitality of a "fundamentalist" outlook on foreign relations, a perspective that would shortly threaten the cultural program as a whole. Three criticisms of the art program in particular boded ill for a cultural program of any sort. One argument emphasized the tradition of passivity and inaction: Who needed to impress foreigners with an art program of any sort? A second complaint bespoke irritation with an action that did not accord with popular standards: Why choose incomprehensible modern art when there were plenty of examples of upstanding democratic painting to choose from? Finally, the incident represented an outburst of anger at what seemed to be bureaucratic irresponsibility and callousness, a resentment not only of what was done and why, but also of the way in which it was accomplished. Perhaps the fact that the incident focused on a relatively trivial matter instead of on an issue of high policy made it all the easier to express arguments in emotional, absolute terms rather than in more cautious rhetoric. But for that very reason it provided a spectacular illumination of the gap that divided prewar and postwar attitudes. Altogether, there could have been no more drastic juxtaposition of old and new approaches to cultural relations. And because these outlooks canceled each other out politically, making impossible any art policy, they were a disturbing omen for other policy areas.

The same attitudes were present in the mid-1947 House debates on the Informational and Educational Exchange Act, the so-called Smith-Mundt Bill. To many congressmen, there seemed to be no compelling reason to sell America. "For more than 200 years – even in the remotest corner of the earth – people have

known that the United States meant freedom in the fullest conno-
tation of the term," argued Congressman John Bennett (R-
Mich.). "Things which are self-evident require no proof."
America's role had always been to serve as an example to the
world. There was also a potent strain of xenophobic apprehensive-
ness, especially evident in discussions of the bill's educational exchange provisions. There was talk of being "swamped by invaders
from Europe" who would no doubt import alien ideologies. As it
was, the explosion in college enrollments caused by the GI Bill
seemed to leave scarcely enough space for deserving Americans.
Finally, some congressmen saw the legislation as "a subtle, sinister
way to Federal control" of private cultural institutions via the back
door of internationalism. The 1946 elections seemed to provide
an anti–New Deal mandate, and throttling the information program seemed a good place to begin. All in all, this mixture of
idealistic isolationism, nativism, and antiradicalism presented an
entrenched opposition to institutionalizing the cultural program.[22]

Besides this substantial hostility to the very idea of an information program, there developed simultaneously a well-orchestrated
campaign to separate totally the cultural and the informational
functions in the pending legislation. Rather than being a struggle
between past and present, in which terms the congressional debate was largely framed, the campaign for separation signaled a
political split between two approaches that had cohabited, uncomfortably at times but on the whole rather peaceably, since the
inception of the cultural program. In 1938 both the national interest advocates and the internationalists accepted the doctrine of
minimal governmental involvement in cultural affairs. Regardless
of their political orientation, they were able to frame a consensus
around voluntarist doctrines. But by 1947 the situation had
changed dramatically. The failure of the multilateral system to
take root following the war and the concomitant rise of a nationalist approach to cultural relations as a competitor to liberal internationalist tenets set the stage for a showdown between once compatible foreign policy outlooks.

The war played the crucial role in bringing about this disjunc-
tion. America's active world role inflated the expectations of both
the pragmatic and the idealistic advocates of cultural relations, a
development further enhanced by the creation of competing bu-

reaucracies eager to impress their version of cultural relations upon foreign policy. The formulation of maximal programs brought to the surface major differences that in prewar days had been submerged by the common agreement that government's role in cultural matters was minor. Attempts to form a new consensus on activist principles simply wound up splitting opinion down the line on major issues. The culturalists continued to hew to the reciprocity theorems of liberalism, whereas the informationalists were more congenial to what was an unashamedly nationalist approach. One group advocated a circumscribed, if active, governmental role, whereas the other saw government as the central policy mechanism. This disagreement regarding administrative forms in turn hinged upon differing estimates of the importance of private participation and of the essential nature of international politics – a point at which the logic of each approach came full circle. The two approaches seemed to be mutually exclusive, and now that institutionalization and the future role of government were at stake, it was vitally necessary to choose between them. Certainly it was odd that once the United States did come close to adopting an activist outlook in its cultural policies – once it "internationalized" – its two inherited outlooks on the form of those relations should turn out to be so fundamentally opposed.

The crusade for separation was headed by Ben Cherrington, who, by virtue of his strategic position in the educational and cultural establishments, was able to cause the State Department grave concern. Writing to his longtime associate Waldo Leland, Cherrington confessed that he was literally losing sleep worrying about the matter. "So to put my conscience at rest," he explained, "I have gone all out in advocating legislation that will divorce once and for all propaganda from cultural cooperation." Basically, Cherrington's position was little changed from his 1940 views on the necessity of maintaining the long-term, short-term distinctions in emergency situations and on keeping cultural relations at arm's length from immediate foreign policy questions. He was not opposed to the existence of information or propaganda programs as such – indeed, he freely acknowledged their indispensability in times of crisis – but he insisted that the cultural function needed to maintain a separate identity.[23]

To charges that his opposition would give succor to the isolationists and defeat the entire informational-cultural program, Cherrington paid no heed whatever. He thought it quite possible, for one thing, to receive separate mandates from Congress. Even if it came down to an all-or-nothing choice between the two programs, he was quite willing to accept the elimination of cultural services – this in the belief that the UNESCO National Commission could successfully elicit the support of the American people and provide a completely private alternative to the State Department–dominated cultural program. "The support for the cultural activities, once the National Commission has found itself, will be irresistible," he prophesied.[24]

The scenario went something like this: As the international situation improved from year to year, it would be possible to make the information programs more cooperative in character or perhaps to phase them out altogether in favor of purely cultural modes of international contact – an unlikely occurrence if long-range cultural activities were not sustained in the interim. Of course, this faith also made necessary a coordinate campaign for the separation of the UNESCO Relations Staff from the State Department, a turn of events that brought Cherrington into direct conflict with a department desperately trying to tighten up its control over UNESCO matters. In any case, by mid-1947 the die was cast. Cherrington was assiduously writing letters to all the members of the Senate Foreign Relations Committee, to the members of the National Commission, to his numerous friends and acquaintances – in fact, to anyone "who might have some influence."[25]

The opposition of Cherrington and his allies stemmed in part from the belief that informational and cultural functions were "fundamentally different." As he explained to the trustees of the Social Science Foundation, one involved "obviously strictly a national function, the other an international and necessarily a reciprocal relationship." Also at stake was the future of the nation's cultural institutions. Writing to Benton's deputy, Howland Sargeant, Cherrington revealed: "To understand my position you should know, Howland, that I am pretty much an old-fashioned nineteenth century liberal . . . I have become allergic toward all trends toward the totalitarian state." Mindful of this danger, George Zook of the American Council on Education argued that it was "a healthy sign and in accordance with American tradition if the voluntary agencies of this country actually administer a substantial portion of this country's educational program." Along these lines, the NEA demanded that the legislation be amended to require that the State Department make use of private bodies. It also insisted that an advisory committee be set up to safeguard the new program, much as the General Advisory Committee, which had withered away in 1945 due to postwar uncertainties, had once restrained the State Department's policy influence.[26]

The unflagging energy with which Cherrington marshaled his forces did not endear him to a department obsessed with the need to obtain passage of the information bill. In Benton's judgment, Cherrington, although possessed of "great charm and personality," did not "think straight on this problem and in . . . many others." Some departmental officers now came to adopt a deprecatory attitude toward Cherrington's liberal pietism. Stressing the need for a united front, the department intimated that much of the demonstrated congressional resentment was aimed at the Smith-Mundt Bill's cultural provisions, when in fact the informational half received its fair share of abuse. The department also argued that no final judgment regarding the relationship between the two approaches need be made until a number of specially commissioned studies of the problem had been completed and digested. The general idea was to close ranks on the passage of the bill, after which the remaining problems could be "worked out at greater leisure." Writing to his friend Edward Barrett of *Newsweek*, Benton confided that "every crack in this united front and every objection, such as those which are being raised by Ben Cherrington, makes us a little more vulnerable, and less able to predict with assurance that we will get this legislation."[27]

The department was reluctant to agree to separation because it had come to consider the two functions as part of a unified approach. "All parts of the program are aimed at the same objective," Benton told Secretary Marshall. "They complement and reinforce each other," he informed Under Secretary Lovett, "they are integrally related." Even Charles Thomson, once the keeper of the liberal flame during the war and now a departmental adviser on UNESCO affairs, was brought into the lists. In a conversation held with Cherrington in late 1947, he went over the old argument that it was impossible to distinguish between informational and cultural relations by media, because any or all "could be used either for nationalistic or for cooperative international purposes." If the information function were to be conducted along liberal lines – as everyone argued that it should – what was the disagreement all about? Then too, separation would be detrimental because it would be a tacit admission of propagandistic intent, making the program a convenient and unjustified target of abuse from unfriendly foreign governments. From this perspective, the two programs were Siamese twins.[28]

Numerous attempts at semantic reconciliation notwithstanding, it was evident that the State Department saw both informational and cultural activities as political tools. A memo by W. R. Tyler of October 4, 1947, acknowledged that the "cycle of fruition" and the methods applied toward each seemed to dictate differing approaches. But there was an important matter of priority to be kept in mind. According to Tyler, a long-term cultural program could never achieve success without the prior success of informational activities – precisely the reverse of Cherrington's logic, which held that world peace would not be reached without first attaining a condition of mutual understanding through the liberal processes of cultural diffusion. "The acid test is not whether political information activities 'contaminate' the purity of cultural projects, but rather whether the latter impede the success of the former," Tyler concluded. A "problem paper" prepared for Sargeant in November drew the appropriate conclusions: Complete separation was "neither feasible nor desirable," policy supervision and control of both activities should remain with the department, and both types of activity should be related integrally to U.S. foreign policy as a whole.[29]

Through the final passage and signature of the Smith-Mundt Bill in January 1948, Cherrington and his cohorts used every possible forum in their drive to bring the bill "into line with American traditions." At the same time, though, private groups also hastened to line up behind its cultural provisions. College educators wrote directly to President Truman affirming their conviction that cultural relations provided "the foundation of world peace," and the Institute of International Education once again was in the forefront of those advocating educational exchanges. The American

Library Association consistently opposed any further reductions in the cultural budget and backed the idea of a comprehensive bill, and the American Book Publishers Council expressed similar sentiments. On behalf of International House in New York City, the aged Henry Stimson added his appeal for the governmental promotion of intercultural contacts. Not to be outdone, the Near East College Association weighed in with influentials such as Joseph Grew and its attorney, Allen Dulles, who pleaded for public support on its behalf. Governmental officials joined the swelling chorus. Added to the favorable presentations delivered by Generals Marshall, Eisenhower, and Bedell Smith, were the imprimaturs of respected diplomats such as Charles Bohlen and W. Averell Harriman. Also, Benton was quite active in securing support for the bill from his acquaintances in the broadcasting, publishing, and advertising communities.[30]

It was clear by mid-1947 that the legislation would pass. After the unruly House debate, it remained only for the Senate to concur. Public opinion was solidly behind the idea. A poll taken in April 1947 by the Public Opinion Research Center disclosed that 69 percent of those polled approved of an information program, whereas only 24 percent disapproved, and of this latter number only 12 percent opposed a program designed to "correct false ideas" of America abroad. The vote taken in the House on June 24 was bipartisan, with more Republicans voting for than against; of the ninety Republican opponents, some sixty came from the Midwest, the traditional home of isolationism. Far from being the Achilles' heel of the entire program, the educational exchange aspects turned out to be among the most popular of the bill's provisions and served as a locomotive to pull along the other provisions. When influential senators such as Robert Taft expressed great interest in student exchanges, the department could only benefit thereby. As Senator Vandenberg explained to one of his constituents, the problem was less with the programs than with the "highly doubtful personnel" who were thought to administer them.[31]

In the course of its deliberations, Congress was gorged with arguments about trade flowering from cultural contacts, the practical value of intercultural understanding, and the extraordinary interest of European powers such as France and Great Britain in this area – all in the hope of raising its consciousness. Benton especially was fond of spreading the idea that his problems with Congress had been caused not so much by intractable policy differences as by a refractory parochialism. "Generally speaking, the attitudes divide according to the experience and observations which members of Congress have had in travelling abroad," he informed Secretary Byrnes in the fall of 1946. Benton actively encouraged representatives to take overseas trips, and over 130 of them took the opportunity to do so in 1947. Thereafter, a minor myth developed that these individuals were somehow "internationalized" by their experiences abroad, much as Saint Paul was born again on the road to Damascus. Whatever conversions did occur took place at the surface level of ideological perceptions rather than at profound spiritual depths. The vexing divisions within Congress were not so much redeemed by a new internationalism as they were superseded by a heightening fear of Communism – a process well under way before the congressmen began their peregrinations. Anti-Communism bridged the gap between fundamentalist and nationalist positions.[32]

The European junket taken in the autumn of 1947 by the joint House-Senate committee established to investigate the problems addressed by the Smith-Mundt Bill illustrated the convergence of ideology and interest. In its visits to U.S. diplomatic establishments in both Eastern and Western Europe, the committee was provided with shock treatment by American diplomatic personnel. In Western Europe, the emphasis was on the pervasiveness of Communist ideology. Ambassador Lewis Douglas in London told them that Communism was an "offensive of ideas" and claimed that the intensifying Soviet anti-American campaign was beginning to have a telling effect upon public opinion in Great Britain. In Paris, the first secretary of the embassy compared the Communist propaganda apparatus in France to a "tremendous symphony orchestra" that was playing all the time. The diplomats stationed in Eastern Europe, by contrast, tended to emphasize the stifling nature of Soviet power. "Unless we devise some special technique we are now in grave danger of being forgotten in this country," they were told in Bucharest by Minister H. Arthur Schoenfeld. "Knowledge of the United States is being systematically blotted out." In Poland, the group was told that the information program hoped to maintain open channels of friendly communication with the Polish people "in order to weaken support for Russia should a decision be forced upon Poland in the future." If there was a logical distinction between Communist expansionism and Soviet imperialism to be drawn here, it was impossible to make it out in fact.

The U.S. program was invariably described as lamentably inferior to that of other nations. Not only were the Russians outspending the Americans in this field, but the committee was embarrassed to discover that the French and British were also outstripping the United States effort by a wide margin. In Poland, the British were said to have an organization approximately ten times larger than that of the United States, and the French operation was said to be five times as large. Prestige was a secondary consideration, however, for everywhere the committee went it was greeted with pleas for greater financial resources to take on the Communists in the battle for minds. The mission staffs were unanimous in their requests for additional monies for both "high level" (cultural) and "low level" (informational) propaganda. Appalled by the "successive nightmares" of its Eastern European experiences, the committee returned to describe the existing information and cultural effort as "woefully inadequate" to deal with "the pattern of Communist infiltration."[33]

Once the fundamentalist perspective was ideologized, so to speak, its elements of nativism and antiradicalism became prominent aspects of the new program. Senator Smith made sure that safeguards were incorporated into the legislation to prevent "the infiltration of these long-haired Communists." The selection of educational entrants to the United States was to be backstopped by a process of ideological as well as intellectual screening. From this narrow perspective, the prescription of Congressman John Davis Lodge (R-Conn.) was typical. "The important thing is to bring the foreigners in here and work them over," he urged. "That is the point in sending our boys over there," replied Senator Smith, thereby adding to the concept of cultural exchange as a two-way process the notion that "foreigners" could be suitably "worked over" in their own milieu. In this ideologically distended form of parochialism, one in which foreign dangers became projections of domestic insecurities, the fundamentalists made their peace with the national interest approach to cultural relations. Their agreement came none too soon. "In the light of the coming debate on the Marshall Plan we have to have this kind of program," argued Senator Carl Hatch (D-N.Mex.). The influential Senator Arthur Vandenberg was even more specific. "It seems to me that the informational function at the moment is almost of emergency importance," he opined, but hastened to add that disinterested cultural relations had "a tremendous utility in a somewhat stabilized and standardized world."[34]

Nevertheless, the legislators were also responsive to the suggestions of those who argued for the separation of the informational and cultural programs. For one thing, it was good politics to pay heed to influential constituents. Besides, for a few it seemed possible to do right by the educators for the wrong reasons. Congressman Mundt, for instance, viewed separation along the lines of the British Council model as a good idea, as too close a linkage of the program to foreign policy and the diplomatic establishment might produce a bad impression overseas. Mundt had been convinced for some time that the world was divided into competing secular religions whose differences were "firm, fast and fixed," and he was a believer in using cultural means as an instrument of evangelical struggle. From this perspective, separation would be more a public relations ploy than a serious disentanglement from the issues of the day. Senator Smith, the other cosponsor, had his own reasons for mollifying the educators. As a one-time member of the Belgian-American Commission and a former instructor at Princeton, he was naturally more familiar with the idea of culture-for-culture's-sake than were some of his colleagues. He was persistently lobbied by Cherrington, George Zook, and, most importantly, by President Harold Dodds of Princeton, all of whom voiced their dissatisfaction with unitary legislation. In one way or another, then, by the end of 1947 Congress was paying a good deal of attention to the internationalist point of view at the same time that its heart was set on an opposing course.[35]

Congress resolved the contradiction by creating a paradox masquerading as a compromise. The Smith-Mundt Bill explicitly recognized the distinction between informational and educational functions, and it also endorsed the corresponding foreign policy objectives of making the United States better understood abroad and increasing international understanding on a mutual basis. Separate advisory commissions on information and educational exchange were to be created, each with the obligation of reporting to Congress every six months, and the State Department was commanded to make full use of private agencies and resources. Separation was also mandated, but as an administrative matter entrusted to the department. "Certainly for the present it is better to keep the umbrella over the whole works," Senator Smith had concluded. In this form, the bill was intended to be a "logical" compromise satisfactory to both sides. Cherrington at one point had indicated that administrative separation would be acceptable as his "last line of retreat," whereas the department had insisted all along that the matter be left to the discretion of the secretary of state without having the requirement written into legislation. Shortly after the passage of the bill in late January 1948, Cherrington optimistically wrote to Robert Redfield that "it looks as if we had won a clear victory so far as legislation is concerned." Unfortunately for Cherrington, there was an underlying administrative logic to the legislation that vitiated its reassuring externalities.[36]

Actually, any sort of compromise or meaningful separation within the department was precluded from the start by its nearly total rejection of the internationalist approach. Beginning first with its political officers, the department had as early as 1946 begun to contract a case of anti-Communism, a virus that circulated to its extremities until, by 1947, it laid hold of the cultural program. Anti-Communism, when combined with a nationalist approach and accelerating bureaucratization, blended quite nicely into something resembling a new activism. Thus when the Truman Doctrine was promulgated, Benton suggested to Acheson that the entire informational-cultural program be stepped up by a factor of two or three, and his staff began to draw up hurried plans for a democratic rehabilitation of the Greek educational system. General Eisenhower, testifying before the Senate Foreign Relations Committee on behalf of the Smith-Mundt Bill, agreed that "the programs could be used to implement the Truman Doctrine." Although only modest results issued from these ideas, they demonstrated that the cultural bureaucracy was now prepared to fight for its slice of the foreign policy pie.[37]

Indeed, the department now told Congress that information and cultural relations comprised "an aggressive program in sup-

port of our foreign policy." Giving instructions to an ambassador
for a speech covering information functions, Benton's personal
assistant typically reminded him that the program "should be regarded as part of our national defense." This line of argument received reinforcement in mid-1947 when the Soviets launched an
ambitious propaganda assault upon the United States. Before
long, the Moscow embassy was recommending as "essential" the
use of "all possible means to counteract the intensive anti-American campaign now being carried out by all Soviet facilities and
those of the Comintern abroad." Suggestions came from within
the State Department as well that the programs needed to be
made increasingly "positive." Benton, for example, upon saying
farewell to a cultural attaché, wholeheartedly endorsed this infusion of ideological zeal. "His statement that he was going to Cuba
as a cultural officer to engage in the real in-fighting on the Communist issue, is the kind of concept we badly need applied to our
cultural relations," Benton commented with evident approval.[38]

The pressure for a positive departmental program in the intellectual sphere intensified as some of the more abstract elements of
Soviet-American relations were given consideration. Benton was
most impressed by a conversation he had with Averell Harriman
in October 1946, in which Harriman reportedly said: "As important as any fact in the field of foreign policy today, and perhaps
much the most important, is the fact that the Russians have declared psychological war on the United States, all over the world.
It is a war of ideology and a fight unto the death." Alive to the
apparently crucial role of ideas, in December 1947 the fledgling
National Security Council (NSC) called for coordinated information programs "to influence foreign opinion in a direction favorable to U.S. interests and to counteract effects of anti-U.S. propaganda." The demands for an active approach grew even stronger a
few months later when the NSC ordered the State Department to
"develop a vigorous and effective ideological campaign." This instruction was amplified later in the year by the NSC's Zoroastrian
view of the relationship between American liberalism and Soviet
Marxism-Leninism: "Plainly, it is not enough that these concepts
should cease to dominate Soviet, or Russian, theory and practice
in international relations. It is also necessary that they should be
replaced with something approximating their converse." Militarily
and politically, U.S. policy may have been operating on the princi-

ple of containment, but at the cultural level it was speeding toward the apocalypse.[39]

Fortified by its new sense of mission, early in 1948 the department fought off a final attempt by Cherrington and his supporters to recapture cultural policy for the private sector. At the fourth meeting of the UNESCO National Commission held in Washington, D.C., in mid-February, Cherrington passionately equated the strict "segregation and autonomy of educational activities on the international scale" with the American way of life. Admitting the necessity of a national information program, he nonetheless looked forward confidently to "a day when the national program will become an implementation of the UNESCO program." Counterattacking, Benton insisted that Cherrington's arguments were based on "fallacies and delusions." Information was not necessarily propagandistic "in its evil or ulterior sense," but a part of a series of "legitimate and potentially educational efforts of peoples speaking to peoples." In the sense of outright distortion, Benton was the first to deny, "flatly and categorically," that the department was engaged in propaganda or psychological warfare. The debates over information strategy centered on the respective merits of the "mirror" versus the "showcase" approach, neither of which involved departing from the truth or aggressively demeaning other nations. The real truth, he maintained, was that the dirtiest propaganda infighting was actually "more prevalent in the so-called cultural areas as conducted today by various countries than in the so-called informational activities." To Benton's mind, Cherrington's arguments "confused the use of both media and caused needless conflicts between individuals involved in both areas." The majority of the National Commission sided with Benton.[40]

The fact was that by this time the policy alternatives represented by the information-cultural relations dichotomy had been emptied of their former significance – the problems involved were "esoteric," as one department officer put it. The State Department bureaucracy had already adopted another foreign policy framework based on an idealized nationalism, a view reminiscent of Ralph Turner's discarded wartime vision, which successfully integrated the concepts of national interest, idealism, and antiradicalism, while simultaneously identifying this outlook with international well-being. "The passage of this legislation," Sargeant argued, "constitutes congressional recognition that the world-wide struggle between democracy and Communism makes it imperative that the United States Government conduct a vigorous information and education program in support of our foreign policy." Given this global confrontation, national ideals needed to be actively projected. The Department's obligation, according to Sargeant, was "to foster the spread and maintenance of the democratic form of life in every country of the world because it is only in this way that the freedom and dignity of the individual human being can be preserved." Americans had finally come to realize, Ralph Block informed Assistant Secretary George Allen, that their democratic traditions constituted "the fundamentals of a faith to be propagated abroad by the government."[41]

From this perspective, information and cultural relations were different administrative devices rather than policy extremes. Sargeant claimed there was "no such thing as 'pure culture' or 'pure educational exchange.'" Once the various cultural programs were defined as "important tools for influencing attitudes in foreign countries," it clearly followed that "policies governing the conduct of such programs must therefore be coordinated with the policies which govern the execution of *informational* programs." Given this insistence on viewing the two categories operationally rather than philosophically, the legislatively mandated separation of culture and information proved to be chimerical. The activist national interest approach had clearly triumphed. "I wish Cherrington would now drop it, because, it seems to me, the battle is in fact over with the passage of the legislation," Benton wrote to Thomson shortly after the National Commission had adjourned its meeting. Although Cherrington continued to make threatening noises following the passage of legislation, the game was indeed up.[42]

The important point is not so much that cultural internationalism was defeated – that was only to be expected, given its ineffectual performance – but the way in which the defeat was accomplished. Theoretically, Congress had endorsed both points of view, leaving separation to the State Department. True separation would have required the institutionalization of competing, mutually antagonistic policies. But the ascendancy of the nationalist ap-

proach, aided by the development of a political consensus centering on anti-Communism and the emergence of bureaucratic
activism ("morally dynamic government" was the phrase that
struck Benton's fancy), clearly made such a course impossible.
Thus a pivotal conflict, evaded by Congress, was"solved" by transforming it into a relatively trivial organizational problem. In effect, a question of policy became a matter of administration. There
could have been no plainer demonstration of the process of bureaucratic rationalization.[43]

The results of this rather disorderly postwar period went a long
way toward forging a new approach to cultural policy that could
satisfy the apparent requirements of the international system and
replace the failed, if not quite discredited, informal system. Anti-
Communism, allied with an idealized conception of national interest, rather than realpolitik, provided the intellectual rationale; the
passage of the Information and Education Exchange Act solved
the problem of political support; and the incorporation of cultural
relations into a managerial foreign policy network furnished the
institutional basis for an active, or "positive," policy. Still, these
developments failed to bring about a total metamorphosis. To the
degree that the complaints of the cultural internationalists had
been handled by administrative legerdemain, instead of being sub-
stantively addressed, the problem of adapting cultural relations to
a new era of foreign policy had been evaded. Nor would it be
resolved until the liberal internationalists, the spiritual progenitors of the cultural program, were somehow made to feel at home
in the new political environment.

CHAPTER 6

The transformation of cultural internationalism

By 1950, American cultural programs of all kinds were deeply committed to waging Cold War. Although it has often been remarked that the programs became somehow more "political," the dynamics of that transition remain unexamined. True, the passage of the Smith-Mundt Bill and the construction of an energetic bureaucratic apparatus provided the institutional base for this departure, but it was clear that neither a reflexive, visceral anti-Communism nor the prospect of selling America to the world provided an intellectual rationale adequate to the task of cultural containment. The American tradition of cultural relations was simply too liberal and too internationalist to readily accept a complete reversal of course. It was necessary not only to nationalize cultural power, but to rationalize it. Legitimation could come only if the new political operations were harmonized with the tenets of American liberalism and if internationalists were included in a new policy consensus. For all the difficulties involved, such a consensus was the result of an ideological compromise between the intractable demands of power realities and the no less compelling call of traditional verities.[1]

The ideological transition was apparent in the field of educational relations, traditionally the core of American cultural concerns. The enrollment of foreign students in American colleges and universities soared from a low of just over 7,000 in 1943–4 to 17,000 in 1947–8, and 26,000 in 1949–50, prompting the Washington *Sunday Star* in 1947 to crown the United States as "the educational capital of the world." As the IIE explained, these figures reflected "a deliberate effort" by the U.S. educational structure to accommodate as many foreign students as possible, despite crowded postwar conditions. "If it is the destiny of the American people to be given the opportunity of serving the world through our educational methods," said Dr. Kendrick Marshall of the Office of Education, "then destiny needs a little shove." Although it was understood that the purpose of exchanges was to promote cross-cultural understanding, there was added the element of national promotion as well. "The facilitating and supplementing program in the Government does not obscure the influences which have flowed out from this country, through all channels, to all points of the earth, since Columbus," claimed Richard Heindel of the State Department.[2]

A major obstacle to the flow of students was the same phenomenon that threatened to undermine Western economic recovery – the dollar gap. A generalized shortage of foreign exchange and a proliferation of blocked currencies disrupted educational patterns no less than trade in physical goods. There was a geopolitical overlap as well, for critical areas such as Western Europe and the Far East were the most adversely affected by the currency problem. An ideal solution would have run along liberal lines. "The interchangeability of the dollar with other currencies is undoubtedly necessary for the broadest possible . . . interchange of persons," one governmental memo stated wishfully. But in the context of an unbalanced global economy, this was impossible. Clearly, what the situation required, according to J. Hall Paxton in Nanking, was a "temporarily disproportionate support" of the educational exchange process; that is, some form of unilateral action by the United States was necessary. Ironically, reciprocity could be attained only by its temporary abandonment.[3]

A painless partial solution to the currency problem came with the signing into law of the so-called Fulbright Bill in August 1946. As an amendment to the Surplus Property Act of 1944 it sailed through Congress with little fanfare. The act made available for educational purposes nondollar currencies derived from the sale of U.S. surplus property abroad, so long as they were used for the benefit of U.S. citizens or American institutions within the country of sale. Overall policy authority was vested in a Board of Foreign Scholarships, in cooperation with the State Department, with programs to be guided by the suggestions of "foundations" to be set up in the various countries. The charter of each binational foundation was to be negotiated through executive agreements. A variety of enthusiastic American educational organizations were placed in charge of the program's selection and placement procedures. The Conference Board of Associated Research Councils, for instance, was charged with the task of screening professional exchange candidates. George Zook of the American Council of Education explained that this was simply "a logical extension" of previous public-private patterns of cooperation.[4]

The first meetings of the Board of Foreign Scholarships in October 1946 set a liberal, if self-interested, tone for the program. The board agreed with Fulbright's desire to emphasize youth and to favor humanistic studies. However, Fulbright's thinking by that time had already incorporated a foreign policy dimension, for he visualized exchanges as "a necessary adjunct to relief and recovery plans if these latter are to be more than stop-gap measures." It was agreed that the U.S. Educational Foundations "should have an American educational flavor," and that the selection of foreign students in their formative years for study in American institutions abroad would "further the aim of greater understanding of the democratic system." The program was also conceived as an adjunct of the "general aims of U.S. foreign policy," although care was to be taken "to avoid all appearances of cultural imperialism."[5]

Whether or not it was admitted, or even recognized, the Fulbright Bill provided for the creation of an overseas American educational imperium through the system of binational "foundations." Many educators were under the impression that the United States was "by no means in a commanding position" to influence the programs initiated abroad. This was not so, for in all cases the United States negotiators were instructed to achieve American majorities on the foundation boards and to keep them free of foreign educational control. Nations sensitive to the slightest hint of cultural inferiority balked at accepting such conditions. The Iranians, for example, favored a formal treaty rather than an executive agreement, doubted the need for a foundation at all, and haggled over its name. The paragons of nationalist resistance were the French, who succeeded in having the foundation retitled a "commission" and in equalizing representation. Not to be outdone by their Latin cousins, the Italians insisted on first signing a bilateral cultural convention to regulate the terms of the agreement. Only after much bickering did they agree to the French model, but on the condition that the United States would enter into discussions on a bilateral convention. And so it went throughout Europe, where nationalist traditions were still in a position to defend cultural sensibilities.[6]

Such was not the case with China. Most officials continued to view the Chinese revolution as a problem of acculturation to liberal values and saw cultural solutions where political methods were out of the question. The areas in which American tutelage was needed seemed endless: The Chinese legal system appeared to require drastic overhauling, economic theory and practice had to be reoriented, American expertise in public administration seemed essential, and exposure to democratic philosophy and literature needed to be increased. But the most pressing perceived need was to inculcate democratic values in China's literate elite. As Embassy Counselor W. Walton Butterworth put it, "The group which seems most calculated to represent a Chinese equivalent of American democratic ideology is the group which we must encourage." It was precisely the intelligentsia whom the Kuomintang was taking care to isolate from foreign influence. "A cloud of fear hangs over Chinese universities," remarked one visitor to China. In mid-1947, student strikes and dismissals of faculty members took place, and it appeared that the Nationalist Government was planning a purge of the universities.[7]

If liberalism in China was disintegrating, the U.S. cultural program was in a poor position to do anything about it. Presidential funding had ceased with the war's end. To make matters worse, American institutions there were in poor financial shape and were clamoring for relief. Thus when the Fulbright Bill was passed, it seemed to be at least a partial solution to some of the cultural program's pressing financial difficulties. As the department cabled to Nanking, one purpose of the program was to give foreign students in the countries concerned the "opportunity to experience and absorb American academic atmosphere and freedoms. This [is] not now possible [in] most institutions [in] China where emphasis is on Kuomintang and Confucian ideologies." Fulbright's advocacy of the liberal arts and humanities also fitted in nicely with the desire to counter the Chinese penchant for technical education. The embassy responded that it was "keenly interested" in a program that could "act as a ferment and a catalyst in Chinese intellectual development."[8]

But first an agreement had to be signed. In May 1947, the Chinese embassy in Washington complained that the proposed foundation to be set up in China would be "completely under American domination." Numerous aspects of the proposed agreement rankled the Chinese – the foundation's name, for a starter. Rather than "U.S. Educational Foundation in China," they suggested the more egalitarian "Sino-American Educational Foundation." In addition to the inevitable disagreements over financing, they also insisted on official Chinese representation on the board of trustees. According to the U.S. embassy, there were two considerations involved: "One is the question of face and the second is that of extremely heavy pressure from the various Chinese organizations to have a hand in expenditures from the fund." The embassy contended that Chinese membership on the board "could only be productive of conflict and embarrassment." The department agreed, urging the embassy to stand firm. By mid-October, the Chinese relented and the first Fulbright agreement was signed. Unlike the agreements to be reached with other nations, Chinese representation was limited to an advisory panel of five whereas the U.S. embassy retained complete operating control. Actually, the Chinese had even less influence under the Fulbright program than they did under the terms of the paternalistic Boxer agreements.[9]

Over the next two years the program made a futile attempt at influencing the course of the Chinese civil war. By mid-1948, concern had spread among American diplomatic personnel over Soviet cultural initiatives, especially in Manchuria. Soviet cultural missions began to turn up in North China and numerous Sino-Soviet Friendship Associations sprang into being. The Soviets also launched a large publications program, flooding bookstores and Chinese universities with pro-Soviet literature. All this activity prompted W. Bradley Connors in Shanghai to write: "We are losing the battle of ideas." Given the seriousness of the political situation, the embassy stressed the need for "further understanding of the essential ideas of democracy in a country which may well be at a political cross-roads." But there was relatively little that the foundation could accomplish. It was at the mercy of mercurial local currency conditions, and narrow legislative provisions restricted its applicability to peripheral needs. Such limitations made it an unreliable instrument of cultural diplomacy.[10]

Even so, members of the Board of Foreign Scholarships continued to believe that the Fulbright program could have a "very salutary" psychological effect. As other American policy levers lost their strength, cultural relations came to be seen as a last-ditch means of preserving American influence. Ambassador Stuart was an especially strong proponent of this view. As a former president of Yenching University in Peking, Stuart looked upon many of his former students-turned-Communists as amenable to cultural suasion. American ideas, he thought, could eventually disabuse the "Chinese student dream of Communist millennium." Moreover, the continuing Communization of the countryside might be arrested by a continued American cultural presence. Stuart argued that the "ease with which they succeed in projecting Communist mythology and converting [the] Chinese mass into propaganda men will be conditioned to a considerable degree by [the] continuation of American-maintained institutions and related cultural exchange activities in China." Although department officials agreed, arguing that "we should do our utmost to emphasize western democratic ideology in our programs with the Chinese," by mid-1949 the cultural program was reduced to ameliorative measures, such as the $500,000 granted by the ECA for the relief of Chinese students stranded in the United States.[11]

Finally, as hopes for turning the situation around faded, cultural relations came to be seen as the last remaining link to China. "It is particularly important that cultural ties must not be allowed to weaken," argued the American Council on Education. Voicing the opinion of many others, Stuart came to feel that "cultural activities might be the least difficult approach to the Chinese Communists." If anything, however, Mao's Communists were to be even more nationalist culturally than were the Kuomintang's neo-Confucian ideologues. To the last, in keeping with the pattern of misunderstanding furthered by a program designed to decrease it, the area of most profound differences between the two nations was perceived as the sphere of greatest mutuality.[12]

In Eastern Europe, by contrast, the importance of power factors produced a decision to curtail, rather than to sustain, cultural contacts. With the passage of the Fulbright and Smith-Mundt bills, the department's problems no longer centered on a lack of funds. But then, neither was there a problem of dollar exchange as far as the Soviets or their satellites were concerned. "Political policy determines the Soviet attitude in this regard," explained the Moscow embassy. "Satisfactory cultural exchange between the United

States and the USSR will be achieved only after a fundamental political settlement is made of the existing areas of conflict between the two." But this accommodation with Soviet power seemed to depend on a prior moderation of Soviet ideology. "It would be unrealistic to expect that our efforts will meet with any success unless the present hostile attitude of the Soviet Government toward all things Western undergoes a profound change," the embassy concluded. In the meantime, the Soviets were rapidly spinning a web of bilateral cultural contacts throughout Eastern Europe. Student exchange agreements, friendship societies, exchanges of cultural artifacts – the full panoply of media devices was employed in cementing Soviet influence throughout the region.[13]

The effect on the Western cultural presence seemed catastrophic. To take one example, in a petition to Congress, American publishers and university presses described aggressive Soviet techniques in distributing their scientific publications, while lamenting the fact that "exports of American scientific books are almost nil." Soviet literature not only furthered the USSR's propaganda interests, but also put it "in a position to influence the buying countries industrially." The Soviet drive was accompanied by efforts to minimize residual Western cultural influences. The Poles, for instance, took care to see that an exhibit of American textbooks and books on education resulted in "a complete fiasco"; American schools were closed down in Bulgaria; and in Czechoslovakia, which before the 1948 coup had sent sizable numbers of students to the United States, the outflow of students ceased abruptly once the Communists seized power. The public affairs officer in Budapest ruefully commented that "socialism is synonymous with Byzantine-Tatar-Mongolian institutions developed in the Soviet Union . . . For the first time in over a thousand years, Hungarian intellectuals, scientists, writers and artists are invited to turn their backs on Western civilization and look toward the East." The setbacks seemed not only political and geographical, but also a reversal of age-old historical patterns.[14]

There were two possible idealist responses to this state of affairs. One view held that the spread of the Soviet miasma called for a continuing U.S. cultural effort in the region. Internationalists on the Board of Foreign Scholarships felt that cultural contacts should be maintained regardless of political difficulties. But for others, cultural relations seemed to be an appropriate ideological counter to the Soviet presence. Rather than being an innocuous nonpolitical activity, cultural relations were perceived as "more penetrating and long lasting" than other policy alternatives then available. Thus, the USIS staffs in Poland and Hungary both advocated an expansion of cultural activities as a means of buttressing democratic tendencies. Ambassador Lawrence Steinhardt in Prague argued that it was "far more desirable to spread our culture in areas where strenuous attempt is made to suppress and dominate it than in countries which are not in Soviet sphere." According to this interpretation, an expanded cultural program was not an implicit accommodation to the fact of Soviet regional hegemony, but an opportunity for preventing its cultural consolidation. Perhaps it could even lay the foundation for the eventual overturn of Soviet power.[15]

But a contrary political interpretation with ideological overtones carried the day. After debating in January 1948 whether or not to press for a Fulbright agreement with Poland, the Warsaw embassy decided against it. "Essential basis for academic exchanges envisaged under plan is favorable atmosphere which does not exist here," the cable explained. Moreover, it raised the possibility that "coldly cynical Polish Government authorities" would use the agreement to ideological advantage, resulting in an "inevitable seepage into U.S. under plan of crypto-Communists, fellow travellers and other undesirable agents." More important than ideological purity, though, was the belief that persistent attempts at initiating cultural contacts would be perceived as a sign of political weakness by the Communists. This had been the consistent position of the Moscow embassy, and now the others began to fall into line. Following the Czech coup, the Budapest embassy argued that beginning Fulbright negotiations "might be interpreted locally as portent of fundamental U.S. weakness and predilection for further appeasements." Continuing to beg for modest cultural favors could appear to be a craven form of accommodation to an illegitimate status quo.[16]

Domestic considerations also pointed in the direction of closure. Although a few officers argued that an "open door policy" paid dividends in terms of public opinion, the liabilities of unrestricted interchange weighed heavily in the department's thinking. Already there were suspicions that Eastern-bloc students admitted to the United States under private exchange programs were secret police spies. Security checks were standard procedure both at the consular end and through the State Department's Security Division (a fact the Board of Foreign Scholarships was not eager to advertise), but the FBI remained critical of the department for its lack of adequate control over the entry of potential subversives from Communist-controlled nations. There was also a formidable array of legislation to enforce. The Immigration Acts of 1917 and 1918 placed restrictions on the entry of Communists into the United States, although they granted some discretionary control to consular officials and the attorney general. The Foreign Agents Registration Act of 1938 also erected barriers to the entry of possible enemy agents. Finally, the Smith-Mundt Act authorized the State Department to "terminate or limit" cultural contacts with nations that failed to show a willingness to cooperate on a reciprocal basis.[17]

Although the Board of Foreign Scholarships wanted to negotiate agreements with Communist nations, the department opposed the idea. In October 1948, this disagreement was referred to the newly created Advisory Commission on Educational Exchange. After enumerating the pros and cons, a compromise was reached that satisfied the State Department's political and ideological needs and maintained the fiction of informal internationalism. It was agreed that the department would stop promoting cultural relations with Eastern Europe. As a quid pro quo, it promised not to hinder private cultural contacts, provided it retained the right to "evaluate critically" such exchange experiences with Communist nations. This decision marked an end to the pursuit of cultural internationalism in Eastern Europe and a victory of the managerial approach to educational exchange.[18]

It did not mark the end of all difficulties, however. Despite the operational consensus, there remained a conceptual dilemma that refused to go away. One administrator of the education exchange program provided some insight into its refractory nature:

Educators are extremely dedicated to the fact that they want education for education's sake and not for political reasons. And, although I ran this program with my eye on politics all the time, international politics and the security of my country – I've had to play it out of both sides of my mouth in a way – but we were spending the taxpayer's money for this, and although I had to placate the educators and get their cooperation, at the same time I had to sharpen our program in such a way that we would score politically abroad. Now, this is a tightrope, but we tried to do it.

A tightrope indeed! On the one hand, the State Department was assiduously integrating educational exchanges into its foreign policy apparatus. Yet, despite this obvious politicization of the program, Advisory Commission Chairman Harvey Branscomb could still declare in 1949 that "probably no nation in history ever had so receptive a field for the establishment of ties of a non-political character with other peoples."[19]

Politics and education had yet to make their peace. Although each would always feel uneasy in the other's presence, their partnership thrived once the Solomonic East European decisions were left behind. The promotion of free-world solidarity provided a task that welcomed the release of American educational energies, whereas Eastern Europe had made uncomfortably plain the subordinate status of cultural activities. In the West, cultural relationships could be pursued along liberal lines, with the not incidental effect of contributing to the overall balance of power. By April 1950, Senator Fulbright indicated that the exchange program's task was "to bring about a much closer association of the people still free from the Iron Curtain."[20]

Internal tensions remained. A proposed "Five Year Plan" of informational and cultural objectives formulated in January 1950 presumed the function of the exchanges was "to bulwark the free and democratic areas against the erosion of revolution and totalitarianism." Consequently, the plan proposed a shift in emphasis away from purely educational targets. The exchange program "must be designed to indoctrinate as well as educate," the document urged. Although the Advisory Commission complained that the plan was based "too heavily on anti-Communist values," it had little to recommend in its stead other than differences of emphasis. For by this time, liberal and anti-Communist principles had become functional equivalents, an identity symbolized by the adoption of a vocabulary that embraced both without offending either.[21]

As the rhetoric of the Cold War grew progressively more abstract – with frequent allusions to the conflict of systems, the antithesis between totalitarianism and democracy, and the struggle between slavery and freedom – contradictions evaporated. Phrases describing the United States as the world's "arsenal of knowledge" testified to the new ideological linkage between politics and education. "In this struggle for free minds we are all engaged," declared William C. Johnstone, Jr., the director of the State Department's exchange programs. Education was now to be part of "a total American effort to build a free world." Former educational internationalists also began to call for cooperation with State Department policy, arguing that liberal educational goals could be attained "only if our universities and colleges can be won over to the sacrificial demands of total diplomacy." Ideology became the balancing bar that stabilized an otherwise precarious high-wire act.[22]

Power politics and ideology also made their entrance on the multilateral stage, as UNESCO was temporarily transformed into a mouthpiece for the expression of American ideological interests. Although many U.S. officials traced UNESCO's politicization to Julian Huxley's leftist leanings, his administration consistently adopted classically liberal positions. Huxley remained optimistic about the Soviet Union eventually joining the organization, fearing, as did some of his friends, that there was a great danger of turning UNESCO into "a cultural alliance against Communism." But Huxley's brand of liberalism was being exorcised from the American body politic, as evidenced by the fate of Henry Wallace's Progressive movement and the concomitant growth of the pragmatic, "anti-ideological" Americans for Democratic Action. In addition, Huxley irritated Americans by insisting that UNESCO was dominated by "Anglo-Saxonism" and by seemingly pro-Communist actions, such as his intercession with the Chilean government on behalf of the politically harassed Communist poet, Pablo Neruda. By late 1947, among Americans interested in UNESCO, Huxley had become "increasingly unacceptable" to succeed himself as director general.[23]

Much time was spent in 1948 searching out a suitable successor. A subtle blend of racial, geographical, and political factors converged to influence the American decision. Implicitly recognizing the force behind Huxley's critique of Anglo-Saxonism, State Department officials decided not to seek the election of an American. An early favorite was the Indian, Ramaswami Mudaliar, but geography was against him. As Waldo Leland pointed out, "It would be difficult for an oriental to be Director General of an international organization which is mainly occidental in composition and which must rely almost entirely on occidental support and interest." Politics also had to be taken into account. Officials like Walter Kotschnig, wary of French influence, warned against the danger of "gallicizing UNESCO." "Any active leadership in UNESCO would have to come from the Anglo-Saxon rather than the French speaking world," it was argued.[24]

The United States finally decided to support Jaime Torres-Bodet of Mexico as its candidate. Torres-Bodet had served as both foreign minister and minister of education, all the while remaining a devoted academician. According to Leland, he was "by far the best of the candidates . . . he has long European tradition and experience and has held very responsible positions in the new world." His political sagacity was important to Arthur H. Compton, Jr., the new State Department UNESCO representative in Paris. "Being a man of no small political experience, he should also be susceptible to political influence (applied appropriately) on the most vital matters," Compton suggested. Only after heavy pressure was exerted on the executive board by Assistant Secretary of State George V. Allen, Benton's successor, was Torres-Bodet nominated over the New Zealander, John Walker. His election at the 1948 Beirut conference was perhaps that gathering's most fruitful achievement.[25]

To American officials, the growing sense of East–West crisis inevitably underscored the political vulnerabiity of UNESCO. "All of us here in Paris continue to work under the shadow of Russia's aggressive policy," Kenneth Holland reported from Paris in 1948. "I believe it essential under present conditions in Europe to see UNESCO against the general political background." In keeping with the spread of this cynical outlook, American representatives to various UNESCO-sponsored East–West conferences were now "selected very carefuly for a tough, hardboiled attitude and carefully briefed." As in the case of meetings of the International Theatre Institute, American officials were alive to "the political importance of having a large number of strong delegations from the Western democracies to counterbalance the possible effect of the strong delegations from the Eastern European countries." As for the Eastern European bloc, Compton suggested that "influence and deals are useless with this group, and the only line to follow in the future with them is to be constantly alert and explain and express our views forcefully and frequently—then vote them down consistently." There was also an increasing worry that UNESCO was becoming linked to numerous Communist "front" organizations through Huxley's zeal for proliferating its informal affiliations.[26]

Nevertheless, many liberals urged UNESCO to take a more daring role, not in heightening antagonisms between East and West, but in bridging them. Eleanor Roosevelt's attitude was typical of this group. "What is UNESCO doing to improve relations between Russia and the satellite countries and the rest of the world?" she demanded of a somewhat embarrassed State Department official. The most articulate advocate of this position was Archibald MacLeish, who insisted that the Cold War was precisely the sort of situation for which UNESCO was designed. "The objectives of the 'cold war' are cultural," he asserted . If culture was associated with nationalism, then it was UNESCO's task to restore the "sense of a common humanity, of a common human experience" that transcended cultural barriers. "The crisis of our time is not a conflict of ideologies," he warned. "It is the destruction in this mechanized and mass-minded time, of the sense of human community." Internationalists like Robert Redfield tended to agree. "We must find ways to think about community and to teach people about it," he wrote to Cherrington.[27]

The academic liberals – those who advocated a purely intellectual role for UNESCO – rejected this cultural definition of the Cold War in favor of a political explanation. Responding to MacLeish, Waldo Leland reminded the National Commission that the experience of the ACLS with the Soviets had resulted in "complete frustration." "We can discuss the reconciliation of ideologies and reach some agreement among ourselves," he predicted, but the real problem lay in "the totalitarian character of the USSR and its refusal to admit the peoples under its control to freedom of information, thought and expression – in short to its denial of intellectual freedom." Luther Evans spoke more to the point. "UNESCO's tools are inoperative in Russia," he declared bluntly. Most in this group downplayed the importance of ideological animosities, preferring to focus on Soviet nationalism as the culprit. Accepting the ideological point of view would have required some political definition of intellect, but people like Richard McKeon were determined to maintain that ideas had "an integrity of their own." This separation of politics and intellect, concerned as it was with preserving UNESCO's intellectual purity, allowed many of these individuals to back American Cold War initiatives outside of UNESCO, at the same time that it made them sympathetic to the department's fears of Communist (political) penetration of UNESCO. As a result, overall relations between the State Department and the National Commission improved markedly during 1948.[28]

There was something decidedly chimerical about this debate in the National Commission, as each side clung desperately to unrealistic premises. MacLeish could resolve what he called a cultural conflict only by asseverating the overriding importance of a universal, supracultural sense of community. On the other side were those who insisted adamantly on the independence of intellect. Among this latter group there remained the hope for cooperation, at least on the basis of the universality of science, if nothing else. But each evaded the basic problem of the political role of ideas: MacLeish by asserting the transcendence of intellect, the others by segregating it altogether from political life. If freedom of ideas was basic to both views – a premise that the Soviets rejected – were not both groups at least implicitly anti-Soviet? Milton Eisenhower, for one, had already come to the conclusion that "UNESCO cannot avoid taking an active part in the 'cold war.'" William Carr was driven to agree, albeit with differing emphasis. "Even if UNESCO should prove unable to bridge the gap between East and West it can nonetheless build a strong foundation for our end of the bridge," he concluded. The problem of politics simply would not go away. As with a Chinese finger puzzle, the more that National Commission members tried to pull ideas and politics apart, the more firmly were the two joined together.[29]

The academicians were left high and dry when influential State Department spokesmen began to argue that political differences, traditionally defined, had little to do with Soviet-American differences. Repeating an old platitude of U.S. diplomatic history, George Allen pointed out to the National Commission that "the strictly national interests of the United States and the Soviet Union come perhaps less in direct conflict than those of any two major powers on earth." Nor was the grave world situation the result of a contest between capitalism and communism, between economic systems. The struggle was "between two political systems, one based on democracy, the dignity and freedom of the individual, and the other based on the police state, the concentration camp, and the negation of human liberty." Although problems of interest, political or economic, could be negotiated, Allen vowed that there would be "no basis for compromise, no 'middle ground,' on the basic principle of democratic freedom." The State Department, by conscripting the principle of freedom, repudiated the distinction between the world of politics and the world of ideas. It remained only to draw the necessary conclusions. As Milton Eisenhower claimed, if UNESCO did not involve itself in current ideological conflicts, "then all the fine words of UNESCO's constitution and of UNESCO speeches must be empty words." Whether it liked it or not, UNESCO was part of the Cold War. Once that was decided, there was no doubt as to which side it would favor.[30]

These tentative ideological formulations were accompanied by calls for a more "practical" role for UNESCO as "an effective instrument of internationalism." People like Deputy Director General Walter Laves complained that UNESCO's basic strategy was not sufficiently clear, and looked for a more purposive role in the international situation apart from naked power politics or illusive idealism. "The support that UNESCO can bring to the U.N. is the yardstick for measuring its work," claimed Byron Dexter in a *Foreign Affairs* article. "The task is political," he concluded, "but its objective is not to strengthen any one nation, but the United Nations organization." Rejecting the plea of Georges Bidault at the General Conference held in Paris in September 1949 that UNESCO remember its "spiritual nature" and steer clear of political shoals, George Allen insisted that international understanding would be effective only in the context of a world political structure, one that was "strong enough to keep the peace." Therefore UNESCO must be operated "as part and parcel of the United Nations." The problem of crass politicization was avoided now by identifying the purposes of UNESCO, the UN, and the United

States. "The goal of UNESCO and the goal of the United States are precisely the same," said Allen. "The goal is to achieve world democracy."[31]

By this time, nationalism and internationalism had been reduced to the same policy through the mediation of ideology. As Allen explained to Davidson Taylor of the Columbia Broadcasting System, the United States was not attempting to make UNESCO a propaganda agency for U.S. foreign policy. It could cooperate easily with UNESCO because it was "based on the idea of free flow of information and thought which are fundamental in our own foreign policy." Whereas earlier, some department officers had inflated national interest to global dimensions, a reverse conflation was now occurring among the department's internationalists. Although this view foresaw a more political role for UNESCO, it was not grounded in realism, for its arguments on behalf of the UN were still premised on that organization's acceptance of common ideals. These were still internationalists with a bridge theory; only, in this case, the bridge from the UN led straight back to the United States.[32]

Benton and the more nationalist officers had already suggested that UNESCO's activities be "developed and expanded to further the cause of United States foreign policy." Despite the interest taken by the department in 1947, its approach to UNESCO through 1949 was largely reactive and negative, more to assure the failure of Communist penetration than American dominance. But then the tempo of change began to quicken. Throughout the first half of 1950, Benton, by then a freshman senator from Connecticut, called for a "world-wide Marshall Plan in the field of ideas." In April, President Truman announced the need for a "campaign of truth" against Communist propaganda. In the same month, Benton informed Under Secretary James Webb that the United States "must decide on its own policy, very clearly and very explicitly. Then decide how UNESCO fits into that policy, and helps us get done – the things we want done. This is the first approach to UNESCO." As there was no veto in UNESCO, and because its constitution explicitly enshrined liberal principles, Benton saw no reason to tread lightly. As his assistant John Howe pointed out, all the United States needed to do was to call on UNESCO "to do better by its constitution . . . with the implicit understanding that the *effect* would be anti-Communistic."[33]

The confluence of national and international policy approaches to UNESCO took place with the help of the Korean War. After the North Korean attack, Waldo Leland and others abandoned the distinction between politics and ideas and proposed that UN-ESCO undertake "an educational and informational campaign in Korea in support of the U.N. police action." Leland broached the possibility of "a complete mobilization – even expansion – of UNESCO's resources to support a total war against enemies of the United Nations." People like Luther Evans now saw "no inconsistency between the ideal of universality and an insistence on the observance of principles and commitments to establish and maintain peace . . . There can be no straddling by UNESCO when the issue of aggression has been so clearly stated by the competent organ of the United Nations." Aggression thus became defined as a violation of universal principles rather than as a pragmatic political problem. Similarly, George Stoddard of the National Commission now argued that UNESCO was "expected to play a leading part in the war of ideas," its role being "to set up a counterforce, as needed against any attempt to win anything through murderous attack." A few idealist holdouts like William Carr and James Marshall deplored this abrupt change of course, but their resistance was easily overtaken by events. A special resolution of an emergency meeting of the National Commission held on July 22 endorsed the new policy.[34]

It remained only to implement a "positive" program for UN-ESCO. At the time it seemed crucial, as a newpaper editor pointed out, to meet Russian propaganda "on a level higher than that of mere national counter propaganda." UN Secretary General Trygve Lie urged Torres-Bodet to take decisive action. "With each passing week, it becomes more obvious that the peoples of the world are in need of informational and educational material with regard to the United Nations action in Korea," he wrote. The State Department also made known its desire that, in Charles Thomson's words, "the educational, scientific, and cultural leaders of the world . . . make plain the menace of aggression in Korea and other possible areas threatened in the future." In late August, the UNESCO executive board condemned the North Korean attack and authorized the director general to use the organization's resources to bring about "a full understanding of the principles of the United Nations action for peace and security." Torres-Bodet, unhappy with this turn of events, had little choice but to acquiesce under pressure. Reviewing these developments, the State Department shortly afterward recommended further initiatives by UNESCO in support of the UN action.[35]

A scholarly observer of this hurly-burly reluctantly concluded that "UNESCO is now involved in power politics." At the operational level, Korean policy certainly seemed like an American manipulation of universalism for political purposes. But it also represented an idealist justification of political action, allowing formerly detached academicians to take part in what had suddenly become a hot war. Reflecting this change was the comment by Chester Barnard of the Rockefeller Foundation that, as things stood, "the ivory tower attitude would be as unreasonable as the iron curtain attitude." This was no descent to the ramparts of realpolitik. The threat of Soviet power was countered by an American-inspired mobilization of national power on behalf of liberal ideals. Realistic consequences flowed from idealistic motives, as it suddenly became clear that the defense of the integrity of ideas required the use of political power. Whether that power was national or international was irrelevant so long as it was in accord with liberal principles. In Eastern Europe the Soviet political presence had forced a nationalization of educational policy, and the use of military power in Korea had harnessed UNESCO to a militant internationalism. It remained to be seen what effect Soviet ideological power would have on the workings of informal internationalism.[36]

Shortly after the war, a profusion of organizations came into being, supposedly for the purpose of promoting transnational friendship. The State Department was under no illusion as to their nature. "USSR has regularly sought to penetrate and utilize international youth organizations, as it has international labor, cultural, and women's organizations," wrote John Paton Davies from Moscow in mid-1946. Indeed, at times it seemed difficult to find any purely cultural groups. As the cultural attaché in Paris reported of some pro-American organizations, "Unfortunately, not all are above suspicion of being motivated by other than disinterested Franco-American amity." The fact was that many of these organizations, in the European fashion, had assumed extreme ideological orientations. Thus, for the Association France-U.S.A., a mirror image counterpart in the form of France-USSR sprang up. The question was: What attitude should the U.S. government adopt and how should it deal with this ostensibly privately organized propaganda?[37]

An obvious course was to encourage informally the formation of moderate, pro-Western groups, but this path was strewn with obstacles. For instance, the Association France-U.S.A. was formed shortly after the liberation of Paris, and was heavily subsidized by French industrialists and bankers with a strong anti-Communist animus. In eighteen months, it grew to 35,000 members. Official Foreign Office approval or open embassy approbation was impossible, however, "because of the political leanings of the leaders of the group and their manner of operating." In an attempt to tone down the right-wing character of the organization, the U.S. embassy in Paris became deeply involved in discussing a reorganization and a possible merger with another pro-America group; in addition, it discreetly encouraged private U.S. business contributions to the organization. Ambassador Caffery went so far as to take "a personal interest in the reorganization of France-U.S.A. in the hope of seeing it strengthen and expand its activities." Still, the embassy would have preferred to exercise more than a moral influence over these groups. When the Smith-Mundt junketeers reached Paris in the autumn of 1947, First Secretary Norris Chipman argued that the "Ambassador should have private funds to assist in combatting Communism and promoting democratic methods." Of course, he meant public funds, secretly disbursed. American diplomats in Italy encountered similar political and ideological difficulties.[38]

The State Department's attention soon shifted to propaganda focuses more visible than the relatively sedate cocktail-lecture circuit. In the autumn of 1945, a World Youth Conference was held in London, called by the World Youth Council, an organization formed in 1941 to represent the youth of Allied and occupied countries. By August 1945 the British government had come to see the World Youth Council as "communist-inspired and fostered by extreme leftist elements in Britain." At the London conference, a World Federation of Democratic Youth (WFDY) was established as a global umbrella organization for national youth movements. Italian youth groups associated with the Christian

Democratic, Socialist, and Communist parties, for instance, all affiliated themselves with the WFDY. But by late 1946, the American embassy in Moscow was forwarding British reports warning of "strong Communist influence" in the organization. Although the department had been originally sympathetic to these youth gatherings (President Truman sent his felicitations to one), by 1947 it was extremely wary of their political purposes.[39]

A youth festival to be held in Prague in July 1947 forced the department to adopt a policy. On a number of occasions the embassy in Prague urged the United States to send "a truly representative organization," that is, one with a minimum of Communist-liners, but the department had no authority to designate official delegations to an informal gathering of this sort. So it decided to sponsor no one. Still, political officers worried about "The impression that might be created when an American delegation, whose travel has been facilitated by the Department, joins in resolutions condemning the Truman Doctrine, American monopoly capitalism, and the like, with much publicity." Because such occurrences were sure to make hairs stand on end in Congress, a few precautionary measures were taken.[40]

The department denied government-facilitated transportation to Europe to groups traveling for "political" purposes. Through the Maritime Commission and the intercession of the White House, the department had received congressional authorization to allocate two former troop ships for the purpose of carrying students to Europe and back on summer holidays. Transportation arrangements were coordinated by the Institute of International Education on behalf of more than thirty-five sponsoring groups. Already some right-wing congressmen demanded to know the connection between the ship program and the festival. Scenting trouble, Benton immediately ordered his staff to see to it that no Communists sailed aboard either of the two vessels. As it happened, a member of the U.S. Youth Committee of the World Youth Festival, Doris Senk, asked for room on board one of the ships, a request that the department hastily denied. Senk had already been labeled a Communist by the FBI, even though her committee had received the backing of some reputable private citizens. In a special meeting held in the department to discuss Senk's protest, she was told: "We fail to understand how you

could even venture to presume that the Department could confer
its blessing on this project . . . We are here to advance the interests of the U.S. – not to defeat the same."[41]

But the Prague embassy was extremely unhappy with the way in
which the affair was handled. Its report on the festival described it
as "a mammoth front, a stunt engineered by Moscow trained
Communists who are using this occasion to propagandize thou-
sands of young people." An American exhibit that particularly
outraged the embassy was a photograph on open display of a Ne-
gro being lynched. "What other country would permit such a dis-
creditable photograph to be sent?" the embassy asked incredu-
lously. Although by no means were all the U.S. delegates
pro-Soviet, neither did they seem to be enthusiastically pro-
American. The embassy's postmortem argued that "a well-bal-
anced U.S. delegation could have played a leading role in the festival and seriously jeopardized Soviet use of [the] festival as [a]
vehicle of Communist propaganda." Other complaints also began
to reach the department to the effect that it would have been better to have no Americans represented. Thus the department was
criticized by some for allowing participation and by others for failing to properly promote it.[42]

Its solution to the dilemma relied on the workings of the informal cultural system. Although official support was legally and politically impossible, it seemed plausible that "large, clean, alert and
representative American delegations" could exert a good deal of
influence on the youth of other nations, perhaps to the point of
"setting up other and more representative youth congresses outside the sphere of Russian influence." Representative Karl Mundt
agreed with Howland Sargeant that it was "wiser to stand up and
attempt to fight this kind of thing than to turn tail and take refuge
in a kind of isolationism."[43]

The plan was to channel the initiative to private organizations.
The department would provide informal encouragement to favored private groups and facilitate their attendance at conferences
abroad when there was any possibility that pro-American delegations could exert some influence, even if only rhetorical. After the
Czech coup, however, the department began to encourage groups
like the National Student Association, which originally had hoped
to wrest control from the Communists, to secede from the Inter-

national Union of Students in favor of an organization free of Communist influence. On the negative side, one means of control adopted was a more stringent exercise of the department's passport powers. For instance, requests from members of American Youth for a Free World to attend an international conference in Warsaw in 1948 were turned down, a pattern of regulation that would become increasingly familiar to suspected radicals.[44]

The concern with youthful allegiances was quickly overtaken by the more serious problem of the political role of independent intellectuals. This new issue arose out of a sweeping Soviet ideological campaign begun in August 1946, when the Central Committee decided to make Soviet art and literature more responsive to party doctrine. The Soviet press soon began to revile "worthless and harmful works devoid of ideological content." Party theoretician Mikhail Suslov defended this new emphasis on ideological partisanship in the humanities with the claim that it provided "immense service in exposing and combating all manifestations of bourgeois influence in the ideological field." Domestic vigilance went so far as to halt Walt Disney's alleged "infiltration" of Soviet animated cartoons. After setting their own house in order, Soviet propagandists turned their cultural sights outward and by mid-1948 were impugning all aspects of Western culture. Theoretically, the campaign was anchored in the distinction between Soviet "realistic" philosophy, with its material base, and the "formalism" of the West which, because it was dissociated from the life of the people, represented only "pseudo-culture." Before long, party organs were assailing the dissociation of ideas in musical composition, architecture, and in the "reactionary, idealistic, formalistic theories of foreign physics." They reached a logical limit in a denunciation of "bourgeois mathematics." The struggle between Lysenkoism and Mendelian genetics was simply the most celebrated aspect of a comprehensive assault on the principle of the autonomy of ideas.[45]

This cultural campaign assumed political dimensions in August 1948 with the staging of a World Congress of Intellectuals in Wroclaw (formerly Breslau), Poland. Although Western liberal participants were aware of its Communist sponsorship, they hoped that the congress could reduce East–West tensions by initiating a dialogue. One of the invitees was Bryn Hovde, chief of the Division of Cultural Cooperation in 1944 and 1945, and in 1948 the president of the New School for Social Research. As a disciple of John Dewey, Hovde was a fervid believer in the exercise of dispassionate reason. "Precisely when international divisions are sharp . . . it pays for people from opposing sides and different viewpoints to sit down together for an exploration of the situation," he argued. "This seems to be the purpose of the Wroclaw Conference." Although the *New York Times* was somewhat more skeptical of the conference's aims, it went along, fingers crossed, with this assessment of its potential.[46]

Hopes for a friendly dialogue were quickly dashed. Alexander Fadeyev, general secretary of the Union of Soviet Writers, delivered a wild diatribe against Western culture, describing its products as "disgusting filth." Major literary figures like T. S. Eliot, Eugene O'Neill, John Dos Passos, and Henry Miller were accused of breeding "aggressive propaganda." Not content with that, Fadeyev quite gratuitously added that "if hyenas could type and jackals use fountain pens, they would write like them." Ilya Ehrenburg continued the assault. "We cannot speak of bourgeois culture. It no longer exists," he said. "Now it is bourgeois barbarism." George Lukacs, the noted Marxist philosopher from Hungary, chimed in with the mysterious assertion that "Russian culture and Soviet culture are beyond Western intelligence." And so it went. Only with some persistence was Hovde grudgingly granted floor time to respond to these orchestrated tirades.[47]

Afterward, British historian A. J. P. Taylor reflected bitingly on the mediocrity of the discussions by insisting, "The first duty of intellectuals is to be intelligent." The partisan tone of the proceedings caused a disgusted Julian Huxley to fire off the caustic remark: "Workers of the world unite! You have nothing to lose but your brains." Soon afterward, the Soviet literary press began to identify him as "the specious director of UNESCO," and to accuse him of taking orders from the British Foreign Office. The American press reacted with repugnance and indignation. "It is hard to see what discussion is possible when one party to the parley insists from the outset that the other party and all his relatives are imbeciles and degenerates," said Margaret Marshall in her *Nation* column. For Hovde, the entire incident was dismaying. "Cultural integration does not involve surrender of the kind sought by the

Communists at Wroclaw," he insisted. "The highest and most universal culture lies in the tolerance of differences and in their unforced adaptations to one another."[48]

Following this debacle, the State Department's antennae sensed signs of trouble when the Wallace-liberal National Council for the Arts, Sciences and Professions (NCASP) called a World Cultural Congress at the Waldorf-Astoria Hotel for the following March. Harlow Shapely, one of the NCASP's organizers, promised Secretary of State Dean Acheson that it would be "an analytical conference on the problems of world peace" attended by eminent scientists, artists, and intellectuals from all nations. In spite of the fact that a number of Soviet and Eastern European intellectuals had been invited, including Fadeyev and Dimitri Shostakovitch, Shapely disclaimed any connection whatever with Wroclaw. These assurances were greeted skeptically. Already the White House had been informed by the FBI of the pro-Communist tilt of the NCASP, a judgment confirmed by the mail reaching the White House and the State Department. "You know as well as I do that this whole schemozzle has nothing to do with art, science, or free speech," an irate Dorothy Thompson wrote to Acheson. "It is a pure Cominform invasion and a propaganda move in the Cold War." The dyspeptic Walter Winchell also denounced the conference on his radio program.[49]

The State Department centered its thinking on visa policy: Should Communists be admitted, and if so, should they be made to register as foreign agents? The denial of visas might produce a "boomerang effect," especially as the Advisory Commission on Educational Exchange had only recently issued its opinion that private contacts with Eastern Europe were to be encouraged. Thus everyone agreed that visas should be issued to the Russians and, contrary to the recommendations of the Moscow embassy, that they should not be made to register as foreign agents. To ease the attorney general's displeasure with this decision, only Communists traveling on official visas were admitted, whereas individual applications from Western European Communists were turned down on the basis of immigration law provisions.[50]

The department's policy originated not from a concern with fostering the exchange of ideas, but from calculations of imagery, public relations, and propaganda advantage. Briefing the president on the department's reasoning, Dean Acheson told him that decisions in this matter were made "from a propaganda point of view." Why score a debating point for the Russians by denying entry? There was no real cause for security concern, because the patently absurd arguments of the Soviet delegates would surely "defeat their own purposes." Then too, the department was in a position to guarantee against a repeat of the Wroclaw farce. Howland Sargeant recommended "a strong public relations offensive," and suggested that the department "discreetly get in touch with reliable non-Communist participants in the New York Conference to urge them to do what they can to assure objective debate and to expose Communist efforts at controlling the Conference." Thus, the conference could safely be publicized as "a dramatic example of the willingness of a democratic country to meet opposition in open, public debate . . . to contrast democratic methods with police state methods in combatting offensive ideologies." As part of its managerial approach, the department's press release attributed its decision to "its unswerving devotion to freedom of information and free speech on any issue however controversial it may be." This was an outright distortion. The department was not so much interested in fostering intellectual freedom as in promoting freedom as propaganda – an altogether different proposition.[51]

The conference itself quickly became a surrealist production, a media event marked by intellectual posturing that swept away any possibility of dispassionate discourse. The public proceedings at the Waldorf were well covered by the press, and the private goings-on, telephonic or otherwise, were monitored by a small army of FBI agents. All of its sessions were marked by inconclusive, if emotional, confrontations of righteous illuminati. The Soviet representatives especially were peppered with embarrassing questions from the floor. Norman Cousins, the politically liberal but literarily conservative editor of the *Saturday Review of Literature,* took the floor at the State Department's behest to deliver a fervent assault on intellectual totalitarianism. Meanwhile, an ad hoc group calling itself "Americans for Intellectual Freedom" staged a counterrally at Freedom House, a memorial for Wendell Willkie. The counterdemonstration was captained by the philosophy professor Sidney Hook, who denounced the Waldorf gathering as an intellectual fraud. Yet, as even a secret report on the conference pointed out, the meetings were "on the whole quite well and fairly chaired," and there was "at no time any attempt by any chairman to choke off speech or to give anything but a fair deal to any speakers from the floor." If the conference deteriorated into a burlesque of its stated purposes, it was in part because the department and its intellectual allies wanted it to turn out that way.[52]

The continuation committee of the Wroclaw conference had scheduled a Congress of World Partisans of Peace for Paris in April, the first in a series of such gatherings. Sidney Hook was once again deeply involved in staging a counterrally, an "International Day Against Dictatorship and War," which received the enthusiastic but secret backing of the department and the Paris embassy. (Knowledge of U.S. backing would, Charles Bohlen warned, "diminish its value.") Hook's enthusiasm notwithstanding, the result was disastrous – "a cross between a political fair and a political bedlam," Hook admitted – because the speakers turned out to be just as much anti-American as anti-Stalinist. As for the Partisans of Peace, they attracted a throng of 100,000 to a stadium rally, and their cause received a stunning symbolic lift from Pablo Picasso's poster drawing of the dove of peace. Their campaign would escalate in intensity and numbers until the issuance of the widely publicized Stockholm Appeal for Peace the following year.[53]

Weary of ad hoc improvisation, the State Department yearned for a permanent solution to the problem. Thus it welcomed a proposal by Arnold Beichman of the Americans for Intellectual Freedom suggesting the formation of an organization called "World Intellectuals for Freedom" to combat Communist propaganda on a global basis. Howland Sargeant was alive to the problems caused by "inadequate organization" in recent months, especially in the Paris fiasco. The department might be in a position to furnish advice and perhaps go so far as to subsidize the transportation and expenses of delegates and support a permanent secretariat. However, he warned that "the Department's assistance should be of a completely covert nature." He realized that this organization might occasionally be critical of the United States. But as the "general line" of American propaganda was to admit U.S. inadequacies, such criticism was part of a "calculated risk" the government would have to take.[54]

The creation of the new organization resulted from the efforts of Melvin Lasky, editor of the German-language journal *Der Monat*. In the immediate postwar years, Lasky was the Berlin correspondent of the vehemently anti-Stalinist *New Leader*. By the end of 1947, he became convinced of the need for greater American initiative in the cultural field in Germany. Ideas needed to be put to organized use in the Cold War. "The mere announcement of fact and truth is not enough," he wrote. "The fact must illustrate, must dramatize, must certainly be *timed;* our truth must be *active,* must enter the contest, it cannot afford to be an Olympian bystander." After convincing the occupation authorities of the soundness of his ideas, he joined the Army's Political Information Branch and oversaw the creation of the high level *Der Monat*.[55]

Lasky conceived the idea for a broadly-based cultural organization in late 1949, at a meeting of the cultural congress of the European Union in Lausanne, Switzerland. It was there that Lasky also discussed the matter with General William ("Wild Bill") Donovan, former head of the OSS. Everyone agreed that Berlin would be an ideal spot for such a conclave, but Sidney Hook argued that the project, instead of being sponsored by *Der Monat,* should be "something undertaken under the *auspices* of a non-government, especially a non-occupying government group." "You are quite right about the sponsorship," Lasky replied. In February 1950, Lasky traveled to Paris and London to secure financial backing for his project. Although the details of the financial arrangements are not clear, subsequent revelations indicate that from the first some funds came from the CIA. Once financing had been assured, Lasky felt that the moment had arrived for "a radical democratic political offensive."[56]

Arrangements at the American end were placed in Hook's hands. Prominent anti-Communists of varying backgrounds, such as James Burnham and Arthur Schlesinger, Jr., were recruited. On the cosmopolitan level, distinguished intellectuals – including Bertrand Russell, Benedetto Croce, Julian Huxley, Karl Jaspers, André Gide, Raymond Aron, and others – were induced to lend their names as sponsors of the meeting. In his promotion of the conference, Lasky welcomed a wide divergence of views (not so wide, however, as to repeat the Paris fiasco), claiming that "the issue of totalitarianism is the litmus-paper test." Arguing "the necessity of a direct ideological assault on the principles of totalitarian Communism," he expressed his hope that the conference would "broaden out into a full-fledged European and world-wide offensive."[57]

If the government's role was not known at the time, it was not for want of indicators, and such a connection was simply assumed by many. The *New Republic,* for instance, characterized the meeting as "unofficially sponsored by the Department of State and its High Commission in Germany." High Commissioner John McCloy was enthusiastic about the project, to the point of offering the use of military airplanes for transportation, and the State Department actively expedited visa clearances and suggested delegate names from the Far East. In addition, the Voice of America, in Director Foy Kohler's words, promised to give the meeting "the full treatment." The revelation of CIA financing would later provide a sinister – and useful – target for criticisms that could have been made years earlier. They were not made at the time because secrecy was a necessary fiction, no matter how flimsily disguised.[58]

The congress convened in Berlin just as the Korean War was breaking out, a circumstance that added an apocalyptic air to its feverish deliberations. More than one hundred delegates from twenty countries were present at what Hook described as "an exciting affair." But the fiery statements of ex-Communists like Arthur Koestler, James Burnham, and Franz Borkenau struck a few sensibilities as being little better than the ones they were supposed to be refuting. H. R. Trevor-Roper, writing in the *Manchester Guardian,* described one session as "a catalogue of personal declamations against Communism." It was, he concluded, "an inverted Wroclaw." There were a few other criticisms in this vein, but on balance the publicity was favorable. Shortly after the Berlin meeting, a permanent secretariat headed by the Russian emigré composer Nicolas Nabokov was established in Paris, a constitution was drawn up, and an American Committee for Cultural Freedom was created. "All that remains is really to build the democratic international," Lasky wrote to Schlesinger, unable to resist the comparison with the enemy. Thus was born the Congress for Cultural Freedom, the "independent" liberal response to Soviet cultural propaganda.[59]

By 1950, then, the cultural relations program had completed a transit from internationalism to nationalism, from an informal to a formal policy system. The world of 1938 had been turned upside down: Public–private relationships had largely been reversed and cultural internationalism was now an instrument of national policy. The educational system was successfully turned to Cold War political uses, UNESCO was pressured to carry out American foreign policy, and independent liberal intellectuals were mobilized into a militant force for ideological combat against their Communist confreres. And yet to claim that there had occurred a complete transformation would be misleading, because such an explanation would fail to account for the most significant aspect of the change: the belief that very little change of consequence had taken place. For, oddly enough, these events went on amidst a nearly unanimous insistence on the continuing validity of the old ways. Did not educators continue to act in the belief that they were being nonpolitical? Were not the UNESCO stalwarts convinced that they were defending internationalism rather than playing the dummy to the State Department's ventriloquist? And did not the liberal intelligentsia believe it was defending cultural freedom rather than the State Department's manipulation of that freedom? Most tellingly, perhaps, why could not the department openly admit to its new role? In 1938, there had existed a correspondence between internationalist beliefs and their political and organizational uses. But now, ideal and reality were held together by illusion.

Conclusion: Freedom, ideology, and culture

During the 1950s, homage continued to be paid to the cultural program's ongoing tradition of public–private cooperation.[1] But if the language had a familiar ring to it, suggesting that the old values still commanded respect, the fact was that in the space of a few years policy rationales and institutional relationships had been radically transformed. Whereas the original Division of Cultural Relations was erected with a scrupulous regard for voluntarist and internationalist principles, by 1950 the cultural programs were pursuing an aggressive new diplomacy in which the rhetoric of idealism masked the pursuit of power. This policy transformation was accompanied by a no less radical shift in the institutional locus of policymaking. Numerous advisory panels notwithstanding, private interests no longer dominated the program. In their place stood an ideologically inspired bureaucracy that was more responsive to managerial imperatives and competitive rationales than to a tradition of liberal idealism for its policy decisions. What remained, then, was only the husk of memory; its kernel had long since disappeared.

Yet memories and traditions continued to exercise a powerful influence on policy. Normally, diplomatic historians have characterized the drastic foreign policy changes of the 1940s as part of a postwar foreign policy revolution in which the United States shed its isolationist cocoon and, as part of its new stage of growth, naturally assumed a position of global responsibility. The transition was not so readily made, however. The evolution of the cultural programs displayed precious little in the way of orderly historical maturation or straight-line progression. Although standard liberal prescriptions were clearly inadequate to treat postwar disorders, the accumulated force of tradition remained, and it was powerful enough to prevent the adoption of alternative policies and institutions based nakedly on the principles of power politics. Given the continuing hold of the past, there was no logical way in which new departures of the required magnitude could be readily accepted. Because a direct transition to power politics was out of the question, the only alternative was an ideological detour in which, paradoxically, a determination to abide by tradition was the precondition of its abandonment.

There exists general agreement on the proposition that the Cold War, in addition to being a struggle between the superpowers, was also an ideological confrontation. One need only to ponder the familiar images triggered by words such as Stalinism and McCarthyism to reaffirm that conviction. But ideology has been used to describe so many different intellectual experiences – among them exotic species of political thought and arcane epistemological phenomena, not to mention ideation in general – that it has more often served to frustrate explanation than to advance it. Its indiscriminate use has prevented fruitful inquiries into what we know, with an ignorance bred of excessive familiarity, as the Cold War. A closer look at some of ideology's possible meanings and their interrelations is necessary if the discontinuities of Cold War cultural policy are to be properly understood.[2]

Of the numerous definitions of ideology, three in particular are relevant to the cultural programs and the Cold War: One is anthropological in approach, another emphasizes sociological factors, and the last provides a symbolic interpretation. Each of these analytical perspectives happens to correspond to a specific aspect of Cold War ideological experience. Each differs substantially from the others, yet ultimately the three are closely related. These ideological categories can be analyzed separately, but they also form a unity when viewed either consecutively or holistically. Thus it is not too farfetched to suggest that the cultural Cold War resembled an ideological triptych.

In normal anthropological parlance, ideology refers to the intellectual and philosophical patterns that give meaning and coherence to a culture. To put it another way, an ideology is a culture's intellectual style. Most American internationalists tended to view the Cold War in this fashion as a conflict between contrasting totalitarian and liberal styles. The popularity of this ideological interpretation of the foreign policy crisis was heavily dependent on a complex of prior liberal assumptions regarding the nature of the

American polity. Many were convinced that there existed a natural affinity between intellectual freedom and their democratic society. Some even went so far as to assert a peculiarly salutary relationship between science, the epitome of liberated thought, and the American environment. "Scholarly inquiry and the American tradition go hand in hand," claimed James B. Conant. "Specifically, science and the assumptions behind our politics are compatible; in the Soviet Union, by contrast, the tradition of science is diametrically opposed to the official philosophy of the realm." This linkage of ideas and their social milieu involved more than mere compatibility, however, for descriptions of the American social order invariably posited a spiritual base. Thus Henry Allen Moe believed an "all-pervading freedom" to be the very essence of the nation, and Willard Thorp of the State Department called freedom of information and discussion "the great bases underlying our social and political structure." Statements stressing the importance of principles could be multiplied. The point is that American ideals were viewed not as epiphenomena, but as causal agencies in their own right.[3]

It was the perception of a causal connection between intellectual liberty and a democratic social order that originally caused the founders of the Division of Cultural Relations to segregate cultural from political affairs. They believed that free intellectual interchange was the basis of social freedom and, reciprocally, that intellectual freedom prospered in a social milieu uncontaminated by political or bureaucratic interference. Their faith in the benignity of natural intellectual and social processes derived from an unquestioning belief in the rationality of man and nature. According to the liberal credo, human reason and natural social processes, when joined together, formed a harmony of interests. The beliefs of the founders seemed to be validated by the existence of a complex system of free intellectual institutions that had developed of its own accord. What was true at home was thought to be equally valid for foreign policy applications. That is why the concept of propaganda, with its artificial manipulation of ideas, was anathema to prewar liberals and to their postwar successors. Not only did propaganda offend against the truth, but it was also identified with authoritarian institutional structures that distorted normal, beneficent domestic and international relationships. For all the naiveté displayed by the cultural pioneers, the relations between ideas and institutions, ends and means, and internal and external behavior all achieved a certain symmetry and balance in their formulations.

If the Soviets did not make a habit of accurately interpreting such American views, they were correct on one point at least: This idealist ("formalist," in the Soviet jargon) philosophical orientation *was* antithetical to the USSR's materialist canons. This difference was commonly thought to be at the heart of Cold War polarization. One interpreter, for instance, saw an "epoch-making shift in the very foundation of international politics, from the nationalistic balance of power to ideology." Even a foreign policy "realist" like Charles Bohlen concluded that "fundamental differences in concept account for the deep cleavage between East and West." Given prevailing idealist assumptions, to many analysts the conflict assumed critical proportions. If the stakes in the struggle of ideologies were no less than the survival of America's basic spiritual values, then idealist logic automatically converted this threat into a danger to American institutions as well. The natural conclusion to be drawn from all this was that U.S. policy was a necessary response on the part of a free society to the threat of totalitarian domination.[4]

That is one picture of the Cold War as an ideological phenomenon. But a look at American liberal ideology from a somewhat narrower sociological focus shows this image of a Manichaean death struggle to be simplistic and misleading. Sociologists can be roughly divided into two groups in their thinking on ideology. One school, following in the materialist tradition of Marx and Karl Mannheim, defines ideology as a conservative phenomenon, a mode of thought peculiar to historically retrograde social strata like the bourgeoisie. An ideologue is a nonprogressive; his habits of thought are conditioned by an attachment to outworn traditions and institutions. By contrast, politically liberal scholars have tended to view ideology as the intellectual hallmark of revolutionary minority segments of society. The image of the ideologue remains pejorative, for his rebellion is frequently associated with or ascribed to idiosyncratic disgruntlement or a pathological alienation. Both groups agree that ideology is a distorted form of thought and perception; they disagree over what forms of social affiliation produce such distortions and on the nature of the distortions themselves. These differences, although important in themselves, need not detain us. We can assume that both are correct to a degree, because both outlooks find historical echoes in the intellectual patterns of the late 1940s.[5]

The postwar years demonstrated that America's commitment to the principle of intellectual freedom could be more rhetorical than real. These were times when the public and numerous intellectuals looked to high culture for a reaffirmation of traditional values and not for individualistic pronunciamentos concerning the autonomy of art or freedom of intellect. Once the careers of artists or intellectual figures became linked, however tenuously, to Fascism or Communism, the legitimacy of their art was instantly brought into question. The smoldering ruins of such confrontations litter the cultural landscape of the era. Kirsten Flagstad, Wilhelm Furtwängler, Walter Gieseking, and others suffered the consequences of the public's aversion to politically tainted art. Genuflections before the principle of freedom notwithstanding, ideas were deemed valid only so long as they supported "democratic," that is to say, populist, cultural values. The fact that many of the suspect ideas and artists were intellectually "internationalist" simply heightened suspicions as to their fidelity to homegrown mores. On the other hand, an influential intellectual minority continued to insist on the separation of intellectual values from social control.[6]

A noisy conflict between the two kinds of ideologues occurred in connection with the decision of the Library of Congress, early in 1949, to grant the Bollingen Prize in Poetry to Ezra Pound for his *Pisan Cantos*. Pound was immured in a mental institution at the time of his selection, having previously been declared unfit to stand trial on treason charges brought in connection with his World War II propaganda broadcasts from Mussolini's Italy. Despite some anti-Semitic and pro-Fascist remarks in the volume, the library's Fellows in American Letters decided bravely if foolishly to award the prize purely on the basis of literary merit. Pound's poetic skills and not his patriotism, they thought, were the sole issue.[7]

The popular *Saturday Review of Literature* soon launched a campaign against this tribute to the "traitor" Pound. In the process, it intimated that the fellows were part of a crypto-Fascist literary cabal dominated by the tenets of the so-called New Criticism, and that American poetry as well as democratic values were being subverted by their strange doctrines. The *SRL's* complaints caught fire and stimulated an astonishing outpouring of emotional popular support. The award to Pound stood, but shortly thereafter the Library of Congress was stripped of all its prize-granting authority. Once the smoke had cleared, it was evident that the *SRL's* rabid insistence that literary values reflect a popular democratic outlook had ignited what Allen Tate called "the most serious literary crisis of our generation."[8]

Loath though they were to admit it, most of the fellows were indeed sympathetic to the doctrines of the New Criticism, an aesthetic theory that gave heavy emphasis to technical and structural analysis as opposed to a reliance on ethical or sentimental criteria of literary judgment. There was also no question that the New Critics were by and large politically conservative, if not reactionary. The odd part of the situation was that they were cast in the role of literary Fascists with their defense of the *intellectually liberal* doctrine of art-for-art's-sake, which was just another way of arguing on behalf of the autonomy of ideas. The opposition, led by political liberals like *SRL* editor Norman Cousins, wrapped itself in the mantle of democracy and egalitarianism while taking a *literarily conservative* position that insisted on artistic fidelity to social mores. This confrontation of liberal and conservative literary ideologues was thus characterized by a political role reversal that has ever since compounded the confusion regarding its significance.[9]

Whatever the political subtleties of this affair, one conclusion emerges with stark clarity: Intellectual freedom in the United States was culturally circumscribed. In what has been described by one intellectual historian as a perennial American struggle between reason and emotion, the latter clearly won the day. There was no love lost on "formalism" here. Indeed, most Americans would have felt more at home with Soviet "realist" premises, which demanded a subordination of art to politically defined mass needs, than with a seemingly incomprehensible aesthetic theory originating in T. S. Eliot's obscure complaints about the "dissociation of sensibility." Radio Moscow could have been speaking for a sizable portion of the American public when it wondered "how low and miserable must be the quality of modern bourgeois poetry in America if even the insane and verified ravings of a madman could win a literary prize."[10]

The Pound imbroglio was not the only instance in the late 1940s in which the freedom of ideas took a populist shellacking. The State Department's cancellation of its art program in 1947 owed much to a similar combination of antiintellectual, antiradical, and nativist sentiments. Thus, in the Marxist terminology, there was no obvious causal connection between the material base and the intellectual superstructure; the relationship was opaque rather than transparent. In defining freedom of intellect as America's spiritual center of gravity, many American liberals confused the part with the whole. To be sure, it was an important part. But in times of crisis, intellectual libertarianism bowed before the force majeure of America's populist temper. America's dominant image of itself, at least the one purveyed for international consumption, was an inaccurate reflection of a more complex social reality. In attacking formalism, then, the Soviets were not striking at America's spiritual foundations; they were attacking an ideological facade.[11]

Despite the passions unleased by the Pound affair, the dichotomy between reason and emotion was not perceived as evidence of a deep-seated cultural schizophrenia. Significantly, the outcry against Pound was raised initially not by populist voices, but by a formidable chorus of liberal intellectuals. In this period of crisis, the bulk of the American liberal intelligentsia (the "vital center") was unwilling, in the last analysis, to concede the complete freedom or autonomy of ideas. If there was a logical contradiction in their simultaneous allegiance to reason and to populism, it was dissolved by the belief, which became the crux of the postwar definition of "pragmatism," that American democratic culture had a rational core. In other words, they idealized the prevailing social structure. Thus Norman Cousins could defend the right to free thought against totalitarian depredations in a speech at the Waldorf conference, and shortly afterward in the Pound imbroglio argue even more eloquently in favor of populist definitions of intellectual responsibility. He swallowed his liberalism whole, never thinking to raise the possibility that its intellectual and social components were not always complementary. Meanwhile, a minority of unregenerate cultural formalists like Archibald MacLeish (who reluctantly defended Pound) was left to wander in the wilderness for its failure to heed the vox populi.[12]

From the standpoint of national cohesion, an internal ideological balance was indispensable if the external balance were to be enforced. Internationalists and fundamentalists were advocates of potentially antagonistic forms of liberty, as the Pound dispute should have demonstrated, because their negative perceptions of the USSR originated in differing concerns: One saw Stalinism as a threat to intellectual, the other to social freedoms. Although the issues raised in the Pound controversy contained the basis for a schism between the two outlooks, the political conservatism of the New Critics providentially saved liberal intellectuals from having to make the hard choice between intellectual freedom and populist democracy. Instead, they were able to preserve the fiction of a harmony of interests by identifying intellectual freedom with the American social order. In this manner, the distorted image of ideological struggle against Stalinism was reinforced by a conservative domestic ideological consensus – conservative in the sense that intellectual novelties perceived as being out of phase with prevailing social pieties were not tolerated. In this de facto alliance, the external proof of unity became unrelenting prosecution of the struggle against Communism whereas the internal test became mutual tolerance, so long as differences between the two outlooks were not pushed to extremes. Too irrational and ferocious an anti-Communism, as in the case of McCarthyism, or too pure an intellectual liberalism, as displayed by many liberal backers of the Wallace crusade, could explode the liberal myth of social harmony. It was proof of the myth's sturdiness that the political storms of the 1950s failed to shatter it. Thus, for the duration, the myth became reality.[13]

Nevertheless, these internal and external ideological rationalizations did not add up to an agreement on the program of the cultural Cold War. Although Stalinism and intellectual liberalism were antithetical, this was purely an abstract confrontation devoid of political substance. The stumbling block, when it came to action, was that purist liberal principles forbade a resort to propagandistic Kulturpolitik. In its horror at being politically manipulated, liberalism was inherently self-denying in its capacity to deal with its Stalinist opposite number on a retaliatory basis. Liberal thought was at bottom an antiideology, and all the "pragmatic" posturing of liberal theoreticians in the late 1940s did nothing to resolve the policy dilemma posed by this political emptiness at its core. In its starkest terms, the problem was how to use intellectual freedom as propaganda without turning it into propaganda in the process.

There were a few hardy souls who argued that the *idea* of freedom was of itself sufficient to smite down Soviet falsehoods. Even the National Security Council, in that blueprint for the Cold War, NSC 68, paid lip service to this view in its assertion that the idea of freedom was "particularly and intolerably subversive of the idea of slavery."[14] But of course, ideas backed by the meager resources of decentralized private interests were not enough to do the job. The inadequacy of purely liberal cultural methods in a political world led inexorably to the development of a system of cultural interchange based on a more practical combination of national interest, anti-Communism, and bureaucratic activism – in all, a "positive" policy mixture suitable for most purposes. But even these were unequal to the task, for by 1950 the Soviet peace campaign seemed to dictate the launching of an aggressive and sustained propaganda counterattack that would effectively promote the concept of freedom. The political logic of this novel situation entailed the covert manipulation of liberal ideals and their proponents.

Two considerations were crucial to this policy departure: effectiveness and legitimacy. There had always existed the assumption that private control of cultural programs enhanced their respectability, and hence their effectiveness, abroad. From a bureaucratic standpoint, the covert approach reflected the adoption of a political motivation in place of idealist ends at the same time that it took advantage of the nonpolitical reputation of idealist means. More important, perhaps, as a determinant of this resort to dissimulation was the fact that secrecy was the only means by which an effective ideological counteroffensive could be legitimated at home. Once again the tension between internal and external demands was central to the policy outcome.

From the standpoint of domestic ideological tranquility, government subsidies to intellectuals were bound to offend funda-

mentalist and liberal alike. Had they been made public, many purist liberals would have condemned them out of hand or severely
questioned their propriety. Whatever the degree of intellectual
freedom actually enjoyed by the recipients, the mere suggestion
of propaganda motivation would have been enough to compromise their independent standing. In addition, the fundamentalists
would have criticized not the appropriateness of such measures,
but the specific recipients of governmental largess – this at a time
when the ideological battle overseas dictated supporting intellectuals. Indeed, in the 1950s and 1960s, government officials argued that secret CIA subsidies were the only domestically feasible
kind; conservative ideologues would certainly have rejected them
otherwise. Consequently, there was a huge gap between the
needed propaganda instrumentality and the possibility of its social
acceptance. It was this domestic breach that ideology had to fill in
order to give political force to the international ideological struggle.

It is at this point that the final definition comes into play. Ideology has also been defined symbolically as a means by which societies make sense out of revolutionary social changes. A common
characteristic of this process is the use of traditional belief systems
to sanction solutions to problems they were not designed to confront. In this way history is given a reassuring measure of continuity that it did not originally possess, and the demands of modernity
are blessed by tradition. But there is a price to be paid for this
otherwise happy union of old and new. The strain between actual
policy and its rationalization in traditional terms results in ideological distortions. If the gap between the two is great enough, this
form of ideology might even amount to a large-scale form of cultural self-delusion.[15]

The United States found itself in such an incongruous situation
by 1950 because, in terms of political philosophy, it remained an
underdeveloped country. Circumstances dictated an effective mobilization of national cultural resources and their use in an international power struggle at the same time that there existed the
equally vital need to maintain the intellectual and organizational
continuity of a nonpolitical, antinationalist tradition. Could one
join opposites by reconciling liberalism and realpolitik? In a world
governed by rationality, it would have been impossible to do so.

Politics has its own logic, however. In this case, the only solution was an ideological one that met the conflicting demands of power and principle by obscuring the actual meaning of each. In its moderate form, the resolution of this dilemma entailed a modicum of self-deception; at its extreme, it required deliberate secrecy from domestic as well as foreign scrutiny. Ironically, to deal with reality was to flee from it.

An exchange between the new Senator William Benton and Secretary of State Dean Acheson in 1950 hinted at the difficulty involved in separating a realistically necessary national policy from ideological legitimation:

Senator Benton: I wonder if you would agree, Secretary Acheson, however, that although perhaps it took the Nazi propaganda and the Communist propaganda to awaken us as a country to the problem, and to awaken the State Department and the Congress, do you not think that we have learned enough about it by now so that we could see that there would be a need, even apart from the Communist propaganda? I ask that question because so many people tend to focus the entire emphasis of this problem on the need of counteracting Communist propaganda. I wonder if you would not discuss for a moment whether the need is not still there and is not one that we should now recognize entirely apart from the activities of the Soviets?
Secretary Acheson: Yes, I think there is that need. It is a little hard to separate it out.
Senator Benton: Yes.
Secretary Acheson: Because two things operate together.
Senator Benton: Yes, but I think we must try to judge them separately.[16]

In his concern with incipient McCarthyism, Benton was attempting to put some distance between anti-Communism and a more realistic conception of national policy.

This made sense if one used only abstract foreign policy criteria, but it ignored domestic political and historical realities. Benton must have forgotten the fundamentalist animosities stirred up by the Smith-Mundt Bill, the seminal role of anti-Communism in getting the legislation passed, and perhaps even his own anti-Communist fervor while assistant secretary of state. What history had joined, abstract logic could not pull asunder. The same was true of more sophisticated reactions to Communism. At the higher intellectual elevations, where a visceral anti-Communism was replaced by an articulated animus, the separation of ideology from policy was equally difficult, for the precondition of the liberals' involvement in the Cold War was a belief that the continued existence of fundamental principles was at stake. To call into question the validity of this motivation would have been to undermine the entire basis of their commitment. With its antiliberal dogmas and social structures, Communism provided an indispensable focus for an urgently required ideological consensus. If Communism had not existed, something like it would have had to be invented.

Ideology was both a means of disguise and a source of comforting reassurance: disguise, because it concealed the unwelcome dynamics of power and institutional change; false reassurance, because it furnished traditional justification for novel and otherwise questionable activities. It rationalized, legitimized, and concealed underlying political and structural transformations, the existence of which originally gave rise to the need for ideological thought. It allowed the United States to undertake policies that it had to adopt, but could not otherwise justify. To put it somewhat perversely, ideology provided a means of violating American beliefs while continuing to defend them. It thereby resolved, at least temporarily, some of the underlying dilemmas of U.S. foreign policy: how to play power politics while rejecting realpolitik as immoral; how to cling to internationalist aspirations while undergoing an intense period of national mobilization; and how to adopt a managerial approach to ideas while continuing to insist on their inherent autonomy.

All three panels in the ideological triptych have some applicability to the cultural Cold War, depending on what aspect of the American experience one chooses to emphasize. The anthropological view highlights the very real conflict of conceptual universes between the United States and the USSR, while concealing its inner contradictions. The sociological perspective significantly qualifies the initial interpretation and demonstrates how ideology provided a means of forging a cultural consensus by unifying drastically opposed points of view. Finally, the conception of ideology as a stopgap means of resolving the tension between cultural tradition and political realities provides at least the beginnings of an understanding of how American liberals could come to treat freedom as propaganda without questioning the integrity of their actions. Because ideology was the deus ex machina of postwar foreign policy, America's global activism could take place only in the context of Cold War, to the exclusion of more realistic and, perhaps, more humane forms of power politics. Unfortunately, such "realistic" responses to the postwar situation, however they might be defined, were ruled out by American cultural realities. That the most important ingredient in America's postwar foreign policy turned out to be a heaping measure of self-delusion was more a matter of historical necessity than of guileful or, as some would have it, conspiratorial manipulation.

Although the perceptual distortion of reality was central to this ideological diplomacy, it would be a mistake to conclude that it was only an intellectual phenomenon. As W. I. Thomas once put it, "If men define situations as real, they are real in their consequences."[17] For all the chimeras involved, the foreign policy revolution of the 1940s was no fantasy. America's domestic structure and the nation's overseas role did change dramatically, even though it all happened as if in a dream. There would come an awakening of sorts once the struggle with the Soviets lost its apocalyptic air and domestic insecurities were drained of urgency. The nation would then be shocked at how far it had strayed from its traditions and would wonder at how this could have come about. This would be a happy ending if one could demonstrate that the awakening was a return to reality. Given the proved strength of American liberal traditions, however, this would be claiming too much. America may have regained its senses, but these had not been realistic to begin with.

Epilog

When Americans spoke of cultural relations, they actually meant intellectual relations – it would not have occurred to them that the two were not identical. "Intellectual" in this context does not refer to "high culture." Liberal definitions of culture, diffusion, and acculturation – all of which habitually emphasized the paramount role of ideas – although frequently elitist, were essentially classless. Culture was defined as a spiritual phenomenon, interchange was viewed as a process intellectual in essence, and acculturation was perceived as the readjustment of opinions through rational means. The endlessly repeated references to the need for "mutual understanding" were rooted in this mentalist imagery. Although the cultural program did not lack for idealism of the do-good variety, its moral imperatives were overshadowed by a persistent philosophical idealism. For at the root of the enthusiasm for cultural relations as a diplomatic pursuit lay a belief in ideas as the determinant cultural reality.

Running parallel to these idealist assumptions was an individualist bias that viewed the human mind as the source of creative ideation and as the fount of cultural change. The mechanics of intercultural adaptation normally were described psychologically rather than in terms of processes that involved entire cultures. The basic purpose of cultural relations was thus to reorient individuals through the noncoercive, rational implantation of ideas. Change the thinking of enough individuals – or better yet, reach the strategically located elites – and cultural progress would automatically ensue. This conception of culture and cultural relations as an atomistic phenomenon – if that is not a contradiction in terms – reflected the regnant individualism inherent in the liberal American conception of political man.

The American emphasis on ideas and rationality was also inherently internationalist in its thrust. If rational thought were liberated thought, it followed that ideas must have universal passports, free from the restraints of diplomatic interference or ideological censorship. "The world of learning is 'One World,'" declared the American Council on Education in 1950. Ben Cherrington meant much the same thing by his remark in the 1930s to the effect that culture was "cosmic" in its essence. Accompanying this faith in the universal scope of rationality and the unimpeded flow of ideas was the conviction that the spread of rationality, knowledge, and understanding provided the basis for an ecumenical world community. There seemed to be hard, physical evidence for this optimism in the proliferation of international communications of all kinds and in the indisputable fact of growing world interdependence. The physical unity of the world would find its ultimate expression in global political institutions reflecting shared values rooted in a common rationality.[1]

This trust in the transcultural capacity of ideas to hasten the arrival of a generalized "understanding" comprised the intellectual core of the U.S. approach to cultural relations. How else explain the pervasive references to principles as the foundation of American society and to cultural relations as the underpinning of world community? Internationalism and an aversion to power politics were only logical extensions of idealist axioms. Inevitably, the faith in ideas as the determining reality considered even culture as only another, if perhaps the final, obstacle to the triumph of rationality. Culture was the last hurdle before universal understanding, rather than its limiting condition.[2]

It is not unreasonable to suggest that advocates of international understanding actually were calling for the elimination of culture altogether. For ultimately, their belief in the universality of ideas was not cultural at all, but supracultural. It was a restatement of the old Enlightenment faith in reason – the belief in a uniform nature and a rational human nature – masquerading in modern anthropological dress. From this view, culture was the social mask thrown over primitive reason rather than the social expression of irrationality. Given the presumption of a common human psychic identity that was rational in essence, one suspects that cultural relativism was so readily acceptable because it was not really a relativism at all. Diverse cultures were thought to be merely particular facets of an underlying intellectual and moral unity – "common values expressed in different modes of behavior," to use the words of Melville Herskovits. Differences were welcomed because all peoples, at bottom, were thought to be alike. Cultural interests did not separate men, but bound them together.³ If the culture concept is to have any meaning, however, it must lie in the affirmation of particularity and irrationality at the expense of a uniformitarian and rationalistic view of human nature.⁴

Although Americans rejected the concept of culture while acting in its name, they had little choice in the matter. If the cultural programs did not confront the basic realities of cultural relations, it was because they were culturally incapable of doing so. As the world was changing rapidly and making new and difficult demands on the United States, Americans could keep pace only by using the traditions available to them. It was inevitable as well as ironic that a cultural diplomacy that prided itself on its ecumenicism and its rationality was prevented by the very expansiveness of its vision from becoming conscious of its parochial limitations. What passed for universalism was only a projection of America's self-image, and a distorted one at that. More inescapable yet was the process whereby the compulsive pursuit of internationalism ended in its unknowing frustration. For in the attempt to universalize culture, Americans were unwitting captives of the very phenomenon they sought to transcend.

Notes

Introduction

1. My thinking on the subject has been most influenced by Marvin Harris, *The Rise of Anthropological Theory* (New York: Crowell, 1968); Julian Steward, *Theory of Culture Change* (Urbana: University of Illinois Press, 1955); and Leslie White, *The Concept of Cultural Systems: A Key to Understanding Tribes and Nations* (New York: Columbia University Press, 1975). Strong arguments for culture as a non-material organizing medium are presented by Marshall Sahlins in *Culture and Practical Reason* (Chicago: University of Chicago Press, 1976).

2. For the somewhat inbred and anemic literature that defines cultural relations as intellectual relations, see Ruth McMurry and Muna Lee, *The Cultural Approach: Another Way in International Relations* (Chapel Hill: University of North Carolina Press, 1947), pp. 1–3; Charles A. Thomson and Walter Laves, *Cultural Relations and U.S. Foreign Policy* (Bloomington: Indiana University Press, 1963), p. 23; Charles A. H. Thomson, *Overseas Information Service of the United States Government* (Washington, D.C.: Brookings Institution, 1948), p. 173n; Philip H. Coombs, *The Fourth Dimension of Foreign Policy* (New York: Harper & Row, 1964), pp. 17–22; Charles Frankel, *The Neglected Aspect of Foreign Affairs: American Educational and Cultural Policy Abroad* (Washington, D.C.: Brookings Institution, 1966), p. 5; Wilma Fairbank, *America's Cultural Experiment in China, 1942–1949* (Washington, D.C.: Government Printing Office, 1976), pp. 1–3; J. Manuel Espinosa, *Inter-American Beginnings of U.S. Cultural Diplomacy, 1936–1948* (Washington, D.C.: Government Printing Office, 1976), pp. 1–4; and the essays in Paul J. Braisted, ed., *Cultural Affairs and Foreign Relations*, rev. ed. (Washington, D.C.: Columbia Books, 1968), passim.

3. For the argument that evolutionary thought and cultural relativism were incompatible, see Elvin Hatch, *Theories of Man and Culture* (New York: Columbia University Press, 1973), pp. 51–3. Although logically impeccable, this argument fails to see that individuals could simultaneously endorse both positions. On this point, see the Epilog, infra.

4. Alexander Goldenweiser, "Diffusionism and the American School of Historical Ethnology," *The American Journal of Sociology* 31 (1925): 38; Introduction by Ivan A. Brady, in Ivan A. Brady and Barry L. Isaac, eds., *A Reader in Culture Change* (Cambridge, Mass.: Schenkman, 1975), vol. II: *Theories,* pp. xi–xiii; Jane Steward and Robert Murphy, eds., *Evolution and Ecology: Essays in Social Transformation by Julian H. Steward* (Urbana: University of Illinois Press, 1977), p. 73; Melville Herskovits, *Franz Boas: The Science of Man in the Making* (New York: Scribner, 1953), p. 66. Marvin Harris, *The Rise of Anthropological Theory*, p. 334, cites the "anti-materialist current" of the Boasian intellectual milieu.

5. Bert F. Hoselitz, "Advanced and Underdeveloped Countries: A Study in

184

Development Contrasts," in William B. Hamilton, ed., *The Transfer of Institutions* (Durham: Duke University Press, 1964), pp. 28–9; Marshall Sahlins, Elman Service, et al., *Evolution and Culture* (Ann Arbor: University of Michigan Press, 1960), pp. 46–57, 89, 118; Leslie White, *The Concept of Cultural Systems*, pp. 49–56.

6. Of the many works from which to choose, Janet L. Dolgin, David S. Kemnitzer, and David S. Schneider, eds., *Symbolic Anthropology: A Reader in the Study of Symbols and Meanings* (New York: Columbia University Press, 1977), despite its preoccupation with praxis theory, is a good place to begin. Marshall Sahlins, *Culture and Practical Reason* (Chicago: University of Chicago Press, 1976) and Clifford Geertz, *The Interpretation of Cultures* (New York: Basic Books, 1973) provide, theoretically and demonstratively, brilliant examples of the view of culture as a system of symbolic meaning.

1 Philanthropic origins of cultural policy

1. For the nineteenth-century explosion of private transnational contacts, see James A. Field, Jr., "Transnationalism and the New Tribe," in Robert O. Keohane and Joseph S. Nye, Jr., eds., *Transnational Relations and World Politics* (Cambridge: Harvard University Press, 1972), pp. 3–22. Two monographic studies of private cultural activities with foreign policy implications are James A. Field, Jr., *America and the Mediterranean World, 1776–1882* (Princeton: Princeton University Press, 1969), and Henry Blumenthal, *American and French Culture, 1800–1900* (Baton Rouge: Louisiana State University Press, 1977).

2. Frederick Lynch, *Personal Recollections of Andrew Carnegie* (New York: Fleming H. Revell Co., 1920), pp. 79–90. The fullest account of the founding of the endowment is David Patterson, *Toward A Warless World: The Travail of the American Peace Movement, 1887–1914* (Bloomington: Indiana University Press, 1976), pp. 141–52. But see also Warren F. Kuehl, *Hamilton Holt: Journalist, Internationalist, Educator* (Gainesville: University of Florida Press, 1960), pp. 98–100, and Joseph Wall, *Andrew Carnegie* (New York: Oxford University Press, 1970), pp. 897–9.

3. Merle Curti, *Peace or War: The American Peace Struggle, 1636–1936* (New York: Norton, 1936), pp. 204–6; Kuehl, *Hamilton Holt*, p. 101.

4. Philip C. Jessup, *Elihu Root*, 2 vols. (New York: Dodd, Mead, 1938), 2:488–9. See also Richard Leopold, *Elihu Root and the Conservative Tradition* (Boston: Little, Brown, 1954), pp. 54–8, 62–7; Andrew Carnegie, *Autobiography* (Garden City, N.Y.: Doubleday, 1933), p. 264.

5. Robert Bacon and James Brown Scott, eds., *Latin America and the United States: Addresses by Elihu Root* (Cambridge: Harvard University Press, 1977), pp. 70–1; Robert Bacon and James Brown Scott, eds., *Men and Policies: Addresses by Elihu Root* (Cambridge: Harvard University Press, 1925), p. 319; Jessup, *Elihu Root*, 2:374; Elihu Root, "A Requisite For the Success of Popular Diplomacy," *Foreign Affairs* 1 (September 1922):6–7.

6. Nicholas Murray Butler, *Across the Busy Years*, 2 vols. (New York: Scribner, 1940), pp. 60–75; Sondra R. Herman, *Eleven Against War* (Stanford, Calif.: Hoover Institution Press, 1969), p. 27; John F. Greco, "A Foundation for Internationalism: The Carnegie Endowment for International Peace, 1931–1941" (Ph.D. diss., Syracuse University, 1971), pp. 10–11, 16–20. James T. Shotwell, in his recollections of the endowment's early years, clearly saw Root as the domi-

nating figure, with Butler as "his right hand man." See Columbia University Oral History Collection, Butler Library, Columbia University, p. 146 (hereafter cited as COHC).

7. Herman, *Eleven Against War*, pp. 26–7; Greco, "A Foundation for Internationalism," p. 12; James T. Shotwell, *Autobiography* (Indianapolis: Bobbs-Merrill, 1961), p. 48; Carnegie Endowment for International Peace, *Report of the Acting Director of the Division of Intercourse and Education, March 31, 1917* (Washington, D.C.: Carnegie Endowment for International Peace, 1917), pp. 1–2 (hereafter cited as CEIP *Annual Report*, with appropriate year given).

8. Nicholas Murray Butler, "The International Mind: How to Develop It," *Proceedings of the Academy of Political Science* 8 (July 1917):16–20; Nicholas Murray Butler, *The International Mind: An Argument for the Judicial Settlement of International Disputes* (New York: Scribner, 1912), passim; Butler to Frederick Delano, 19 April 1932, cited in Greco, p. 27; Butler to Carnegie, cited in Burton J. Hendrick, *The Life of Andrew Carnegie*, 2 vols. (Garden City, N.Y.: Doubleday, 1937), 2:340; Nicholas Murray Butler, "The Carnegie Endowment for International Peace," *The Independent*, 27 November 1913, pp. 399–400.

9. Paul Reinsch, *Public International Unions* (Boston: Ginn & Co., 1911), pp. 1–11; CEIP *Annual Report, 1930*, p. 7.

10. For early endowment activities, Memorandum by Butler, 26 October 1911, in Papers of the Carnegie Endowment for International Peace, Butler Library, Columbia University, indexed bound volumes, 1911, vol. I, no. 208 (hereafter cited as CEIP MSS); Charles W. Eliot, *Some Roads Toward Peace* (Washington, D.C.: CEIP, 1914), passim; Hamilton Wright Mabie, *Educational Exchange with Japan* (Washington, D.C.: CEIP, 1914), passim; Robert Bacon, *For Better Relations with Our Latin American Neighbors* (Washington, D.C.: CEIP, 1915), passim; Harry Edwin Bard, *Intellectual and Cultural Relations Between the United States of America and the Other Republics of America* (Washington, D.C.: CEIP, 1914), pp. 3–4, 21. For the endowment's wartime attitudes, see Butler to Root, 18 January 1915, Papers of Elihu Root, Library of Congress, Manuscript Division, Box 136; Root to Colonel Edward House, 16 August 1918, ibid., Box 129; CEIP, *Yearbook, 1918*, pp. 65–6.

11. James R. Mock and Cedric Larson, *Words That Won the War: The Story of the Committee on Public Information, 1917–1919* (Princeton: Princeton University Press, 1939), pp. 288–90, 293–6; George Creel, *How We Advertised America* (New York: Harper & Row, 1920), pp. 244–5; *Complete Report of the Chairman of the Committee on Public Information 1917:1918:1919* (Washington, D.C.: Government Printing Office, 1920), pp. 161–3, 170–2, 193; Barry D. Karl, *Charles E. Merriam and the Study of Politics* (Chicago: University of Chicago Press, 1974), pp. 89–93.

12. CEIP, *Annual Report, 1923*, p. 5; Stephen Duggan, "The Kyoto Conference," Institute of International Education *News Bulletin* 5 (October 1929):1 (hereafter cited as IIE *News Bulletin*); Stephan Duggan, *A Professor at Large* (New York: Macmillan, 1943), p. 36; Reinsch, *Public International Unions*, p. 6.

13. There is no satisfactory historical study of corporate philanthropy's role as a nongovernmental planning institution. Robert H. Bremner's judgment in his *American Philanthropy* (Chicago: University of Chicago Press), p. 121, that the new foundations were designed "to put large-scale giving on a business-like basis," is the standard interpretation. But see also the following: F. Emerson Andrews, *Philanthropic Foundations* (New York: Russell Sage Foundation, 1956); Raymond B. Fosdick, *The Story of the Rockefeller Foundation* (New York:

Harper & Row, 1952), passim; George W. Gray, *Education on an International Scale* (New York: Harcourt Brace Jovanovich, 1941); Allan Nevins, *John D. Rockefeller: The Heroic Age of American Enterprise,* 2 vols. (New York: Scribner, 1940), 2:614–65; Raymond Fosdick, *Chronicle of a Generation* (New York: Harper & Row, 1958), pp. 251–88; Waldemar Nielsen, *The Big Foundations* (New York: Columbia University Press, 1972), pp. 31–7; Peter Collier and David Horowitz, *The Rockefellers: An American Dynasty* (New York: Holt, Rinehart and Winston, 1976), pp. 48–65, 99–107, 135–50; Merle Curti, *American Philanthropy Abroad: A History* (New Brunswick, N.J.: Rutgers University Press, 1963), esp. pp. 301–38 for activities in cultural relations.

14. Rockefeller Foundation, *Annual Report, 1919,* pp. 45–6; ibid., *1922,* p. 59; ibid., *1935,* p. 216; John Simon Guggenheim Memorial Foundation, *Reports of the Secretary and Treasurer, 1929–1930* (New York: Guggenheim Foundation, 1930), pp. 15–21.

15. Raymond Fosdick, *John D. Rockefeller, Jr.: A Portrait* (New York: Harper & Row, 1966), pp. 388–90. Fosdick's internationalist views are readily evident from a perusal of the following of his works: *The Old Savage in the New Civilization* (Garden City, N.Y.: Doubleday, 1928); *Letters on the League of Nations* (Princeton: Princeton University Press, 1966); *Chronicle of a Generation: An Autobiography* (New York: Harper & Row, 1958).

16. Carnegie Corporation of New York, *Report of the President and Treasurer for the Year Ending September 30, 1928* (New York: Carnegie Corporation, 1928), p. 31; Frederick P. Keppel, *The Foundation: Its Place in American Life* (New York: Macmillan, 1930), p. 103; Henry Allen Moe, "The John Simon Guggenheim Memorial Foundation," *The Educational Record* 6 (July 1925): 264–8.

17. Joseph E. Kiger, *American Learned Societies* (Washington, D.C.: Public Affairs Press, 1963), pp. 160–2, 190–8; Waldo Leland Interview, COHC, pp. 46–7; Waldo Leland, "The International Union of Academies and the American Council of Learned Societies," *International Conciliation* 154 (September 1920): 442–57; American Council of Learned Societies (hereafter ACLS) *Bulletin* 1 (October 1920):3; Papers of the American Council of Learned Societies, Library of Congress, Manuscript Division, correspondence in Box A-5 (hereafter cited as ACLS MSS). For a summary of private interest in internationalism, see David Allan Robertson, "International Educational Relations," *The Educational Record* 7 (January 1926):46–58.

18. Memorandum by Edward C. Armstrong, 16 April 1926, ACLS MSS, Box A-5; Memorandum by John Franklin Jameson, 28 March 1921, ibid.; Harold Josephson, *James T Shotwell and the Rise of Internationalism in America* (Rutherford, N.J.: Fairleigh Dickinson University Presses, 1975), pp. 48–64; Shotwell, *Autobiography,* p. 167; George T. Blakey, *Historians on the Homefront: American Propagandists for the Great War* (Lexington: University Press of Kentucky, 1970), pp. 16–21.

19. Waldo Leland, "The International Union of Academies and the American Council of Learned Societies," pp. 442–57; Waldo Leland Interview, COHC, p. 50; ACLS *Bulletin* 4 (June 1925):38; Correspondence of Charles H. Haskins in ACLS MSS, Box A-1; Leland Interview, COHC, pp. 61–2. See the various ACLS *Bulletins* for progress reports in area studies.

20. Memorandum, "Discussion of International Library Cooperation," 22 October 1926, Papers of the American Library Association, University Archives, University of Illinois, Urbana, Series 7/1/6, Box 1 (hereafter cited as ALA MSS); "Proceedings of the 57th Annual Conference," ALA *Bulletin* 29 (September

1935):638; "Report of the Subcommittee on Library Cooperation With Latin America," ALA MSS, Series 7/1/50, Box 1; "Final Report of Informal Conference on Library Interests," in Carnegie Corporation, *Report of the President and Treasurer* (New York: Carnegie Corporation, 1931), pp. 47, 59; CEIP, *Annual Report, 1935,* p. 44.

21. Butler to James Bertram, 9 December 1918, CEIP MSS, unindexed bound volume, IIE, 1918.

22. Duggan, *A Professor at Large,* pp. 14–15, 25–31; Butler to Duggan, 10 February 1919, CEIP MSS, IIE 1919–20, vol. II. See also the correspondence in IIE Historical Files (microfilmed), Institute of International Education, New York City, Roll 18, Side 1, Indexes 10 and 11; C.R. Mann, "International Educational Relations," *The Educational Record* 9 (January 1928):26–31; Stephen Halpern, "The Institute of International Education" (Ph.D. diss., Columbia University, 1969), pp. 103–24.

23. Jan Kolasa, *International Intellectual Cooperation: The League Experience and the Beginnings of UNESCO* (Wroclaw: Zaklad Narodowy, 1962), pp. 9–125; H. R. G. Greaves, *The League Committees and World Order* (London: Oxford University Press, 1931), pp. 111–38; Charles Hodges, "The World Union of Intellectual Forces," *Current History* 24 (June 1926):411–15; Alfred Zimmern, *Intellectual Foundations of International Cooperation* (n.p., n.d.), pp. 8, 16–18.

24. Josephson, *James T. Shotwell,* pp. 190–3; Vernon Kellogg, "American National Committee on Intellectual Cooperation," *The Educational Record* 8 (January 1927):7–27; ACLS "Proceedings," in ACLS *Bulletin* 4 (June 1925):34; Ursula P. Hubbard, "The Cooperation of the United States With the League of Nations and With the International Labour Organization," *International Conciliation* 274 (November 1931):726–8; Malcolm Davis Interview, COHC, pp. 134–5, 137–8; CEIP, *Annual Report, 1928,* p. 10. For Rockefeller's private contributions, see Vernon Kellogg to Root, 24 March 1926, Root MSS, Box 141.

25. Josephson, *James T. Shotwell,* pp. 191–2; Walter Kotschnig, "Toward an IOEDC: Some Major Issues Involved," *The Educational Record* 25 (July 1944):264; CEIP, *Annual Report, 1934,* p. 47.

26. James T. Shotwell, "International Understanding and International Interdependence," in National Society for the Study of Education, *International Understanding Through the Public School Curriculum* (Bloomington, Ill.: Public School Publishing Company, 1937), pp. 5, 12; James T. Shotwell, "Foundation of Good Will," *THINK* 4 (December 1938):9 ff.

27. IIE, *Fifteenth Annual Report of the Director* (New York: IIE, 1934), p. 9; Nicholas Murray Butler, "World Conditions We Are Facing," *International Conciliation* 350 (May 1939):275–83. See also "Committee on an International Auxiliary Language, Preliminary Report, 25 April 1922," ACLS *Bulletin* 2 (December 1922):32–3. Stephen Duggan became president of the International Auxiliary Language Association in 1940.

28. CEIP, *Annual Report, 1927,* p. 7; Fosdick, *The Old Savage in the New Civilization,* pp. 135–41; CEIP, *Annual Report, 1935,* pp. 9–10; Stephen Duggan, "Moral Disarmament and International Education," IIE *News Bulletin* 9 (November 1933):1; CEIP, *Annual Report, 1922,* p. 5.

29. For studies of voluntarist theory and its relevance to domestic affairs, see Joan Hoff Wilson, *Herbert Hoover: Forgotten Progressive* (Boston: Little, Brown, 1975), pp. 55–62; Craig M. Lloyd, *Aggressive Introvert: Herbert Hoover and Public Relations Management, 1912–1932* (Columbus: Ohio State University Press,

1972), pp. 109–12; and Ellis Hawley, "Herbert Hoover, the Commerce Secretariat, and the Vision of an 'Associative' State, 1921–1928," *Journal of American History* 61 (June 1974):116–40.

30. My view of the 1920s has been most influenced by Joan Hoff Wilson, *American Business and Foreign Policy, 1920–1933* (Boston: Beacon Press, 1973); Carl Parrini, *Heir to Empire: United States Economic Diplomacy, 1916–1923* (Pittsburgh: University of Pittsburgh Press, 1969); and Michael J. Hogan, *Informal Entente: The Private Structure of Cooperation in Anglo-American Economic Diplomacy, 1918–1928* (Columbia: University of Missouri Press, 1977). Although the concept of the Open Door, especially in the structural sense advanced by Hogan, presents a compelling analytical tool for U.S. diplomacy of the 1920s, the concentration upon economic relations by these authors is too restrictive. The Open Door concept possesses a larger cultural significance that not only deepens the issues but also, I should hope, complicates them. In particular, simplistic notions of economic determinism require rethinking.

31. Cordell Hull, *Addresses and Statements by the Honorable Cordell Hull* (Washington, D.C.: Government Printing Office, 1937), p. 6; IIE, *Seventeenth Annual Report of the Director* (New York: IIE, 1936), p. 4; McMurry and Lee, *The Cultural Approach*, pp. 39–126; Paul Gordon Lauren, *Diplomats and Bureaucrats* (Stanford, Calif.: Hoover Institution Press, 1976), passim.

32. Sumner Welles, *The Roosevelt Administration and Its Dealings With The Republics of the Western Hemisphere,* Department of State Publication No. 692, Latin American Series No. 9 (Washington, D.C.: Government Printing Office, 1935), pp. 1, 16; Sumner Welles, *Pan American Cooperation,* Department of State Publication No. 712, Latin American Series No. 10 (Washington, D.C.: Government Printing Office, 1935), pp. 2, 7.

33. Sumner Welles to Norman Davis, 11 May 1935, Norman Davis Papers, Library of Congress, Manuscript Division, Box 63; Sumner Welles, *The Way to Peace on the American Continent,* Department of State Publication No. 877, Latin American Series No. 13 (Washington, D.C.: Government Printing Office, 1936), pp. 8–9; Inter-American Conference for the Maintenance of Peace, *Special Handbook for the Delegates* (Washington, D.C.: Pan American Union, 1936), pp. 100–7; Unsigned Memorandum, "Concerning Intellectual Cooperation," in Records of the Delegation to the Inter-American Conference for the Maintenance of Peace, Record Group 43, National Archives, Box 1; "Report of the Subcommittee," 19 May 1936, ibid., Box 3; Memorandum by Concha Romero James, "The Work of the Pan American Union in the Field of Inter-American Cultural Relations," 1 June 1938, Papers of Samuel Guy Inman, Library of Congress, Manuscript Division, Box 37.

34. Undated Memorandum by Samuel Guy Inman, circa 1936, and Inman to Dean Howard Lee McBain, 10 March 1934, both in Inman MSS, Box 14; Samuel Guy Inman, *Inter-American Conferences, 1826–1954* (Gettysburg, Pa.: Times & News Publishing Co., 1965), p. 163; Address by Inman before the Centro Pro Paz, Argentina, 10 December 1936, Delegation Records, Box 10; Inman Diaries, Lima Conference Notes, in Inman MSS, Box 2.

35. Samuel Guy Inman, *Building an Inter-American Neighborhood* (New York: National Peace Conference, 1937), p. 49; Sumner Welles, *The Practical Accomplishments of the Buenos Aires Conference,* Department of State Conference Series No. 29 (Washington, D.C.: Government Printing Office, 1937); Samuel Guy Inman, "An Appraisal of the Buenos Aires Conference," Address before a Town

Hall Club luncheon, New York City, 4 February 1937, in Conference Records, Box 10.

36. Inman, *Building an Inter-American Neighborhood,* p. 49; Inman to Welles, 31 December 1937, Decimal Files, General Records of the Department of State, National Archives, Record Group 59, 810.4271 1/460 (hereafter all numbered citations refer to the decimal files); Inman to Welles, 2 March 1937, Inman MSS, Box 14; Inman to Hull, 13 August 1937, ibid.; Memorandum, Selden Chapin to Laurence Duggan, 23 March 1938, Files of the Division of American Republics, General Records of the Department of State, Record Group 59, National Archives, Box 2 (hereafter identified as RA Lot Files); Laurence Duggan to Inman, 8 March 1938, Inman MSS, Box 14. Donald R. McKale, *The Swastika Outside Germany* (Kent, Ohio: Kent State University Press, 1977), pp. 141–53, suggests that the most ferocious aspect of the *Auslands-Organisation* in Latin America was a threatening image which, ironically, mobilized a more than effective opposition to its inefficient operations.

37. U.S., Congress, House, Subcommittee of the Committee on Appropriations, *Hearings, Second Deficiency Appropriation Bill, 1938,* 75th Cong., 3rd sess., 1938, pp. 654–7.

38. See the characterizations of Messersmith in Arnold Offner, *American Appeasement: United States Foreign Policy and Germany, 1933–1938* (Cambridge: Harvard University Press, Belknap Press, 1969), pp. 94–5; and Willard R. Beaulac, *Career Ambassador* (New York: Macmillan, 1951), p. 149. See John Morton Blum, ed., *The Price of Vision: The Diary of Henry A. Wallace, 1942–1946* (Boston: Houghton Mifflin, 1973), p. 473, for a description of Messersmith as "a narrow minded martinet with a 19th-century outlook."

39. Undated Memorandum by Richard Pattee, "Intellectual Cooperation Between the United States and Latin America," 810.4271 1/492-3/4.

40. Memorandum, Laurence Duggan to Welles, 3 January 1938, 810.4271 1/471; Welles to Inman, 10 January 1938, Inman MSS, Box 14; Memorandum, Laurence Duggan to Kelchner and Pattee, 26 April 1938, Records of the Interdepartmental Committee on Technical Cooperation and Its Predecessors, Record Group 353, National Archives, Box 2 (hereafter cited as IDC).

41. Verbatim minutes of meeting, 23 May 1938, Records of the War History Branch Project, Record Group 59, National Archives, Box 52 (hereafter cited as WHB); U.S., Congress, House, Subcommittee of the Committee on Appropriations, *Hearings, Second Deficiency Appropriation Bill, 1938,* 75th Cong., 3rd sess., 1938.

42. Sumner Welles, "Radio News and Comments by the Under Secretary of State," Department of State *Press Releases* 19 (30 July 1938):64; Speech given by Laurence Duggan at the Army War College, 5 January 1938, 110.72/80; Radio interview broadcast over WOL, 6 July 1937, Conference Records, Box 1.

43. Memorandum by Gordon Johnstone, attorney for the Social Science Foundation, 27 June 1945, citing a letter written by James H. Causey of 1 May 1923, in the Robert Redfield Papers, Regenstein Library, University of Chicago, Box 29; Morison Shafroth, *The Social Science Foundation of Denver* (Denver: Social Science Foundation, 1946), pp. 9–10, 15; Ben M. Cherrington, *Methods of Education in International Attitudes* (New York: Teachers College, Columbia University, 1934), pp. 4–5; Ben M. Cherrington, *The Social Science Foundation of the University of Denver* (Denver: Social Science Foundation, 1976), passim.

44. "Address by the President, June 30, 1938," Department of State *Press*

Releases 19 (2 July 1938):9; Sumner Welles, "Practical Pan-Americanism," ibid., 20 (24 June 1939):544–5; Radio address by Welles delivered over NBC, 6 November 1938, in ibid., 19 (12 November 1938):318.

45. Ben Cherrington, "The Role of Education in International Relations," Department of State *Bulletin* 1 (8 July 1939):19 (hereafter cited as *DOSB*); General Advisory Committee of the Division of Cultural Relations, Minutes of meeting, 21 November 1938, 111.46 Advisory Committee/13.

46. Verbatim minutes of meeting, 23 May 1938, WHB, Box 53, pp. 7–8, 43–4.

47. Despatch from Tangier, 19 July 1939, 111.46/196; Memorandum, Richard Pattee to Laurence Duggan, 11 March 1938, 810.42711/492.

48. Introduction to Memorandum, "Outline of Tentative Program for the Division of Cultural Relations," 1 June 1939, 111.46/135B; Statement by Cherrington, General Advisory Committee minutes, 21 November 1938, 111.46 Advisory Committee/13, p. 28; Précis of speech by Cherrington, 7 July 1939, delivered before the Northern California Conference for Cultural Relations with Latin America, Inman MSS, Box 37; Henry Grady, "The Role of the United States in International Cultural Relations," *DOSB* 1 (2 December 1939):614; Address by Sumner Welles, 9 November 1939, in "Principal Addresses – Conference on Inter-American Relations in the Field of Education," WHB, Box 54 (mimeographed).

49. Statement by Cherrington, "The Division of Cultural Relations of the Department of State," November 1939, Redfield MSS, Box 33; Ben Cherrington, "The Division of Cultural Relations of the Department of State," IIE *News Bulletin* 8 (May 1939):6; Verbatim minutes of Conference on Inter-American Library Relations, 29 November 1929, ALA MSS, Series 7/1/50, Box 3.

50. General Advisory Committee minutes, 21 November 1938, 111.46 Advisory Committee/13; Memorandum of conversation by Carl Milam, 22 July 1938, ALA MSS, Series 7/1/50, Box 3; Statement by Cherrington, General Advisory Committee minutes, 21 November 1938, 111.46 Advisory Committee/13, pp. 28–9. For a contrary interpretation, see Espinosa, *Inter-American Beginnings*, pp. 79, 122; Thomson and Laves, *Cultural Relations and U.S. Foreign Policy*, p. 35. Samuel Bemis, *The Latin American Policy of the United States* (New York: Norton, 1967), pp. 326–30, and Edward O. Guerrant, *Roosevelt's Good Neighbor Policy* (Albuquerque: University of New Mexico Press, 1950), pp. 116–17, similarly overplay the supposed influence of Axis cultural penetration as a spur to the creation of a U.S. cultural program. The common error appears to be a reading of the atmosphere of 1940 into the events of 1936. J. Fred Rippy's *Latin America in World Politics*, 3rd ed. (New York: F. S. Crofts & Co., 1938), pp. 288–9, is one contemporaneous work that correctly minimizes the dangers arising from totalitarian cultural policies.

51. Memorandum, Warren Kelchner to Laurence Duggan, 1 July 1938, IDC, Box 3.

52. Memorandum by Cherrington, "Implementing the Division of Cultural Relations," 7 October 1938, 111.46 Advisory Committee/1. See also 111.46/27 through 32 and 111.46/61½; Memorandum by Cherrington, 21 November 1938, 111.46 Advisory Committee/12; see the Memoranda of conferences dated 31 March 1939, WHB, Box 52; "Outline of Tentative Program for the Division of Cultural Relations, March 16, 1939," 111.46/107½; Undated Memorandum by Ellis O. Briggs, 111.46/107½.

53. Memorandum, Cherrington to Welles, 25 July 1939, 811.42710 Washington/14 and attachments; Laurence Duggan to Welles, 26 July 1939, IDC, Box 3; Remarks by Adolf Berle, "Conference on Inter-American Relations in the Field of Music," *DOSB* 1 (21 October 1939):412. For conference planning see "Progress Report of the Division of Cultural Relations, June 1940," WHB, Box 56; Waldo Leland, "The Role and Work of the United Nations Educational, Scientific, and Cultural Organization," American Association of University Professors *Bulletin* 35 (Summer 1949):278. Digests of proceedings, copies of speeches, and reports are available in WHB, Box 54.

54. Cordell Hull, "For Closer Cultural Contacts," *THINK* 4 (December 1938):6 ff.

2 Wartime departures from tradition

1. Memorandum, Cherrington to Messersmith and Welles, 25 August 1939, WHB, Box 53; Memorandum by Cherrington, 27 May 1940, ibid., Box 57.

2. U.S., Office of Inter-American Affairs, *History of the Office of the Coordinator of Inter-American Affairs* (Washington, D.C.: Government Printing Office, 1947), p. 7n; U.S., Congress, House, Subcommittee of the Committee on Appropriations, *Hearings, Second Deficiency Appropriation Bill for 1941*, 77th Cong., 3rd sess., 1940, pp. 684–92. See also William L. Schurz, *Latin America: A Descriptive Survey* (New York: Dutton, 1941), p. 291, and Nicholas J. Spyman, *America's Strategy in World Politics: America and the Balance of Power* (New York: Harcourt Brace Jovanovich, 1942), p. 247.

3. CIAA Policy Board minutes, 27 September 1940, Papers of William Benton, privately held, Box 5712; Minutes of meeting in Charles Thomson's office, 30 September 1940, in ACLS MSS, Box B-95.

4. Memorandum, Robert G. Caldwell to Nelson Rockefeller, 4 October 1940, Benton MSS, Box 5712; James T. Shotwell to Waldo Leland, 4 March 1939, ACLS MSS, Box B-61; Remarks by Adolf Berle, General Advisory Committee minutes, 5–6 November 1941, 111.46 Advisory Committee/175; Archibald MacLeish, "Toward An Intellectual Offensive," ALA *Bulletin* 36 (July 1942):425; Adolf A. Berle, "Fundamental Values in American Foreign Policy," *DOSB* 3 (12 October 1940):297; Waldo G. Leland, "The International Role of American Scholarship," Address before the Graduate School Convocation, Brown University, 15 June 1940 (Providence, R.I.: The University, 1940). Some of these comments came near to advocating hemispheric cultural autarchy. For just such a contemporaneous argument, see Charles Wertenbaker, *A New Doctrine for the Americas* (New York: Viking Press, 1941), pp. 160–5.

5. Collier and Horowitz, *The Rockefellers*, pp. 213–14, 228–34. I am indebted to an unpublished paper by J. Scott Hauger that traces Rockefeller's reliance upon his philanthropic and artistic background in forming policies for and staffing the CIAA.

6. Waldo Leland to William Berrien, 13 May 1941, ACLS MSS, Box B-75; CIAA Policy Committee minutes, 14 October 1940, Benton MSS, Box 5712; General Advisory Committee minutes, 10 October 1940, 111.46 Advisory Committee/78.

7. William Benton to Rockefeller, 17 December 1940, Benton MSS, Box 5712; Memorandum, Laurence Duggan to Welles, 30 September 1940, 710.11/2599½; Leland to Thomson, 24 May 1941, ACLS MSS, Box B-95; Memoran-

dum, "Opportunities for Development of the Cultural Relations Program," attachment to letter from Rockefeller to Laurence Duggan, 9 September 1940, 810.42711/9–940. For a survey of Rockefeller's operations during World War II, see Gerald K. Haines, "Under the Eagle's Wing: The Franklin Roosevelt Administration Forges an American Hemisphere," *Diplomatic History* 1 (Fall 1977):373-88. My understanding of early State Department–CIAA relationships has been aided by a reading of the draft chapter on cultural relations from Irwin Gellman's recently published *Good Neighbor Diplomacy: United States Policies in Latin America, 1933–1945* (Baltimore: Johns Hopkins Press, 1979).

8. Franklin D. Roosevelt to Rockefeller, 22 April 1941, attachment to 810.42711/2310½; "Memorandum of Agreement," 5 June 1941, attachment to Memorandum from Thomson to Berle, 810.42711/1615½; Draft history of the Department of State's wartime activities, Chapter 49, pp. 181-2, in WHB, Box 5.

9. Memorandum, Messersmith to Cherrington, 8 June 1939, 121.53/47.

10. Wesley Frost to Hull, Despatch 3147 from Asunción, 2 October 1941, 810.42711/4237; Unsigned Memorandum to Thomson, 2 June 1941, WHB, Box 55; Departmental circular instruction from G. Howland Shaw, 29 August 1941, WHB, Box 10; Memorandum, Thomson to Duggan, 28 April 1943, WHB, Box 10; Circular instruction from Shaw, 11 October 1943, ibid.; "Report of the Trip of Charles Thomson, October 18–December 24," IDC, Box 1; Memorandum, Thomson to Welles, 28 April 1943, FW120.31 Auxiliary/68½; Memorandum, Duggan to Welles, 5 January 1943, ibid.; Herschell Brickell, in Carleton Beals, Bryce Oliver, Herschell Brickell, and Samuel Guy Inman, *What the South Americans Think of Us* (New York: R. M. McBride & Co., 1945), p. 246, alludes to the Foreign Service's resistance to specialized representation.

11. Memorandum by G. W. Ray, 1 July 1940, RA Lot Files, Box 3; General Advisory Committee minutes, 26 February 1942, 111.46 Advisory Committee/181; Undated Memorandum from Selden Chapin to Duggan, Daniels, Dreier, and Bonsal, WHB, Box 55; Claude Bowers to Hull, enclosure No. 1 to Despatch 4415 from Santiago, 11 September 1942, 811.42715/175.

12. Memorandum, William L. Schurz to Thomson, 14 May 1942, WHB, Box 55; Ellis Briggs to Laurence Duggan, 29 April 1942 and Duggan to Briggs, 1 June 1942, 810.42711/6895; Briggs to Duggan, 18 June 1942, 810.42711 Journalists/152; Memorandum, Philip Bonsal to Duggan, 28 June 1941, RA Lot Files, Box 4; Duggan to Rockefeller, 26 June 1942, WHB, Box 52; Laurence Duggan, *The Americas: The Search for Hemisphere Security* (New York: Holt, Rinehart and Winston, 1949), p. 160; Ellis O. Briggs, *Farewell to Foggy Bottom* (New York: McKay, 1964), p. 296.

13. Thomson to Henry A. Wallace, 7 January 1942, Henry Wallace Papers, Franklin D. Roosevelt Library (microfilmed), Reel 54, No. 0049; Charles A. Thomson, "The Role of Cultural Exchange in Wartime," *DOSB* 4 (3 January 1942):29-32.

14. Memorandum of conversation between Thomson and Philip Jessup, 24 April 1941, WHB, Box 57; Memorandum, Thomson to Shaw, 1 May 1941, 111.46/350B; Memorandum, Pierre L. de Boal to Laurence Duggan, 15 May 1941, RA Lot Files, Box 5; Henry B. Haskell to Waldo Leland, 25 June 1941, CEIP 66542.

15. National Education Association, *Among Us*, No. 11, December 1943, p. 3; *Proceedings of the Inter-American Educational and Cultural Conference, Gainesville,*

Florida, April 14–17, 1940 (Gainesville: University of Florida Press, 1940), passim; A. Randle Elliott, "Inter-American Educational Activities in the United States," IIE *News Bulletin* 19 (December 1943):6–8; Cherrington, *The Social Science Foundation*, pp. 19–20; W. Rex Crawford, "Cultural Relations in 1941," in Arthur P. Whitaker, ed., *Inter-American Affairs – 1941* (New York: Columbia University Press, 1943), pp. 97–131. See also the annual wartime volumes of *Inter-American Cultural Relations* (Austin: University of Texas Press, variable dates).

16. Rockefeller Foundation, *Annual Report, 1940 and 1941*, pp. 310 and 249; for SSRC minutes see Charles Merriam Papers, University of Chicago, Regenstein Library, Box 141; for the Joint Committee on Latin American Studies, of which Redfield was chairman, see Redfield MSS, Boxes 17 and 18; David Stevens to Leland, 19 October 1943, ACLS MSS, Box B-71.

17. Memorandum by Edith E. Ware, May 1941, James T. Shotwell Papers, Columbia University, Butler Library, Box 127; Undated Memorandum from Henri Bonnet, ACLS MSS, Box B-61; Edith E. Ware, Memorandum of conversation with Henry Allen Moe, 1 October 1940, Shotwell MSS, Box 127; Edith E. Ware to Charles Stevens, 19 February 1941, ibid., Box 131; Malcolm Davis and James T. Shotwell, "Report on the Havana Meeting of the Inter-American Committees on Intellectual Cooperation," ALA MSS, Series 7/1/6, Box 4; Malcolm Davis Interview, COHC.

18. Thomson to Shaw, 18 December 1941, WHB, Box 53.

19. Halpern, "The Institute of International Education," pp. 238, 243; Guggenheim Foundation, *Reports of the Secretary and Treasurer, 1941 and 1942*, p. 16; Espinosa, *Inter-American Beginnings*, pp. 164–72; Memoranda by Philip Bonsal, William L. Schurz, and Laurence Duggan, October 1942, 810.42711 S.E./3075.

20. IIE, *Report of the Conference of Foreign Student Advisers, April 28-30, 1941, Cleveland, Ohio* (New York: IIE, 1942), p. 11; Joint Policy Committee minutes, 11 December 1942, ACLS MSS, Box B-96; Memorandum, "What Has the Department of State Done to Eliminate Axis Influence in the Other American Republics?" 1 May 1942, WHB, Box 53; *Report* of the Division of Cultural Relations, July 1942, IDC, Box 23, p. 3; Memorandum, Bonsal to Long, 27 February 1941, RA Lot Files, Box 4; Josephus Daniels to Hull, Despatch 6869 from Mexico City, 10 January 1943, 811.42725 S.E./821; Memorandum, Welles to Duggan, 24 June 1943, 810.42711/16710.

21. Memorandum by Thornton Wilder, attachment to 810.42711 S.E./1757; Copy of project authorization attached to Telegram 893 to Rio de Janeiro, 5 April 1942, 810.42711/6035; Memorandum, John C. Dreier to Bonsal, 8 October 1942, RA Lot Files, Box 7; Memorandum by J. F. Griffiths, 28 September 1942, attachment to Despatch 6414 from Buenos Aires, 3 September 1942, 810.42711/9208; Waldo Frank, *South American Journey* (New York: Duell, Sloan and Pearce, 1943), pp. 204–20, 385–9. Frank makes no mention of his travel subsidy from the CIAA in this work.

22. Rodolfo A. Rivera, "The A.L.A. and Latin America," ALA *Bulletin* 34 (December 1940):672; Lewis Hanke, "Is Cooperation With Latin American Libraries Possible?" ibid., 35 (December 1941):668–9; Francis O. Wilcox, "The Libraries and the War Effort of the Americas," ibid., 36 (September 1942):6; "Libraries and the War: A Statement of Policy," ibid., 36 (January 1942):5.

23. Memorandum by William Haygood, 27 September 1939, ALA MSS, Series 7/1/50, Box 9; Haygood to George Lusk, 21 March 1940, ibid.; Haygood to

Milam, 17 February 1941, ibid., Box 16; Joint Policy Committee minutes, 22 October 1941, WHB, Box 54; Rodolfo Rivera to Milam, 18 July 1941, ALA MSS, Series 7/1/50, Box 11; Undated, unsigned Memorandum, "Statement on the American Libraries Program," ACLS MSS, Box B-6; Memorandum, "The Luncheon for Mr. Tschudy," 26 November 1943, ALA MSS, Series 7/1/6, Box 3.

24. Herschell Brickell, *What the South Americans Think of Us*, p. 242; Memorandum, Thomson to Laurence Duggan, 14 May 1941, WHB, Box 55. For a detailed study of the operations of one institute, see Donald H. Scott, "The Cultural Institute in Mexico City as an Example of United States Policy in Cultural Relations" (Ph.D. diss., University of Southern California, 1959), pp. 540-941.

25. Undated, unsigned Memorandum, "Importance of Cultural Institutes in the Cultural Program," WHB, Box 55; Memorandum, Bonsal to Thomson, 7 January 1941, RA Lot Files, Box 4; Memorandum, Louis J. Halle to Bonsal, 18 March 1943, ibid., Box 8; Harley Notter, Memorandum of meeting with Charles Thomson, Duggan, Trueblood, and Otterman, 29 April 1941, RA Lot Files, Box 4; Briggs to Laurence Duggan, 29 April 1942, 810.4271 1/6895.

26. General Advisory Committee minutes, 27 February 1941, 111.46 Advisory Committee/96, p. 14; ACLS, "Memorandum Respecting Assistance to Cultural Institutes in Latin America," circa December 1941, WHB, Box 51; Leland to William Berrien, 7 May 1941, ACLS MSS, Box B-75; General Advisory Committee minutes, 18–19 February 1944, Files of Harley Notter, Record Group 59, National Archives, Box 18; Joint Policy Committee minutes, 1 December 1941, WHB, Box 54.

27. Harley Notter, Memorandum of conversation with McClintock and Duggan, 16 May 1941, RA Lot Files, Box 4; Norman Armour to Hull, Despatch 11032 from Buenos Aires, 4 July 1943, 810.42711/16847; General Advisory Committee minutes, 9 May 1941, 111.46 Advisory Committee/111; Joint Policy Committee minutes, 18 June 1941, WHB, Box 54; Memorandum, Philip W. Powell to Thomson, 6 November 1941, WHB, Box 55; Memorandum, Thomson to Shaw, 15 December 1941, ibid.; Memorandum, Thomson to Shaw and Welles, 17 December 1941, ibid.; Memorandum, Shaw to Thomson, 17 December 1941, ibid.; Joint Policy Committee minutes, 18 December 1941, WHB, Box 54.

28. Arthur A. Compton, Jr., Memorandum of conversation with Thomson and Rockefeller, 28 February 1942, RA Lot Files, Box 6; Memorandum, Thomson to Laurence Duggan, 28 May 1942, FW810.42711/6895.

29. Kenneth Holland, "The Program of the Inter-American Educational Foundation," *The Educational Record* 27 (January 1946):80–7; Statement by Andrew Corry, Joint Policy Committee minutes, 15 July 1941, WHB, Box 54; Philip Powell, Memorandum of conversation, 19 August 1941, 810.42711/4107.

30. Kenneth Holland, "A United States School Program for the Other American Republics," attachment to Joint Policy Committee minutes, 15 January 1942, WHB, Box 54; Joint Policy Committee minutes, 15 July 1941, ibid.; General Advisory Committee minutes, 17–18 September 1941, 111.46 Advisory Committee/154.

31. Joint Policy Committee minutes, 15 January 1942, ACLS MSS, Box B-96; General Advisory Committee minutes, 25–26 February 1942, 111.46 Advisory Committee/181; Andrew Corry, "Memoir Proposing American Sponsored School Program, 1942-1943," in ACLS MSS, Box B-96.

32. Joint Policy Committee minutes, 4 May 1942, WHB, Box 54; Joint Policy Committee minutes, 7 December 1942, ACLS MSS, Box B-96; Report of the Subcommittee on American schools, "Recommendations for Policy Concerning Schools Sponsored by U.S. Citizens in the Other Americas," ibid.; CIAA, Educational Advisory Committee minutes, 18 December 1942, ibid.

33. Harry H. Pierson, "Notes on the Problem of American Schools in the Other American Republics," and "Comments on the Foregoing Basic Memorandum" by the department's political officers, both undated, in ACLS MSS, Box B-97. See also Arthur A. Compton to Dreier, Bonsal, and Duggan, 3 November 1942, RA Lot Files, Box 7, and Bonsal to Laurence Duggan, 5 November 1942, ibid.

34. Laurence Duggan to Rockefeller, 27 July 1943, photostat in files of USIA Historian, 1750 Pennsylvania Avenue, Washington, D.C.; Roy Tasco Davis, "American Private Schools in Latin America," *The Educational Record* 25 (October 1944):327–36; American Council on Education, Memorandum of March 16, 1944 Conference on Financial Aid to U.S. Sponsored Schools Abroad, ALA MSS, File 7/1/6, Box 1.

35. U.S., Congress, House, *Official Trip of Examination of Federal Activities in South and Central America, Report of the Subcommittee of the Committee on Appropriations*, 77th Cong., 1st sess., 1941, pp. 27, 30, 39; Memorandum, G. W. Ray to Thomson, 27 October 1941, 810.42711/4657; U.S., Congress, House, Subcommittee on Appropriations, *Hearings, Department of State Appropriation Bill for 1943*, 77th Cong., 2nd sess., 1941, p. 471.

36. Minutes of staff meeting, 29 September 1941, WHB, Box 55; Memorandum, Thomson to Shaw, 15 January 1942, WHB, Box 53; Memorandum by Michael J. McDermott, 20 September 1943, 811.42790/18.

37. Thomson, Memorandum of conversation with Harley Notter, 4 October 1941, WHB, Box 55; Memorandum by Theodore C. Achilles, 22 January 1942, 811.42741/120.

38. Memorandum, Stuart E. Grummon to Thomson, 6 April 1942, WHB, Box 55; Memorandum, W. C. Ferris to Shaw, 26 December 1942, FW811.42700/121; Memorandum, L. C. Frank to Shaw, 31 December 1942, ibid.; Memorandum by Grummon, 6 April 1943, WHB, Box 55; Memorandum, Wallace Murray to Hull, 25 May 1943, ibid., Box 48; Summary Memorandum by H. Arnold Quirin, 25 August 1943, 800.42711/212; Alexander Kirk to Hull, Despatch 407 from Cairo, and enclosures, 1 June 1942, 811.42790/14; Memorandum, Paul Alling to Wallace Murray with attached comments by Ralph Turner and Stuart Grummon, 6 July 1942, 811.42700/70642.

39. General Advisory Committee minutes, 9–10 June 1943, Notter Files, Box 18; Wallace Murray to Hull, 25 May 1943, WHB, Box 55. For the missionary antecedents of the U.S. cultural program in the Near East, consult Field, *The U.S. and the Mediterranean World*, passim, and Robert L. Daniel, *American Philanthropy in the Near East, 1820–1960* (Athens: Ohio University Press, 1970), passim.

40. Memorandum, Thomson to Shaw, 10 May 1943, 811.42700/5-1043; General Advisory Committee minutes, 9–10 June 1943, Notter Files, Box 18; Memorandum, Paul Alling to Leo Pasvolsky and Notter, 10 March 1943, WHB, Box 48.

41. Robert L. Daniel, "From Relief to Technical Assistance in the Near East, a Case Study: Near East Relief and Near East Foundation," (Ph.D. diss., Univer-

sity of Wisconsin, 1953), pp. 259–60; General Advisory Committee minutes, 9–10 June 1943, Notter Files, Box 18; Memorandum, William A. Eddy to Harry H. Pierson, 1 February 1944, FW811.42783/328.

42. Memorandum, Gordon P. Merriam to Paul Alling, 19 May 1943, WHB, Box 48; Haldore Hanson, comp., *The Cultural Cooperation Program, 1938–1943*, Department of State Publication 2137 (Washington, D.C.: Government Printing Office, 1944), pp. 30–1.

43. Attachment to Memorandum, Paul Alling to Wallace Murray, 6 July 1942, 811.42700/7-642; Memorandum, Donald Webster to Bryn Hovde, 10 February 1945, in Department of State Lot Files, Federal Records Center, Suitland, Maryland, Manifest number FRC63A788, Lot number 53D339, one box only (hereafter all references to the State Department Lot Files will be cited by Manifest, Lot, and Box numbers); Gordon Merriam to Bryn Hovde, 3 March 1945, ibid.

44. Van Engert to Hull, Telegram 85 from Kabul, 20 April 1943, *Foreign Relations of the United States: Diplomatic Papers, 1943*, vol. IV, *The Near East and Africa* (Washington, D.C.: Government Printing Office, 1964), p. 57 (hereafter all references to this series will be cited as *FRUS* with appropriate volume and year); Engert to Hull, 3 May 1943, ibid., p. 58.

45. Memorandum by C. W. Lewis, 29 April 1943, WHB, Box 48; Memorandum, Alling to Thomson, 21 May 1943, ibid.; Memorandum, Alling to Shaw, 21 June 1943, 811.4279OH/63.

46. Memorandum by Daniel C. Dennett, 15 June 1944, enclosure to Despatch 405 from Beirut, 15 June 1944, 811.4279OE/16; Col. Harold Hoskins, Memorandum of conversation with William Eddy, John Wilson, and Foy Kohler, 18 January 1944, FW811.42700/134; Thomson to Donald Webster, 9 March 1944, 111.76/3-944.

47. Copy of contract with the Phelps-Stokes Fund, 16 March 1944, in IDC, Box 1; Undated, unsigned Memorandum, "Cultural Relations With China and the Near East," ibid.; U.S., Congress, House, Subcommittee of the Committee on Appropriations, *Hearings, State Department Appropriation Bill, 1946*, 79th Cong., 1st sess., 1945, pp. 217–18; Memorandum by Irene Wright, 31 October 1944, 811.42790/10-3144; John A. Wilson to Frances Roberds, 10 October 1944, 811.42790H/10-1044 and attachments.

48. On the relationship between missionary interest in the Near East and in the Far East, see James A. Field, Jr., "Near East Notes and Far East Queries," in *The Missionary Enterprise in China and America*, ed. John King Fairbank (Cambridge: Harvard University Press, 1974), pp. 23–55. See also Kuang-Ching Liu, *Americans and Chinese: A Historical Essay and Bibliography* (Cambridge: Harvard University Press, 1963), pp. 13–40; "Reports of Arthur E. Bostwick's Mission to China as ALA Delegate," ALA *Bulletin* 20 (January 1926):35–48; ACLS *Bulletin* 10 (April 1929):3–4, 44–5; Rockefeller Foundation, *Annual Reports, 1938, 1939, 1940*, pp. 69, 72, and 70; IIE, *Sixth Annual Report of the Director* (New York: IIE, 1925), p. 7; Stephen Duggan, *A Professor at Large*, pp. 309–12; and the essays in Chi-Pao Cheng, ed., *Chinese-American Cultural Relations* (Taiwan: n.p., 1965), pp. 134–84. For Fosdick's statement, see Rockefeller Foundation, *Annual Report, 1939*, p. 70.

49. Memoranda by Willys R. Peck, 22 May 1941, 811.42793/461½, and 10 June 1941, 811.42793/464½; Memorandum, Alger Hiss to Stanley Hornbeck, 3 September 1941, 811.42793/480½; Memorandum, Thomson to Shaw, 11 September 1941, 811.42793/481½; Fairbank, *America's Cultural Experiment in*

China, pp. 9–13, 46–55, 113-20; Memorandum, Grummon to Thomson, 13 January 1942, WHB, Box 53; Haldore Hanson, *The Cultural Cooperation Program, 1938–1943*, pp. 12–13, 19–22, 35–8. Currie's pragmatic approach to cultural relations corresponds to what Tang T'sou, *America's Failure in China, 1941–1950* (Chicago: University of Chicago Press, 1963), pp. 89–109, describes as the Roosevelt administration's policy of "unconditional support" for China in the early stages of the Pacific War.

50. Hull to Clarence E. Gauss, Telegram 55 to Chungking, 29 January 1942, and Gauss to Hull, Telegram 113 from Chungking, 12 February 1942, both in *FRUS*, 1942, *China*, pp. 697–702; Hull to Gauss, Telegram 130 to Chungking, 24 February 1942, ibid., pp. 703–4.

51. Chiang Kai-shek, *China's Destiny* and *Chinese Economic Theory*, with notes and comment by Philip Jaffe (London: Dennis Dobson, 1945), p. 205; Gauss to Hull, Despatch 1832 from Chungking, 18 November 1943, 893.00/15195; Tang T'sou, *America's Failure in China*, p. 190; John King Fairbank, *The United States and China*, rev. ed. (New York: Viking Press, 1962), pp. 193–4.

52. Gauss to Hull, Despatch 761 from Chungking, 1 December 1942, 811.42793/924; Fairbank, *America's Cultural Experiment in China*, pp. 83–96, 126–8; Gauss to Hull, Airgram A-69 from Chungking, 7 October 1943, *FRUS*, 1943, *China*, pp. 750–1; Gauss to Hull, Despatch from Chungking, 16 November 1943, ibid., "Embarassment of a Confucian," *Time*, 24 April 1944, pp. 34–6.

53. Gauss to Hull, Despatches 1914 and 1915 from Chungking, 15 December 1943, *FRUS*, 1943, *China*, pp. 759–63; Gauss to Hull, Despatch 1916 from Chungking, 15 December 1943, 811.42793/1468; "Notes," IIE *News Bulletin* 18 (January 1943):11; John King Fairbank to Peck, 30 October 1943, 811.42793/10-3043; Fairbank to Lauchlin Currie, Telegram 579 from Chungking, 28 April 1943, 811.42793/1100.

54. Memorandum by John King Fairbank and T. L. Yuan, enclosure to Despatch 907 from Chungking, 20 January 1943, 811.42793/1006; Memorandum by Fairbank, 19 November 1943, enclosure to Despatch 1858 from Chungking, 24 November 1943, 893.00/15207.

55. Memorandum by J. Hall Paxton, 10 July 1944, enclosure to Despatch 2785 from Chungking, 18 July 1944, 811.42793/7-1844; General Advisory Committee minutes, 23–24 February 1944 and 9–10 June 1943, Notter Files, Box 18.

56. For the Redfield project, see the correspondence in the Redfield MSS (University of Chicago, Regenstein Library), Box 6. SSRC minutes are in the Merriam MSS, Box 142. On the ALA project: John King Fairbank to Carl Milam, 2 February 1944, ALA MSS, Series 7/1/51, Box 1; Correspondence relating to White's trip is in Box 2.

57. Correspondence in Carl Ackerman Papers, Library of Congress, Manuscript Division, Box 63; Edward Stettinius to Patrick Hurley, Telegram 321 to Chungking, 24 February 1945, 811.42793/2-2445; Enclosure to Despatch 586 from Chungking, 1 August 1945, 811.42793/8-145.

58. Paul Braisted to Ralph Turner, 2 August 1944, 811.42700/8-244; Memorandum by Wilma Fairbank, 7 August 1944, 811.42700/8-744.

3 Planning the liberal ecumene

1. Spykman, *America's Strategy in World Politics*, pp. 255–6; Bemis, *The Latin American Policy of the United States*, p. 313.

2. Memorandum, Selden Chapin to Laurence Duggan, 31 March 1942, WHB, Box 55; Undated extract of speech delivered by Thomson at the University of Texas, Austin, circa May 1942, ibid.; Charles A. Thomson, "Intellectual Freedom as a Basis for World Understanding," *International Conciliation* 383 (October 1942):425.

3. Samuel Guy Inman, "Backgrounds and Problems in Intellectual Exchange," in University of Texas, Institute of Latin American Studies, *Inter-American Intellectual Exchange* (Austin: University of Texas Press, 1944), p. 15.

4. Charles A. Thomson, "A Free Mind for a Free World," *DOSB* 8 (20 March 1943):233; Pierre L. de Boal, "Security," *DOSB* 12 (15 April 1945):711; Pierre L. de Boal, "The Substance of Foreign Relations," *DOSB* 12 (18 February 1945):244–6; Charles A. Thomson, "The Basis for Inter-American Cooperation," address delivered before the American Library Association, 20 June 1941, 810.42711/2637½.

5. U.S., Congress, House, Subcommittee of the Committee on Appropriations, *Hearings, Department of State Appropriation Bill for 1943*, 77th Cong., 2nd sess., 1942, p. 473; General Advisory Committee minutes, 18 September 1941 and 4 February 1942, 111.46 Advisory Committee/154 and 181; Henry Wallace to Thomson, 3 January 1942, Wallace MSS, Reel 54, No. 0053; Wallace to Thomson, 11 March 1942, ibid., Reel 47, No. 1237.

6. Minutes of staff meeting, Division of Cultural Relations, 9 February 1942, WHB, Box 57; Memoranda, Richard Pattee to Thomson, 20 March and 1 April 1942, WHB, Box 55.

7. Carl Milam to Thomson, 28 May 1942, Wallace MSS, Reel 54, No. 149; Charles A. Thomson, "The Bases for Inter-American Cooperation," 810.42711/2632½; Adolf Berle, "Address Before the Conference on Inter-American Relations in the Field of Music," *Digest of Proceedings – Principal Addresses*, Washington, 1939 (mimeographed); Sumner Welles, "Blueprint for Peace," in Sumner Welles, *The World of the Four Freedoms*, with a foreword by Nicholas Murray Butler (New York: Columbia University Press, 1943), pp. 99–100.

8. Statement by Ben Cherrington, General Advisory Committee minutes, 18 September 1941, 111.46 Advisory Committee/154, pp. 58-60.

9. Statement by Harley Notter in ibid., pp. 61–6; Memoranda, Laurence Duggan to Notter, 30 September 1941, Philip Bonsal to Duggan, 26 September 1941, and Notter to Bonsal and Duggan, 26 September 1941, all in Notter Files, Box 17.

10. General Advisory Committee minutes, 18 September 1941, 111.46 Advisory Committee/154; Memorandum by Waldo Leland, 12 March 1942, ACLS MSS, Box B-93.

11. Division of Cultural Relations, *Monthly Report*, March 1942, WHB, Box 56; Memorandum, Thomson to Pasvolsky et al., 9 February 1942, 811.42700/140½ and attachments. See also the memorandum by Thomson, 15 January 1942, WHB, Box 53.

12. Memorandum of conversation between Thomson and G. Howland Shaw, 4 March 1942, WHB, Box 55; Memorandum, Thomson to Shaw, 16 May 1942, ibid.; Ralph E. Turner, *The Great Cultural Traditions: The Foundations of Civilization*, 2 vols. (New York: McGraw-Hill, 1941) and *America in Civilization* (New York: Knopf, 1925), p. 392; General Advisory Committee minutes, 19–20 June 1942, Notter Files, Box 18. The other two studies were published as McMurry and Lee, *The Cultural Approach* and Isaac Kandel, *Intellectual Coopera-*

tion: *National and International* (New York: Teachers College, Columbia University, 1944).

13. General Advisory Committee minutes, 19–20 June 1942, Notter Files, Box 18.

14. The following discussion is based on three memoranda by Turner, sent as enclosures to a memo from Turner to Thomson, 28 September 1942, in ACLS MSS, Box B-98. From their appearance, these are only rough drafts, but I have been unable to find any other copies of these memoranda in the State Department files or in any other depository.

15. Memorandum, Louis J. Halle to Philip Bonsal, 13 February 1943, RA Lot Files, Box 8; Memorandum, John Melby to Arthur Compton, 20 February 1943, ibid.; Memorandum, Henry S. Villard to Thomson, 26 August 1943, WHB, Box 48. See also the Memorandum by P. N. Jester, 30 March 1942, 800.42711/213.

16. Memorandum, Notter to Thomson, 24 March 1943, Notter Files, Box 18.

17. Memorandum, Bonsal to Thomson, 25 February 1943, RA Lot Files, Box 8; Memorandum, Welles to Thomson, 22 February 1943, 811.42700/2-2243.

18. General Advisory Committee minutes, 23–24 February 1943, IDC, Box 29. For an exception among this group see Carl Milam to Thomson, 2 February 1943, ALA MSS, Series 7/1/6, Box 20.

19. Proceedings of the annual meeting of the ACLS, in ACLS *Bulletin* 36 (December 1944):32–3; Isaac Kandel, "Memorandum on the Organization of Intellectual Cooperation," CEIP 78384; Notes on motions approved by the Executive Committee of the National Committee of the USA on Intellectual Cooperation, New York City, 6 June 1943, CEIP 78366; Statement of Drafting Committee, 28 June 1943, CEIP 78452.

20. Thurston J. Davies, "The Arts and the Crisis," *The Educational Record* 23 (January 1942):30–1; Minutes of the Advisory Committee on the Adjustment of Foreign Students, 14–15 December 1944, FRC63A217, Lot 52-86, Box 299; "Report Number One of the Special Committee on International Cultural Relations," ALA *Bulletin* 36 (October 1942):755; Walter Kotschnig, "International Education," *The Educational Record* 22 (October 1941):500; Max Lerner, "American Leadership in a Harsh Age," *The Annals* 216 (July 1941):122; Esther Caukin Brunauer, "Power Politics and Democracy," ibid., p. 115.

21. Stephen Duggan, "Sovereignty," IIE *News Bulletin* 16 (November 1941):4; Duggan, *A Professor At Large*, pp. 428–31; Milton E. Lord, "Postwar Relationships and International Cultural Relations," ALA *Bulletin* 36 (September 1942):15; Rockefeller Foundation, *Annual Report, 1944*, p. 10; Esther Brunauer, "The Development of International Attitudes," in National Society for the Study of Education, *International Understanding Through the Public School Curriculum*, p. 25.

22. Lura G. Camery, "American Backgrounds of the United Nations Educational, Scientific, and Cultural Organization" (Ph.D. diss., Stanford University, 1949), pp. 216–17; "Education and the People's Peace," National Education Association *Journal* 32 (September 1943):165–8. See also William G. Carr, *Only By Understanding* (New York: Foreign Policy Association, 1945), p. 26.

23. Walter Kotschnig, *Slaves Need No Leaders* (New York: Oxford University Press, 1943), pp. 256–7.

24. Walter Kotschnig, "Toward an IOECD: Some Major Issues Involved," *The Educational Record* 25 (July 1944):265–6; Malcolm W. Davis, "The League of Minds," in Harriet Eager Davis, ed., *Pioneers in World Order, An American Ap-*

praisal of the League of Nations (New York: Columbia University Press, 1944), pp. 248–9.

25. Philip Jessup, remarks at a round-table discussion at the Palo Alto World Peace Forum, 23 September 1942, Jessup MSS, Box 216; Lester A. Kirkendall, "Education and the Postwar World," *The Educational Record* 24 (January 1943):48; John M. Fletcher, "Human Nature and World Peace," NEA *Journal* 34 (May 1945):102; Minutes of the SSRC Board of Directors, 11–12 September 1943, Merriam MSS, Box 141; James Marshall, *The Freedom to be Free* (New York: John Day Co., 1943), pp. 211–14; Comment by Leland on the grant proposal submitted by the Liaison Committee to the Columbia Foundation, in Papers of Waldo Leland, Library of Congress, Manuscript Division, Box 106.

26. Ben Cherrington to Sumner Welles, 15 January 1943, 800.42/204. See also Henry S. Curtis, "Education for Permanent Peace," *School and Society* 58 (17 July 1943):34; Grayson Kefauver to Thomson, 10 March 1943, 800.42/212; Grayson Kefauver, "Peace Aims Call for International Action in Education," *New Europe* 3 (May 1943):15–19; Henry Merritt Wriston, *Subsoil of Peace*, The Hazen Pamphlets, No. 6 (Haddam, Conn.: Hazen Foundation, 1942), pp. 9–14.

27. Camery, "American Backgrounds of [UNESCO]," pp. 219–33, 240; Grayson Kefauver to Welles, 1 June 1943, 800.42/234. See also the correspondence in ACLS MSS, Box B-61:International Education, for the Council on Education in World Citizenship and its connection to the U.S. National Committee on Intellectual Cooperation.

28. The best treatment of the Conference of Allied Ministers of Education, drawing on conference documents, is James P. Sewell, *UNESCO and World Politics* (Princeton: Princeton University Press, 1975), pp. 33–70; Winant to Hull, Despatch 9364 from London, 31 May 1943, 800.42/231.

29. Division of Cultural Relations, *Monthly Report*, April 1943, 111.46/502; Memorandum, Turner to Thomson, 20 January 1943, Notter Files, Box 17; Memorandum, Notter to Thomson, 4 March 1943, ibid.; *New York Times*, 8 April 1943, pp. 1 and 9; General Advisory Committee minutes, 9–10 June 1943, Notter Files, Box 18. These minutes are particularly interesting for the views they reveal on the problem of German reeducation.

30. Hull to Winant, Telegram 4991 to London, 1 September 1943, 800.42/256; Winant to Hull, Telegram 5863 from London, 4 September 1943, *FRUS, 1943, General*, pp. 1153–4; Memorandum of conversation between Turner and Allardyce Nicoll, 17 May 1943, 800.42/228; Winant to Hull, Despatch 9364 from London, 31 May 1943, 800.42/238.

31. Harry D. Gideonse to Benjamin Gerig, 29 October 1943, Notter Files, Box 17; Winant to Hull, Telegram 6797 from London, 7 October 1943, *FRUS, 1943, General*, pp. 1156–7; Isaac Kandel to Thomson, 10 January 1944, 800.42/444; Ralph Turner and Hope Sewell French, *Conference of Allied Ministers of Education*, Department of State Publication 2221, Conference Series 59 (Washington, D.C.: Government Printing Office, 1944), p. 3; Minutes of Advisory Committee on Adjustment of Foreign Students, 10–11 February 1944, FRC63A217, Lot 52–86, Box 299; Memorandum, Thomson to G. Howland Shaw, 7 January 1944, Notter Files, Box 17; Ralph Turner, "The Conference of Allied Ministers of Education," *The School Executive* 63 (March 1944):38.

32. Memorandum by Ralph Turner, November 1943, attachment No. 1 to Despatch 12183 from London, 11 November 1943, 800.42/306.

33. Unsigned, undated Memorandum, "The Planning That Led to the Estab-

lishment of UNESCO," FRC72A1739, Lot 65D423, Box 19; Memorandum, Esther Brunauer to Notter, 24 March 1944, Notter Files, Box 17. See also Harley Notter, *Postwar Foreign Policy Preparation 1939–1945*, Department of State Publication 3580 (Washington, D.C.: Government Printing Office, 1950), p. 237.

34. Stephen Duggan to Thomson, 4 January 1944, 800.42/364.

35. Memorandum, Thomson to Shaw, 24 December 1943, 800.42/330; Précis of informal discussion, 7 January 1944, notes taken by James T. Shotwell, CEIP 76733; "Statement of Findings Adopted By the Conference on International Educational Relations, 7 January 1944," ACLS MSS, Box B-61; Memorandum by Dorothy Fosdick, 25 January 1944, Notter Files, Box 17; Memorandum, Shaw to Berle, 17 December 1943, 800.42/344.

36. Washington *Post*, 4 May 1944, extract in Notter Files, Box 18; Grayson Kefauver to Harley Notter, 26 April 1944, 800.42/576; Press Release No. 159, 3 May 1944, 800.42/545.

37. Enclosure, Grayson Kefauver to Thomson, 27 June 1944, 800.42/6-2744; James Marshall to Shaw, 23 June 1944, 800.42/6-2344; *I.O.E. News* 1 (June 1944), attachment to 800.42/6-144; William G. Carr to Hull, 7 August 1944, 800.42/8-744 and attachment; Carr to Leland, 17 August 1944, Leland MSS, Box 106; Memorandum, John S. Dickey to Shaw, 9 May 1944, 111.76/5-944.

38. Hull to Harriman, Despatch 219 to Moscow, 13 July 1944, 800.42/7-1344; W. J. Gallman to Hull, Despatch 13013 from London, 30 December 1932, *FRUS*, 1943, *General*, pp. 1160–1.

39. Memorandum by Grayson Kefauver, 21 June 1944, Notter Files, Box 17; Harriman to Hull, Airgram A-109 from Moscow, 29 August 1944, 800.42/7-1344; Memorandum, Kefauver to Thomson, 9 November 1944, FW800.42/8-744.

40. Leland to Carr, 17 August 1944, Leland MSS, Box 106; Memorandum, John S. Dickey to Shaw, 9 May 1944, 111.76/5-944; Ralph Turner to Kefauver, Telegram 7658 to London, 20 September 1944, 800.42/9-2044; U.S., Department of State, *The Defense of Peace*, Part 2, Publication 1475, Conference Series 81 (Washington, D.C.: Government Printing Office, 1946), p. 7.

41. Memorandum by Kefauver, 24 November 1944, 811.42700/11-2444.

42. Memorandum, Bryn Hovde to Archibald MacLeish, 16 December 1944, FW811.42700/12-1244; Memorandum, MacLeish to Dickey, 2 January 1945, MacLeish MSS, Box 5; U.S., Congress, House, *Hearings Before the Committee on Foreign Affairs on H. Res. 215 Urging the Formation of an Organization to be Known as the International Office of Education*, 79th Cong., 1st sess., 1945, p. 49.

43. Leland to Thomson, 23 May 1944, ACLS MSS, Box B-93; National Research Council, Division of Foreign Relations, "Memorandum on the Activities and Future Plans of International Scientific Organizations, 1919–1944," FRC63A217, Lot 52–86, Box 299; Agenda, the Conference on Problems of Restoring International Scientific and Cultural Cooperation, 13 December 1944, attachment to 111.76/11-2244; Sewell, *UNESCO and World Politics*, pp. 47–52; Joseph Needham, "The Place of Science and International Scientific Cooperation in Post-War World Organization," *Nature* 156 (10 November 1945):558–61.

44. Secretary's Staff Committee, minutes of meeting, 2 February 1945, National Archives, Record Group 353, Lot File 122, Box 88G; Memorandum of conversation, Joseph Grew and James Marshall, undated, Leo Pasvolsky Papers, Library of Congress, Manuscript Division, Box 4.

45. William G. Carr Interview, COHC; Liaison Committee Memorandum by Carr, 11 May 1945, Leland MSS, Box 107; William G. Carr, "The NEA at the San Francisco Conference," NEA *Journal* 34 (October 1945):123; Unsigned Memorandum, "Principal Proposals by Other Governments and Arguments Against Them," 23 April 1945, Pasvolsky MSS, Box 5; George Zook, "The President's Annual Report," *The Educational Record* 27 (July 1946):302.

46. General Advisory Committee minutes, 18–19 July 1944, 111.46 Advisory Committee/7-2144; Memorandum by Kotschnig of meeting among Kefauver, Peck, Brunauer, Kotschnig, Harry Warfel, and Herschell Brickell, 30 March 1945, 811.42700/3-3045.

47. Robert M. MacIver, "The Fundamental Principles of International Order," *International Postwar Problems* 1 (December 1943):18.

4 The failure of internationalism

1. Memorandum by Charles J. Child, 23 February 1945, FRC62A624, Lot 21, Box 201; Carl M. White to Archibald MacLeish, 8 March 1945, ALA MSS, Series 7/1/6, Box 16. See also Frank Loescher, *Pathways to Understanding: Overcoming Community Barriers to International Cultural Cooperation* (Haddam, Conn: Hazen Foundation, 1946), p. 6; Universities Committee on Post-War International Problems, "Summaries of Cooperating Groups," *International Conciliation* 405 (November 1944):695.

2. Arthur Judson to William Benton, 9 January 1946, FRC62A624, Lot 21, Box 201; André Mertens to MacLeish, 31 January 1945, ibid.

3. Memorandum, Charles Thomson to Ruth Shipley, 7 July 1944, ibid.; Copy of Despatch from Caracas written by Joseph Flack, 20 April 1945, ibid.; Memorandum, Child to Bryn Hovde, 25 October 1944, ibid.; Charles Seeger to Howard Hanson, 14 January 1947, ibid.

4. Memorandum, Child to Hovde, 22 January 1945, ibid.; Memorandum, Child to Haldore Hanson, 4 January 1946, ibid.; Memorandum, Hanson to Child, 20 November 1946, 811.42700 (M)/11-2046; *The Story of ASCAP: An American Institution, 1914–1944* (n.p., n.d.), p. 13; Minutes of meeting with John Paine, General Manager of ASCAP, 16 January 1946, FRC62A624, Lot 21, Box 201.

5. George Brett et al., *The Role of Books in Inter-American Relations* (New York: Book Publishers Bureau Inc. and the American Textbook Publishers Institute, 1943), passim; Memorandum by Harry Warfel, 24 October 1944, FRC62A624, Lot 21, Box 200; Unsigned Memorandum, notes of 14 March 1944 meeting of Publishers Foreign Trade Committee, ibid.

6. George Brett to Edward Stettinius, 26 May 1944, 811.42741/6-1444.

7. Walter G. Harrap to Malcolm Johnson, 24 April 1944, 811.42741/7-1844; The Publishers Association, *Report on the United States and Canada* (London: n.p., 1943), pp. 57–64.

8. Winant to Hull, Despatch 18259 from London, 28 September 1944, 811.42741/9-2844; George Brett to James A. Ross, 1 November 1944, 811.42741/11-144; Winant to Hull, Despatch 24803 from London, 14 August 1945, 811.42700/8-1445; Winant to Hull, Despatch 19615 from London, 2 December 1944, 811.42741/12-244.

9. Memorandum by Warfel, 17 February 1944, FRC62A624, Lot 21, Box 200; Memorandum by Warfel, 29 January 1944, FRC68A1414, Lot 52–84, Box

1045; Copy of document AME/B/50 from the Conference of Allied Ministers of Education in London, undated, FRC62A624, Lot 21, Box 200; Horatio Smith to MacLeish, 17 April 1945, 500.CC/4-1745. See also the Memoranda from E. R. Schaeffer to Grayson Kefauver, 1 and 6 March 1945, FRC63A217, Lot 52–86, Box 300.

10. Memorandum, Richard Heindel to William T. Stone, 28 October 1946, FRC68A1414, Lot 52–84, Box 1045; Memorandum of OWI-CIAA-State Book Conference, 3 October 1944, FRC62A624, Lot 21, Box 200; Minutes of OWI meeting, 20 November 1944, ibid.

11. USIBA Prospectus, FRC68A1414, Lot 52–84, Box 1045; Memorandum by James S. Thompson, McGraw-Hill, "U.S. Technical Books in International Relations," FRC63A217, Lot 52–86, Box 300; Memorandum, Heindel to Stone, 10 January 1945, FRC68A1414, Lot 52–84, Box 1045; Speech of Eugene Reynal at annual membership meeting, Princeton, New Jersey, 18 January 1946, ibid.; Memorandum by Warfel, 13 March 1945, 811.42700/3-1345.

12. Eugene Reynal to Heindel, 1 April 1946, FRC68A1414, Lot 52-86, Box 1045; Robert L. Wood to Heindel, 26 November 1946, ibid.; Telegram 273 to Praha, 3 April 1946, 811.42700 (B)/4-346; Edward Crane to Heindel, 10 January 1947, FRC68A1414, Lot 52–84, Box 1045; Memorandum, Heindel to William Benton, 14 January 1947, 811.42700/1-2447.

13. Memorandum, Carl Sauer to Lawrence S. Morris, 16 June 1947, 811.42700(B)/4-1047; Harry F. West to George Marshall, 2 April 1947, FRC70A4521, Lot 587, Box 401; Memorandum by American Textbook Publishers Association, American Textbook Publishers Council, and American Association of University Presses, "Books For World Rehabilitation," FRC63A217, Lot 53D247, Box 146; Memorandum, Benton to Robert Lovett, 19 September 1947, FRC70A4521, Lot 587, Box 401; Memorandum, Carl Sauer to Howland Sargeant, 25 August 1947, ibid. Subsidies for overseas publishing operations would begin in 1948 with the Informational Media Guaranty Program, part of the European Recovery Program.

14. Bryn Hovde, "UNESCO From the Point of View of Political Science," *The School Executive* 66 (October 1946):82; Henri Bonnet, "UNESCO: Spearhead of the United Nations," *American Association of University Professors Bulletin* 32 (Winter 1946):611; MacLeish on NBC from London, 10 November 1945, transcript in Leland MSS, Box 107; Charles J. Child, "UNESCO and You," Music Teachers National Association, annual *Volume of Proceedings, 1946*, series 40 (February 1946), p. 26; Thomas Hobbes, *Leviathan* (New York: Washington Square Press, 1946), p. 85.

15. Grayson Kefauver to Benjamin Cohen, 11 December 1945, FRC70A4521, Lot 587, Box 400; George Kennan to James Byrnes, Telegram 3439 from Moscow, 3 October 1945, ibid.; Memorandum, Bryn Hovde to Benton, 6 October 1945, 501.PA/10-545; Memorandum, Thomson to Benton, 4 February 1946, MacLeish MSS, Box 19.

16. William G. Carr, "The London Conference on Education and Cultural Organization," NEA *Journal* 34 (October 1945):124.

17. Edith E. Ware, "National Committee on International Intellectual Cooperation, 1926–1943," typescript in Leland MSS, Box 45, p. ii; James Marshall, Speech delivered 18 August 1945 over radio station WABC, 501.PA/8-1845; James Marshall to Byrnes, 20 November 1945, 501.PA/9-1045; Robert MacIver, "Intellectual Cooperation in the Social Sciences," paper presented before

the American Philosophical Society, 19 April 1946, FRC72A1739, Lot 65D423, Box 19.

18. Report, "Meeting of Consultants on the Program of UNESCO in the Fields of Humanities and Arts, January 26, 1946," Redfield MSS, Box 36; Minutes of meeting, 23 January 1946, Leland MSS, Box 111; Press Release by James Marshall, FW501.PA/2-2146; Memorandum, Thomson to Benton, 29 March 1946, 501.PA/3-2946; Charles Thomson, "The Role of Government in UNESCO," *Proceedings of the American Philosophical Society* 90 (1946):303.

19. Leland to Chester E. Merrow, 8 April 1946, Leland MSS, Box 111; Herbert J. Abraham to Leland, 26 September 1947, ibid., Box 113; Leland to Abraham, 29 September 1947, ibid.; Edward Shils to Robert Redfield, 3 June 1946, Redfield MSS, Box 36; Luther Evans Interview, COHC, p. 310.

20. Memorandum by William G. Carr, "Priorities for UNESCO," Leland MSS, Box 111; Statement by Miss Marcie Southall, National Commission document NC/Plen 2/1, ibid.; Stephen Duggan to Leland, 30 October 1945, ibid.; Robert MacIver, "Intellectual Cooperation in the Social Sciences," *Proceedings of the American Philosophical Society* 90 (1946):310.

21. Waldo Leland, "The Background and Antecedents of UNESCO," *Proceedings of the American Philosophical Society* 90 (1946):296; Memorandum by Benton, November 1947, US Del/117/Prog/Channels/8, Benton MSS, Box 5825; Memorandum, Benton to Charles Fahy, 9 October 1946, FRC70A4521, Lot 587, Box 401; Speech delivered by Benton before the National Commission, 23 September 1946, in Leland MSS, Box 111.

22. Memorandum, Benton to James Byrnes, 5 December 1945, 501.PA/12-545; Memorandum, Thomson to Benton, 19 November 1946, FRC72A1739, Lot 65D423, Box 29.

23. Matt Connelly to Byrnes, 17 October 1946, and Benton to Byrnes, 28 October 1946, both in FW501.PA/10-1746; Memorandum, Benton to Francis Russell, 2 October 1946, FRC72A1739, Lot 65D423, Box 29.

24. Memorandum, Benton to Byrnes, 21 November 1946, FRC70A4521, Lot 587, Box 400; Memorandum, Benton to Acheson, 1 November 1946, ibid.; Memorandum, Benton to MacLeish, 27 November 1946, MacLeish MSS, Box 41; Memorandum, Benton to Byrnes, 12 November 1946, 501.PA/11-1246.

25. Memorandum, Benton to Byrnes, 27 November 1946, and Thomson to George Allen, 26 September 1948, both in FRC72A1739, Lot 65D423, Box 29; Memorandum by Acheson, phone conversation with Benton, 3 December 1946, 501.PA/12-346; MacLeish to Acheson, Telegram 5962 from Paris, 5 December 1946, 501.PA/12-546; MacLeish to Acheson, Telegram 6008 from Paris, 7 December 1946, 501.PA12-746.

26. *Proceedings* of the 1st General Conference, Paris, 21 November 1946, pp. 38–41, 501.PA/-Box 2317; Walter Bedell Smith to Byrnes, Telegram 4260 from Moscow, 29 November 1946, 501.PA/11-2946; "Ideologies," *Time*, 2 December 1946, pp. 27–8.

27. Benton to Byrnes, Telegram 6009 from Paris, 7 December 1946, 501.PA/12-746; Memorandum, Arthur H. Compton, Jr. to Byrnes, 28 December 1946, 501.PA/12-2846; Memorandum by Grayson Kefauver, undated, Leland MSS, Box 107; USD/208, Paris Conference, comments by Charles S. Johnson, ibid., Box 110; Memorandum, Benton to Byrnes, 23 December 1946, 501.PA/12-2346. On French thinking, see William R. Pendergast, "UNESCO and French Cultural Relations, 1945–1970," *International Organization* 30 (Summer 1976):454–78.

28. Memorandum, Benton to George Marshall, 10 February 1947, 501.PA/2-547; Memorandum, Benton to Byrnes, 23 December 1946, 501.PA/12-2346; Memorandum by Edward Trueblood, 22 January 1947, 501.PA/1-2237.

29. Charles Thomson to Walter Laves, Telegram 162 to Paris, 14 January 1947, 501.PA/1-1446; Memorandum, Acheson to Truman, 14 May 1946, 501.PA/5-1446; Lewis Douglas to Byrnes, Telegram 1968 from London, 31 March 1947, 501.PA/3-3147; Caffery to Marshall, Telegram 910 from Paris, 28 February 1947, 501.PA/2-2847; USD/208, Comments by George Shuster, March 1947, Leland MSS, Box 110.

30. Memorandum, M. J. McWilliams to Acheson, 28 February 1947, 501.PA/ 2-2847; Memorandum, Benton to Acheson, 11 March 1947, 811.42700/3-1147; Memorandum, Howland Sargeant to Benton, 7 April 1947, FRC72A1739, Lot 65D423, Box 29; Memorandum, Benton to Acheson, 3 March 1947, 501.PA/3-347; Smith to Marshall, Telegram 976 from Moscow, 24 March 1947, 501.PA/3-2447.

31. Caffery to Marshall, Telegram 1386 from Paris, 1 April 1947, 501.PA/4-147; Marshall to Gallman, Telegram 960 to London, 27 February 1947, 501.PA/ 2-2747; Benton to Caffery, Telegram 989 to Paris, 15 March 1947, 501.PA/3-1547; Memorandum of conversation between Thomson and Julian Huxley, 7 June 1947, FRC72A1739, Lot 65D423, Box 19.

32. Memorandum, G. H. Raynor to John Hickerson, 21 April 1947, 501.PA/ 4-2147; Memorandum of conversation, Henry Villard, Richard Johnson, and Richard McKeon, 13 February 1947, 501.PA/2-1347.

33. Draft memorandum by Esther Brunauer, FW501.PA/4-2947; Memorandum, Brunauer to Sargeant, 26 August 1947, 501.PA/8-2647; NC/ExComm/ S.C. Ex.Bd./1, 5 September 1947, in FRC72A1739, Lot 65D423, Box 32; Draft report of the subcommittee on the status of the UNESCO Executive Board, undated, 501.PA/8-2247; Albert H. Rosenthal, *Administrative Problems in the Establishment of UNESCO* (Washington, D.C.: Department of State, 1948), p. 156 (mimeographed).

34. Richard McKeon to Julian Huxley, 11 March 1947, 501.PA/3-1147; Memorandum of conversation, Karl Mundt, Saxton Bradford, and Howland Sargeant, 10 July 1947, 501.PA/7-1047.

35. Marshall to Caffery, Telegram 2530 (Nesco 252) to Paris, 10 July 1947, 501.PA/7-1047; Julian Huxley, *Memories II* (London: George Allen and Unwin, 1973), pp. 22–3; Memorandum, "Policy of the Department With Respect to Appointments of U.S. Nationals by Intergovernmental Organizations to Participate in Meetings or Serve in Various Posts," 501.PA/7-1847; Minutes of conference with Walter Laves, 9 September 1947, Records of the U.S. Senate, National Archives, Record Group 46, H.R. 3342, Box 15, volume I.

36. Memorandum, Thomson to George Allen, 13 April 1948, FRC70A4521, Lot 587, Box 401; Memorandum, Benton to Marshall, 22 September 1947, Leland MSS, Box 113; James Marshall, "Citizen Diplomacy," *American Political Science Review* 43 (February 1949):83–90; Press Release statement by Milton Eisenhower, 24 November 1947, US Del/132, in Benton MSS, Box 5825.

37. Ben Cherrington to John Peurifoy, 15 August 1947, 501.PA/8-1547; Memorandum, Benton to Lovett, 31 July 1947, FRC70A4521, Lot 587, Box 401; Memorandum, Richard A. Johnson to Thomson, 23 May 1947, 501.PA/5-2347.

38. Memorandum by Loy Henderson, 21 October 1947, 501.PA/10-2147; Undated Memo in Leland MSS, Box 112.

39. Memorandum, W. Walton Butterworth to Sargeant, 14 October 1947, FRC72A1739, Lot 65D423, Box 20; Memorandum, Benton to Lovett, 25 September 1947, 501.PA/9-2547; Memorandum, Benton to Marshall, 22 December 1947, FRC72A1739, Lot 65D423, Box 16.

40. Memorandum, Sargeant to Benton, 29 April 1947, Benton MSS, Box 5825; Luther Evans Interview, COHC, p. 320; Memorandum, Benton to Marshall, 21 May 1947, 501.PA/5-2147; Memorandum, John Howe to Benton, 17 October 1947, FRC72A1739, Lot 65D423, Box 19; NC 5/47 SM/45, 29 September 1947, in Benton MSS, Box 5825.

41. Memorandum, Benton to Marshall, 22 December 1947, FRC72A1739, Lot 65D423, Box 16; Memorandum by Alice T. Curran, 2 October 1947, ibid.; Luther Evans, "Notes on Meetings of the U.S. Delegation, Meeting at American Embassy, October 31, 1947," ibid., Box 16; George D. Stoddard, "Fresco, UNESCO, and Mr. Wierblowski," *School and Society* 67 (6 March 1948):177–80; Memorandum, Benton to Sargeant, 9 February 1948, Benton MSS, Box 5818.

42. Ben Cherrington to Melvin A. Schlesinger, 12 July 1945, Redfield MSS, Box 29.

43. For brief surveys of Soviet-American cultural contacts, see "Soviet-American Cultural Exchanges: A Review Since 1917," IIE *News Bulletin* 32 (October 1956):16-22; Robert F. Byrnes, *Soviet-American Academic Exchanges, 1958–1975* (Bloomington: Indiana University Press, 1976), pp. 10–31; Peter G. Filene, *Americans and the Soviet Experiment, 1917–1933* (Cambridge: Harvard University Press, 1967), pp. 56–8, 256–8; Lewis S. Feuer, "Travellers to the Soviet Union, 1917–1932," *American Quarterly* 14 (Summer 1962):119-49. The Moe quotation is from Milton Lomask, *Seed Money: The Guggenheim Story* (New York: Farrar, Straus & Giroux, 1964), pp. 267–8; Stephen Duggan to Sir Hector Hetherington, 8 July 1943, ACLS MSS, Box B-61. See also Philip E. Mosley, "The Growth of Russian Studies," in Harold Fisher, ed., *American Research on Russia* (Bloomington: Indiana University Press, 1959), pp. 1–8.

44. Memorandum, George Kennan to W. Averell Harriman, 4 October 1944, and attachment, U.S. Department of State, Post Files, Record Group 84, Washington National Records Center, Suitland, Maryland, Moscow-1944, Box 1361C (hereafter cited as Post Files with appropriate city, year, and box information); Telegrams 4166, 4183, and 5065 from Moscow, all in ibid.; Harriman to Hull, 6 September 1944, ibid.

45. Press conference transcript, 9 February 1944, Leo Pasvolsky Files, National Archives, Record Group 59, Box 6; Keyes D. Metcalf to MacLeish, 12 March 1945, FRC63A788, Lot 52-249, Box 4028; Stephen Duggan to MacLeish, 13 June 1945, 811.2222 (1940)/6-1345; Despatch 1 from Helsinki, 5 February 1945, 861.4276OD/2-545; MacLeish to Harriman, 13 July 1945, FRC63A788, Lot 52-249, Box 402. For Hellman's visit to the USSR, see Lillian Hellman, *An Unfinished Woman: A Memoir* (New York: Bantam Books, 1974), pp. 99–142; Haldore Hanson to MacLeish, 26 May 1945, MacLeish MSS, Box 9, 861.42700/1-645.

46. Kennan to Edward Stettinius, Despatch 1732 from Moscow, 23 May 1945, 811.42761/5-2345; Memorandum by Bryn Hovde, 24 July 1945, FRC63A788, Lot 52-249, Box 4028.

47. Harlow Shapely to Elbridge Durbrow, 11 August 1945, 811.427618-1145; Rockefeller Foundation, *Annual Report, 1946*, pp. 10–11; Memorandum, Harold Lasswell to Benton, 22 October 1945, FRC68A1414, Lot 52-48, Box 1042; Memorandum, Durbrow to H. Freeman Matthews, 14 November 1945, 811.4276111-1445; Memorandum by Charles Bohlen, 7 December 1945, 811.4276112-745; Memorandum, James B. Conant to Byrnes, 6 December 1945, 811.4276112-645; Benton to Kennan, Despatch 840 to Moscow, 5 October 1945, 811.4276110-545.

48. Memorandum by Durbrow, 21 May 1946, 811.427615-2146; Despatch 499 from Moscow, 26 October 1946, 811.4276110-2646; Despatch 259 from Moscow, 25 July 1946, 811.427617-2546; George F. Kennan, *Memoirs, 1925–1950* (Boston: Little, Brown, 1967), p. 564; Minutes of meeting, 27 February 1946, IIE Historical Files, Reel 14, Side 2, Index 9; Walter Bedell Smith to Byrnes, Telegram 37 from Moscow, 16 April 1946, 811.427614-1646.

49. Stephen Duggan to Anson Hoyt, 18 October 1946, IIE Historical Files, Reel 14, Side 2, Index 10; Edgar J. Fisher to William J. Carr, 6 March 1946, ibid.; Thomas L. Woody, "Faults and Futures in American-Soviet Cultural Relations," *School and Society* 64 (28 September 1946):209-11; Durbrow to Byrnes, Telegram 3969 from Moscow, 25 October 1946, Post Files, Moscow-1946, Box 1385; Durbrow to Byrnes, Telegram 3353 from Moscow, 29 August 1946, 861.427958-2946; Durbrow to Byrnes, Telegram 8281 from Moscow, 25 November 1946, 861.427009-2546.

50. Marginal notation by Smith on Telegram 2038 to Moscow, 25 November 1946, Post Files, Moscow-1946, Box 1385.

51. Acheson to Smith, Telegram 2066 to Moscow, 3 December 1946, 811.42761 SE12-346; Laurence Duggan to Benton, 7 March 1947, 811.42761 SE3-747; Smith to Marshall, Telegram 1222 from Moscow, 7 April 1947, 811.42761 SE4-747; Durbrow to Marshall, Telegram 1314 from Moscow, 2 May 1947, 811.42761 SE5-147.

52. Memorandum, R. H. Davis to Llewelyn Thompson, 21 May 1947, FW811.427005-1547; Ernest J. Simmons, "Negotiating on Cultural Exchange, 1947," in Raymond Dennett and Joseph E. Johnson, eds., *Negotiating With the Russians* (Boston: World Peace Foundation, 1951), pp. 254-5, 268; Memorandum, Mose Harvey to Howland Sargeant, 10 October 1947, 811.4276110-1047; Smith to Marshall, Telegram 852 from Moscow, 7 May 1948, 811.42700 (B)5-748.

5 The politics of institutionalization

1. Memorandum, John C. Dreier to Charles Thomson, 20 December 1043, 810.4271117706 and attachment; General Advisory Committee minutes, 18–19 February 1944, Notter Files, Box 18. A Carnegie Corporation survey of ACLS operations complained that some of its governmental chores seemed "of doubtful appropriateness for a Council of Learned Societies," in ACLS MSS, Box B-75.

2. General Advisory Committee minutes, 18–19 February 1944, Notter Files, Box 18; Minutes of meeting, American Council on Education Committee on Cultural Relations, 25–26 February 1944, CEIP 65861, 65856; Waldo Leland, "The Organization of International Educational Relations," paper presented to the Conference on International Education, Washington, D.C., 21 March 1943,

ACLS MSS, Box B-61; Waldo Leland to Thomson, 23 May 1944, ACLS MSS, Box B-93.

3. G. Howland Shaw to Leland, 12 June 1944, 810.4271118441; Leland to Thomson, 31 May 1944, ACLS MSS, Box B-95; Memorandum, Carl Sauer to Fitzhugh Granger, 25 September 1946, FRC68A1414, Lot 52-84, Box 1045; Memorandum, Bryn Hovde to Archibald Macleish, 28 December 1944, IDC, Box 13; "Summary Report of Conferences on Cultural Relations Contracts," 31 March and 4 April 1944, ALA MSS, Series 716, Box 1; Circular Despatch, 14 March 1946, FW810.427113-1446; see the correspondence in ALA MSS, Series 7150, Boxes 4 and 9.

4. Halpern, "The Institute of International Education," pp. 181–90; Laurence Duggan to Benton, 2 December 1946, 811.42700 SE/10-2496; Kenneth Holland to Duggan, 11 June 1947, IIE Historical Files, Reel 15, Side 1, Index 33; a copy of the "Sargeant Report" is in IDC, Box 1; Milam to Benton, 23 May 1947, ALA MSS, Series 7/1/6, Box 19.

5. General Advisory Committee minutes, 18–19 February 1944, Notter Files, Box 18; Memorandum, Thomson to Shaw, 4 February 1944, 111.46 Advisory Committee/260; Cherrington to Senator Edward C. Johnson, 18 March 1944, 811.42700/3-1844; Cherrington to Cordell Hull, 9 October 1944, ACLS MSS, Box B-94; Minutes of dinner session of General Advisory Committee, 29 June 1944, IDC, Box 1. On the reorganization, see the essay on Stettinius by Walter Johnson in Norman Graebner, ed., *An Uncertain Tradition: American Secretaries of State in the Twentieth Century* (New York: McGraw-Hill, 1961), pp. 212–13, and Walter H. C. Laves, "The Reorganization of the Department of State," *American Political Science Review* 38 (April 1944):289–301.

6. Stettinius "Record," General Records of the Department of State, National Archives, Record Group 59, Vol. I, Section II, pp. 6, 13–15; Advisory Committee on Art, minutes, 2–3 February 1945, ACLS MSS, Box B-92; MacLeish to John Dickey, 19 December 1944, MacLeish MSS, Box 5; Undated Memorandum, MacLeish to James Byrnes, FRC68A1414, Lots 52–48, Box 1042.

7. Archibald MacLeish, "Statement Before Senate Foreign Relations Committee," *DOSB* 11 (10 December 1944):692–3; Speech draft by Hovde, "The Problems and Tasks of International Education," Papers of Bryn J. Hovde, Truman Library, Box 4.

8. Memorandum, MacLeish to Dickey, 2 January 1945, MacLeish MSS, Box 5; Benton to Thomson, 18 December 1945, FRC71A1739, Lot 65D423, Box 19. The identification of radio technology with democracy is readily visible in S. E. Frost, Jr., *Is American Radio Democratic?* (Chicago: University of Chicago Press, 1937), pp. xi, 302, and Llewelyn White, *Peoples Speaking to Peoples* (Chicago: University of Chicago Press, 1946), p. 9.

9. Chester Williams to Leland, 29 October 1943, ACLS MSS, Box B-78; Memorandum of meeting, Advisory Committee on Libraries Abroad, 29 October 1943, ALA MSS, Series 7/1/6, Box 9; Memorandum by Edward Barrett, 24 March 1945, FRC63A788, Lot 52-249, Box 4028; Memorandum, Chester Williams to Vincent Petrillo, 16 June 1944, ALA MSS, Series 7/1/6, Box 18; Undated OWI Memorandum, "Information Program for Europe," ibid.

10. Minutes of meetings of the Joint OWI-State Committee on Cultural Relations and Information, 12 and 19 January 1945, FRC63A788, Lot 52-249, Box 4028; Draft Memorandum of 30 March 1945, in ibid.; Memorandum of meeting on government-owned libraries abroad, 30 July 1045, ibid. The decision to

merge was formally made on the basis of the so-called MacMahon Report. See Arthur W. MacMahon, *Memorandum on the Postwar International Information Program of the United States* (Washington, D.C.: Government Printing Office, 1945).

11. Extract from article by Henry Flannery, "Selling U.S. Preferred," *Free World* (October 1945) in Benton MSS, Box 5818; Espinosa, *Inter-American Beginnings,* p. 225; Memorandum, William L. Schurz to "Colleagues," 5 September 1945, ACLS MSS, Box B-94.

12. Sidney Hyman, *The Lives of William Benton* (Chicago: University of Chicago Press, 1969), pp. 129–262; CIAA Policy Committee minutes, 9 December 1940, Benton MSS, Box 5712; Memorandum, Benton to Acheson, September 1945, ibid. I am indebted to Marc Hilton's unpublished essay, "Experts on the Air," for illuminating the nature of Benton's interest in educational broadcasting.

13. William Benton, "A New Instrument of Foreign Policy," *DOSB* 15 (13 October 1946):673.

14. See Chapter 2, pp. 36–9, supra.

15. Memorandum by C. D. Jackson, 27 September 1945, and Benton Memorandum of 1 October 1945, FRC68A1414, Lot 52-327, Box 1043; Benton to DeWitt Wallace, 1 November 1945, FW811.42700/10-3045; Memorandum, Benton to George C. Marshall, 15 May 1947, 811.42700 SE/5-1547.

16. On Truman's probable ignorance of the issues, see Charles A. H. Thomson, *Overseas Information Service,* p. 196n; Foreign Service circular 597, 1 August 1946, Post Files, Moscow-1946, Box 1385; Circular Telegram, 9 August 1946, 810.42711/8-946; Memorandum, "Summary of Reports from Missions in the Other American Republics Concerning Post-War Cultural Relations Program," 2 February 1944, RA Lot Files, Box 9.

17. 87 Cong. Rec. 2992 (1943); 87 Cong. Rec. 3008 (1941); 87 Cong. Rec. 2917 (1941); Memorandum by Thomson, 7 December 1943, 811.42700/12-743; Carl Milam to Charles Brown, 13 November 1944, ALA MSS, Series 7/1/6, Box 20.

18. New York *Herald-Tribune,* 15 February 1946, p. 7; William Benton Interview, COHC, pp. 172–3; Hyman, *The Lives of William Benton,* pp. 350–1.

19. H.R. Rep. No. 336, 80th Cong., 1st sess. 6 (1948); a legislative history describing some of these obstacles is available in H. Rowland Ludden, "The International Information Program of the United States: State Department Years, 1945–1953" (Ph.D. diss., Princeton University, 1966), pp. 52–89.

20. Benton Interview, COHC, pp. 152, 168–9; Memorandum, Benton to Francis Russell, 22 August 1946, Benton MSS, Box 5818; Memorandum, Benton to Acheson, 27 January 1947, 811.42700/1-2747; H.R. Rep. No. 336, 80th Cong., 1st sess. 7 (1948).

21. On the art incident, see Frank Ninkovich, "The Currents of Cultural Diplomacy," *Diplomatic History* 1 (Summer 1977):215–37; Hyman, *The Lives of William Benton,* pp. 378–82. The term "cultural fundamentalist" is taken from Jane DeHart Matthews, "Art and Politics in Cold War America," *American Historical Review* 81 (October 1976):762–87.

22. 98 Cong. Rec. 6742, 6756, 6572, 6625, 6748, 6752, 6969, 6981 (1947).

23. Cherrington to Leland, 4 June 1947, Leland MSS, Box 113. In addition to his position as head of the Social Science Foundation in Denver, Cherrington was by this time an influential member of the National Education Association's Educational Policies Commission, chairman of the NEA's International Relations Committee, a member of the UNESCO National Commission, and a trustee of the Carnegie Endowment.

24. Cherrington to Howland Sargeant, 20 June 1947, Leland MSS, Box 113.
25. Cherrington to Senator Arthur Vandenberg, 27 May 1947, copy in Redfield MSS, Box 30.
26. Memorandum, Thomson to Sargeant, 7 April 1947, FRC68A1414, Lot 52-48, Box 1048; William G. Carr to Senator H. Alexander Smith, 3 July 1947, Senate Records, H.R. 3342, Box 14; Social Science Foundation, minutes of meeting of board of trustees, 25–26 April 1947, Redfield MSS, Box 30; Cherrington to Sargeant, 20 June 1947, Leland MSS, Box 113; George Zook, "The President's Annual Report," *The Educational Record* 27 (July 1946):305.
27. Memorandum, Benton to Sargeant, 22 December 1947, Benton MSS, Box 5818; Sargeant to Cherrington, 16 June 1947, FRC68A1414, Lot 52-48, Box 1042; Memorandum, Sargeant to Benton, 17 July 1947, ibid.; Benton to Edward Barrett, 5 September 1947, 501.PA/9-547. Studies were underway at this time by the Brookings Institution, the UNESCO National Commission, and the Foreign Policy Association.
28. Memorandum, Benton to Marshall, 10 February 1947, 111.12 Benton, William/2-1047; Memorandum, Benton to Robert Lovett, 26 September 1947, 501.PA/9-2647; Memorandum by Thomson, 12 December 1947, FRC72A1739, Lot 65D423, Box 19.
29. Memorandum, W. R. Tyler to Stone and Sargeant, 4 October 1947, 811.42700/10-447; Attachment to Memorandum, Stone to Sargeant, 26 November 1947, files of USIA historian; Memorandum, Sargeant to Benton, 17 July 1947, FRC68A1414, Lot 52-48, Box 1042.
30. Telegram from eight university presidents to President Truman, 17 May 1946, Truman Papers, Truman Library, President's Official Files, 20-E; ALA MSS, Series 7/1/6, Box 20; American Book Publishers Council to Senator Styles Bridges, 6 May 1947, Benton MSS, Box 5712; Laurence Duggan to George Marshall, 6 May 1947, 811.42700 SE/5-647; Henry Stimson to John Taber, 21 May 1947, files of USIA historian; Memorandum, Carl Sauer to Sargeant, 24 March 1947, FRC70A4521, Lot 587, Box 401; Dwight D. Eisenhower to H. Alexander Smith, 2 July 1947, Senate Records, H.R. 3342, Box 14.
31. Benton to Robert Taft, 25 March 1947, files of USIA historian; Arthur Vandenberg to Irving Lieberman, 28 May 1947, ALA MSS, Series 7/1/6, Box 22. Results of the poll are in Senate Records, H.R. 3342, Box 15.
32. Memorandum, Benton to Byrnes, 28 September 1946, 811.20200 (D)/9-2846; Benton to Truman, 25 October 1947, Truman MSS, President's Personal Files, 3394. For the myth of internationalization through travel, see Edward W. Barrett, *Truth Is Our Weapon* (New York: Funk & Wagnalls, 1953), pp. 61–2; Wilson P. Dizard, *The Strategy of Truth: The Story of the U.S. Information Service* (Washington, D.C.: Public Information Press, 1961), p. 37; Hyman, *The Lives of William Benton,* p.384.
33. This account is based on the two-volume Record of the Joint Committee's trip, in Senate Records, H.R. 3342, Box 15. See also Sen. Rep. No. 855, 80th Cong., 1st sess. (1948).
34. Records of the U.S. Senate Committee on Foreign Relations, Truman Library, minutes of executive session, 15 July 1947, 16 December 1947, and 7 January 1948, Box 2.
35. Memorandum by William Stone, conversation with Karl Mundt, 14 October 1947, FRC70A4521, Lot 587, Box 401; Karl Mundt, "The United States and Russia – World Leaders," NEA *Journal* 35 (October 1946):390; Senate Committee on Foreign Relations, Truman Library, minutes of executive session, 15 De-

cember 1947 and 7 January 1948, Box 2; Memorandum, Jesse MacKnight to Sargeant, 9 December 1947, files of USIA historian.

36. Senate Committee on Foreign Relations, minutes of executive session, 16 December 1947, Truman Library, Box 2; H. Alexander Smith to Sargeant, 30 December 1947, 811.42700/12-2637; Cherrington to George Zook, 1 October 1947, CEIP 65982; Sargeant to Cherrington, 12 December 1947, Benton MSS, Box 5818; Cherrington to Redfield, 25 February 1948, Redfield MSS, Box 30. See also minutes of meeting of Board of Trustees, Social Science Foundation, 2–4 May, 1948, ibid., Box 31.

37. Memorandum, Benton to Acheson, 12 March 1947, 811.42700/3-1247; Summary of Hearings before the House Foreign Affairs Committee, Subcommittee on Information and Educational Exchange, 20 March 1947, in Senate Records, H.R. 3342, Box 14. On the departmental consensus, see Daniel Yergin, *Shattered Peace: The Origins of the Cold War and the National Security State* (Boston: Houghton Mifflin, 1977), pp. 165–71, and Robert L. Messer, "Paths Not Taken: The United States Department of State and Alternatives to Containment, 1945–1946," *Diplomatic History* 1 (Fall 1977):297–319.

38. Memorandum, Charles Hulten to Benton, 13 May 1947, 811.42700/5-1347; John Howe to Richard C. Patterson, 31 January 1947, Papers of Richard C. Patterson, Truman Library, Box 3; Memorandum, Victor Hunt to Benton, 25 July 1947, Benton MSS, Box 5818; Memorandum, Benton to Stone, 14 April 1947, FRC70A4521, Lot 587, Box 1043.

39. Memorandum, Benton to Acheson, 7 October 1946, 811.42761/10-746; NSC-4, 9 December 1947; NSC-7, 30 March 1948; NSC-20/1, 18 August 1948 – all in the Modern Military Branch, National Archives.

40. Minutes of National Commission meeting, 18 February 1948, Benton MSS, Box 4825; Thomson, *Overseas Information Service*, pp. 309–12; Press Release 489, 13 June 1947, text of letter from Benton to Kent Cooper, executive director of the Associated Press, 13 June 1947, in Senate Records, H.R. 3342, Box 14; Benton to Thomson, 7 March 1948, Benton MSS, Box 5756.

41. Memorandum, Saxton Bradford to Sargeant, 1 December 1947, FRC70A4521, Lot 587, Box 401; Howland Sargeant, "Helping the World to Know U.S. Better," *DOSB* 19 (28 November 1948):672; Sargeant to Benton, 25 June 1948, Benton MSS, Box 5818; Memorandum, Ralph Block to George Allen, 8 September 1948, 811.42700/9-848. Sargeant's aggressive blend of idealism and national self-interest is evident in his essay, "Information and Cultural Representation Overseas," in The American Assembly, *The Representation of the United States Abroad* (New York: The American Assembly, 1956), pp. 96–102.

42. Memorandum, Sargeant to George Allen, 25 October 1948, FRC70A4521, Lot 587, Box 401; Memorandum, Thomson to Allen, 11 March 1948, ibid.; Memorandum, Sargeant to Lovett, 18 January 1948, 811.42700/1-548; Benton to Thomson, 7 March 1948, Benton MSS, Box 5756.

43. Benton to Donald Stone, 28 August 1947, 501.PA/8-2847; Robert K. Merton, *Social Theory and Social Structure,* rev. ed. (New York: Free Press,1957), p. 485; Karl Mannheim, *Ideology and Utopia,* trans. Louis Wirth and Edward Shils (New York: Harvest Books, n.d.), pp. 113–17. Max Weber, in *The Theory of Social and Economic Organization,* trans. Talcott Parsons and A. M. Henderson (New York: Free Press, 1964), p. 340, refers to this bureaucratic trait as the "tendency to substantive rationality." For an assessment of the relationship between the Cold War and the ideology of the Soviet bureaucracy, see Reinhard

Bendix, "Industrialization, Ideologies, and Social Structure," *American Sociological Review* 24 (October 1959):623.

6 The transformation of cultural internationalism

1. Scott, "The Cultural Institute," pp. 120–1, 1034–6; Thomson and Laves, *Cultural Relations and U.S. Foreign Policy,* pp. 81–4. Apparently some authors like Espinosa, *Inter-American Beginnings,* pp. 319–21, fail to discern any discontinuity at all – a fundamental error, to my mind.

2. IIE, *Education For One World* (New York: IIE, 1949), pp. 7–9; *The Sunday Star* (Washington, D.C.), 11 May 1947, C-3; Laurence Duggan, "Fellowships for International Reconstruction," IIE *News Bulletin* 22 (February 1947):3–4; Marshall is quoted in ibid., 1 June 1947, p. 6; Richard J. Heindel, "Understanding the United States Abroad," *Social Education* 11 (February 1947):56.

3. Alan Blaisdell, "New Crisis in Cultural Relations," IIE *News Bulletin* 23 (January 1948):4; Attachment to Memorandum, John McAfee to Francis J. Colligan, 7 May 1948, FRC43A217, Lot 52-86, Box 301; Memorandum by Oliver J. Caldwell, 4 September 1947 ibid.; Unsigned Memorandum, OEX/S Document 41, 3 May 1949, ibid., Box 300; John McAfee, "Student Exchange and the Dollar Shortage," IIE *News Bulletin* 24 (November 1948):5–12; Memorandum, J. Hall Paxton to John Caldwell, 2 July 1946, IDC, Box 22.

4. The standard account is Walter Johnson and Francis Colligan, *The Fulbright Program* (Chicago: University of Chicago Press, 1965); Haynes Johnson and Bernard Gwertzman, *Fulbright the Dissenter* (Garden City, N.Y.: Doubleday, 1968), p. 109; Conference Board of Associated Research Councils, minutes, 18 December 1947, Merriam MSS, Box 142; "The President's Annual Report," *The Educational Record* 29 (July 1948):231.

5. Memorandum, Kenneth Holland to Benton, 28 October 1946, FRC70A4521, Lot 587, Box 400; Board of Foreign Scholarships, summary minutes of 1st, 2nd, and 3rd meetings, 8–9 October 1947, 13 December 1947, and 17 January 1948, in U.S. Department of State, Bureau of Educational and Cultural Affairs (CU), History Files. Unfortunately, all verbatim minutes of early BFS transactions have unaccountably been destroyed by the department.

6. Telegram 666 to Tehran, 8 March 1948, 811.42700 SE/3-848; Telegram 975 from Tehran, 7 October 1948, 811.42791/10-748; Telegram 150 from Tehran, 23 November 1948, 811.42791/10-2348; Airgram A-126 from Tehran, 811.42791 SE/5-549; Telegram 609 from Tehran, 5 May 1949, 811.42791SE/5-549; Despatch 1292 from Paris, 25 October 1948, 811.42751 SE/10-2548; Despatch 1139 from Rome, 26 July 1948, 811.42765 SE/7-2648; Memorandum, Frederic O. Bundy to Colligan, 10 September 1948, FW811.42765/9-1648; Despatch 414 to Rome, 9 December 1948, Post Files, Rome-1948, Box 196. The French Left ridiculed the Fulbright program by comparing its terms to the indignities of the Boxer indemnities. See Telegram 101 from Paris, 7 January 1948, 811.42700 SE/1-748.

7. Memorandum, J. Hall Paxton to John C. Caldwell, 2 July 1946, IDC, Box 22; Undated, unsigned Memorandum, "China Policy and Information," 26 February 1946, FRC62A624, Lot 21, Box 202; W. Walton Butterworth to Marshall, Despatch 468 from Nanking, 31 January 1947, 811.20200 (D)/1-3147; Memorandum by Nathaniel Peffer, attachment to Despatch 475 from Nanking, 893.4212/2-447

8. Roger Sherman Greene to Harry Pierson, 24 May 1946, 811.42793 SE/5-2446; Telegram 493 to Nanking, 16 April 1947, 811.42700 SE/4-1647; Telegram 966 from Nanking, 4 May 1947, 811.42700 SE/5-447.

9. Memorandum of conversation between Arthur Ringwalt and T. L. Tsui, 2 May 1947, 811.42700 SE/5-247; Telegram 710 to Nanking, 6 June 1947, 811.42700 SE/6-647; Telegram 1350 from Nanking, 20 June 1947, 811.42700 SE/6-2047; Telegram 1155 from Nanking, 27 May 1947, 811.42700 SE/5-2747; Telegram 1483 from Nanking, 8 July 1947, 811.42700 SE/7-847; Telegram 939 to Nanking, 8 July 1947, ibid. For an overly harsh critique of the Boxer indemnity that fails to detect the philosophical idealism in U.S. policy, see Michael Hunt, "The American Remission of the Boxer Indemnity, A Reappraisal," *Journal of Asian Studies* 31 (May 1972):539–59.

10. Despatch 38 from Mukden, 8 September 1948, 861.42793/9-848; O. Edmund Clubb to Acheson, Despatch 120 from Peiping, 18 August 1949, 861.42793/8-1849; W. Bradley Connors to John Paton Davies, 3 August 1948, 811.42793/8-348; G. L. Harris to Marshall, Despatch 333 from Nanking, 3 August 1948, 811.42700 (B)/8-348; Stuart to Marshall, Telegram 359 from Nanking, 25 February 1948, 811.42793/2-2548.

11. Board of Foreign Scholarships, summary minutes, 26 April 1949, CU Historical Files; O. Edmund Clubb Interview, Truman Library Oral History Collection, p. 75; Stuart to Acheson, Airgram A-90 from Nanking, 23 July 1949, 893.4212/702349; Stuart to Acheson, Telegram 1342 from Nanking, 21 June 1949, 893.42/6-2149; Memorandum, Howland Sargeant to John Paton Davies, 26 April 1949, FRC70A4521, Lot 587, Box 404.

12. Theodore Hsi-En Chin, "All Is Not Lost In China," *The Educational Record* 30 (October 1949):481; Pardee Lowe to Howard P. Backus, 9 August 1949, 811.42700 SE/8-949; Thomas A. Metzger, *Escape From Predicament: Neo-Confucianism and China's Evolving Political Culture* (New York: Columbia University Press, 1977), p. 233.

13. Smith to Marshall, Airgram A-215 from Moscow, 3 March 1948, 811.42700 SE/3-348; Despatch 424 from Warsaw, 25 November 1947, 811.42700 SE/11-2547; Memorandum by E. Lewis Revey, 22 September 1947, Post Files, Budapest-1947, Box 161; Telegram 234 from Budapest, 5 April 1949, 861.42764/4-549; Despatch 867 from Belgrade, Post Files, Belgrade-1947, Box 43; Telegram 149 from Sofia, 18 February 1946, 811.20200 (D)/2-1846.

14. "Books in World Rehabilitation, 1948," Memorandum by the American Textbook Publishers Institute, American Book Publishers Council, Inc., and Association of American University Presses, ALA MSS, Series 7/1/6, Box 4; Despatch 635 from Bern, 16 August 1948, 811.42700 (B)/8-1648; Airgram A-946 from Warsaw, 3 August 1949, 811.42700 (B)/8-349; Circular Airgram, 16 December 1947, Post Files, Belgrade-1947, Box 43; Joseph E. Jacobs to Acheson, Despatch 442 from Prague, 14 July 1949, FRC63A217, Lot 52-84, Box 297; Despatch 229 from Prague, 26 March 1948, 811.4276OF/3-2648; Cumulative Report by Lewis Revey, 1 November 1948, Post Files, Budapest-1948, File 842-OIE.

15. USIS Report, Trieste, November 1948, Supplement (A), Post Files, Belgrade-1948, Box 54; Telegram 1351 from Praha, 9 October 1947, 811.4276OF/10-947.

16. Telegram 91 from Warsaw, 20 January 1948, 811.42700 SE/1-2048; Tele-

gram 776 from Budapest, 7 May 1948, Post Files, Budapest-1948. See also Board of Foreign Scholarships summary minutes, 17 January and 22 May 1948, CU Historical Files.

17. Memorandum by Donald Cook, 4 March 1948, FRC70A4521, Lot 587, Box 401; Memorandum, Colligan to Jack Neal, 19 April 1948, FRC63A217, Lot 52086, Box 298; Airgram A-547 from Prague, 28 June 1948, 811.42760OF/6-2848; Circular Despatch, 23 July 1946, 811.42700 SE/7-2346; Board of Foreign Scholarships, summary minutes, 8–9 October 1947, CU Historical Files; Memorandum, H. H. Pierson to Oliver Caldwell, 6 February 1947, FRC63A217, Lot 52-86, Box 300; Memorandum, Colligan to H. J. L'Heureux, undated, ibid.

18. Memorandum, Colligan to Holland and Allen, 23 April 1948, FRC70A4521, Lot 587, Box 401; Memorandum, "Educational Exchange with Central and Eastern European Countries," 7 September 1948, attachment to 811.42700/10-1348; Harvey Branscomb to George Marshall, 10 November 1948, 811.42760 SE/11-1048.

19. Russell A. Riley Interview, Truman Library Oral History Collection, pp. 54–5; Memorandum by Harvey Branscomb, "USIS in Certain Countries of Europe and Near East," 811.42740 SE/12-1249.

20. U.S., Congress, Senate, Subcommittee of the Committee on Appropriations, *Hearings, Departments of State, Justice, Commerce and the Judiciary, Appropriations for 1951,* 81st Cong., 2nd sess., 1950, p. 1065.

21. Memorandum, "U.S. Informational and Educational Exchange Objectives in Next Five Years," January 1950, FRC63A217, Lot 52-86, Box 300; OEX/S, Document 53, 12 January 1950, ibid.; Memorandum, William C. Johnstone, Jr., to Sargeant, 9 January 1950, ibid.

22. Transcript of address by William C. Johnstone, Jr., at University of Pittsburgh, 11 December 1948, ibid.; William C. Johnstone, Jr., "Exchange Programs in American Foreign Relations," *DOSB* 21 (19 December 1949):929; Alan Blaisdell, "Educational Relationships with the Near East," IIE *News Bulletin* 25 (June 1950):5–6; Kenneth Holland, "Fear of the 'Little Hot War,' " IIE *News Bulletin* 26 (October 1950):8.

23. Stephen Spender, "UNESCO: Impressions of the First General Conference," *Britain To-Day* 131 (March 1947):14–18; Julian Huxley to Arthur A. Compton, Jr., 501.PA/10-1147; Telegram 3377 to Paris, 27 August 1947, 501.PA/8-2747; Howard Wilson to Benton, 17 October 1947, FRC68A1414, Lot 52-48, Box 42.

24. Memorandum, Dorothy Fosdick to Thomson, 6 February 1948, 501.PA/2-648; Telegram 1751 to Paris, 21 May 1948, 501.PA/5-2148; Walter Kotschnig to Benton, 13 September 1948, Benton MSS, Box 5754.

25. Waldo Leland to Thomson, 16 September 1948, Leland MSS, Box 113; Undated Memorandum by Compton, Post Files, Paris-1948, Box 1570.

26. Kenneth Holland to Thomson, Despatch 69 from Paris, 25 March 1948, ibid.; Memorandum of conversation by Thomson, 21 April 1948, FW501.PA/2-648; Telegram 115 from Paris, 29 April 1948, 501.PA/4-2948; Compton to George Allen, Confidential Report on Beirut Conference, 501.PA/2-3149.

27. Memorandum, Holland to Jaime Torres-Bodet, 28 April 1949, 501.PA/5-549; Summary minutes of the Fifth Meeting, in Benton MSS, Box 5825; Archibald MacLeish, "How Can We Contribute to Peace?" *American Association of University Professors Bulletin* 34 (Autumn 1948):542; MacLeish to Thomson, 5 January 1948, Benton MSS, Box 5756; Redfield to Cherrington, 16 August

1949, Redfield MSS, Box 30. See also *University of Chicago Round Table* 503 (9 November 1947).

28. Verbatim minutes in Leland MSS, Box 113; Memorandum by Leland, 13 September 1948, ibid.; Richard McKeon, "UNESCO In Its Second Year," *The Educational Record* 29 (April 1948):137–44; Richard McKeon, ed., *Democracy In A World of Tensions* (Chicago: University of Chicago Press, 1951), p. ix; William Sanders to Dean Rusk and Durward Sandifer, 501.PA/11-1948.

29. U.S. National Commission for UNESCO, *Summary Minutes of the Fifth Meeting,* Boston, Mass., September 27–28, 1948, document NC5/47 SM.

30. Address by George Allen, "The Opportunity of the National Commission," 27 September 1948, Benton MSS, Box 5825; Text of speech by Milton Eisenhower at the American University of Beirut, undated, FRC72A1739, Lot 65D423, Box 20.

31. Byron Dexter, "Yardstick for UNESCO," *Foreign Affairs* 28 (October 1949):62; Memorandum by Thomson, 23 December 1949, FRC72A1739, Lot 65D423, Box 20; George Allen to Acheson, Telegram 3899 from Paris, 21 September 1949, 501.PA/9-2149; George Allen, "Clarity of UNESCO's Central Purpose Needed in Peacemaking of United Nations," *DOSB* 21 (10 October 1949):536–7; George Allen, "The Place of UNESCO in American Foreign Policy," *DOSB* 21 (3 October 1949):498.

32. George Allen to Davidson Taylor, 501.PA/2-1949.

33. *New York Times,* 21 April 1950, p. 1; Memorandum, Benton to John Howe, 29 April 1950, Benton MSS, Box 5825; Memorandum, John Howe to Benton, 25 April 1950, ibid.

34. Discussion Paper, "UNESCO's Responsibility In the World Crisis," 20 July 1950, Leland MSS, Box 111; Luther Evans to Count Jacini, chairman of UNESCO Executive Board, 16 August 1950, Leland MSS, Box 114; Speech by George Stoddard before National Student Association, Ann Arbor, 30 August 1950, ibid.; Letter to the editor by James Marshall, *New York Times,* 25 June 1950, IV, p. 8; William G. Carr, "Five Years of UNESCO," NEA *Journal* 39 (October 1950):531.

35. 90 Cong. Rec. A4985 (1950), remarks by Karl Stefan; Trygve Lie to Torres-Bodet, 24 August 1950, Benton MSS, Box 5825; Thomson to William McKenna, 29 August 1950, ibid.; Thomson to National Commission members, 30 August 1950, ibid.; Introduction by Percy Bidwell to Frederic S. Dunn, *War and the Minds of Men* (New York: Harper & Brothers, 1950), p. vii; Edward Barrett to Benton, 25 September 1950, Benton MSS, Box 5825.

36. Walter R. Sharp, "The Role of UNESCO: A Critical Evaluation," Academy of Political Science, *Proceedings* 24 (1950–2):112; Chester Barnard, "The President's Review," Rockefeller Foundation, *Annual Report, 1949,* p. 22; George Shuster, *UNESCO: Assessment and Promise* (New York: Harper & Row, 1963), p. 11.

37. Airgram A-360 from Moscow, 2 July 1946, Post Files, Moscow-1946, Box 1385; Telegram 143 from Moscow, 8 June 1946, ibid.; Quarterly Report by Charles A. Page, Despatch 3928 from Paris, 8 January 1946, 811.42751/1-846; Memorandum by Jason Paige, Jr., liaison officer of War Department's Strategic Services Unit, to Jack Neal, 24 April 1946, 851.00B/4-2446.

38. Despatch 9491 from Paris, 20 August 1947, 851.43/8-2047; Memorandum, Willard Hill to Lee Brady, 3 November 1947 and attachments, Post Files, Paris-1947, Box 1567; Jefferson Caffery to Henri Torres, undated, ibid.; Rec-

ords of the Joint Committee on the Smith-Mundt Bill, Senate Records, H.R. 3342, Box 15, vol. 1, France, 9 September 1947, p. 3.

39. Telegram 6943 from London, 10 July 1945, 800.4089/7-1045; Despatch 12625 from Bowers, Santiago, 19 July 1945, 800.4089/7-1945; Copy of British Despatch 303, 8 August 1946, Post Files, Moscow-1946, Box 1385.

40. Telegram 484 from Prague, 6 May 1947, 800.4089/5-647; Memorandum, Coburn Kidd to John Hickerson, 6 May 1947, 800.4089/5-647.

41. Helen Ripley, "Special Ship Project," IIE *News Bulletin* 23 (November 1947):23–4; Memorandum, Francis Colligan to Oliver McKee, 2 June 1947, FRC63A217, Lot 52-86, Box 298; Verbatim minutes of meeting in office of Eric Bellquist, 22 May 1947, ibid.

42. Informal Report from cultural attaché in Prague to Bellquist, 29 July 1947, ibid.; Telegram 1099 from Prague, 20 August 1947, 800.4089/8-2047; Bryn Hovde to William Stone, 15 October 1947, Hovde MSS, Box 1; Memorandum, Holland to Sargeant, 6 October 1947, 800.4089/11-747.

43. Proposed Policy Paper by Saxton Bradford, 29 January 1948, FRC70A4521, Lot 587, Box 401; Memorandum, Sargeant to Bradford, 9 February 1948, ibid.

44. Unsigned, undated Memorandum, "American Participation in International Youth Meetings: A Proposed Policy," FW800.4089/9-2448; Memorandum by Don B. Cook, 25 November 1947, FRC63A217, Lot 52-86, Box 300; Circular Despatch, 7 April 1948, 811.42700 SE/4-748; Memorandum, Colligan to Stone, 30 March 1948, FRC63A217, Lot 52-86, Box 298; Memorandum, Johnstone to Jesse MacKnight, 8 July 1948, ibid.; Telegram 1106 from Warsaw, 20 August 1948, 811.42740 SE/8-2048.

45. Copy of British Despatch 649 written by F. K. Roberts, 27 August 1946, Post Files, Moscow-1946, Box 1385; Telegram 137 from Moscow, 2 February 1948, 861.415/2-248; "Walt Disney Influence Must Go, Says Russian," *New York Times,* 2 October 1948, p. 4; "Quotations From the Soviet Press and Radio," annex to OIR-4629, in Papers of Charles Hulten, Truman Library, Box 9; New York *Herald-Tribune,* 25 November 1948, in Hovde MSS; *New York Times,* 27 September 1948, p. 6, and 22 March 1949, p. 16; Despatch 1373 from Moscow, 11 June 1948, 811.42761 SE/6-1148. On music see Nicholas Nabokov, "Russian Music After the Purge," *Partisan Review* 16 (August 1949):842–51; for a summary of the Soviet ideological campaign, see U.S. Department of State, Office of Intelligence Research, *Communist Offenses Against the Integrity of Education, Science and Culture* (Washington, D.C., 1951), pp. 21–60 (mimeographed).

46. Notarized Memorandum by Hovde, 20 August 1948, Hovde MSS, Box 2; *New York Times,* 12 August 1948, p. 5.

47. Norbert Muhlen, "A Political Circus," *The New Leader,* 18 September 1948, p. 6; "Building a Barricade of Sneers," *Newsweek,* 6 September 1948, p. 28; "Statement of Dr. Bryn J. Hovde at the World Congress of Intellectuals," *New School Bulletin,* 20 September 1948, in Hovde MSS, Box 2.

48. Bryn Hovde, "The Congress of Intellectuals," *The New Leader,* 11 December 1948, p. 6; Conference notes by Hovde, undated, in Hovde MSS, Box 2; Julian Huxley, *Memories II,* pp. 62–4; M. Kharlamov, "The Beginning of a Great World Movement," *Soviet Literature* 12 (1948):154; Telegram 1980 from Moscow, 15 September 1948, 501.PA/9-1548; Margaret Marshall, "Notes By The Way," *Nation,* 18 September 1949, p. 319.

49. Harlow Shapely to Dean Acheson, 5 February 1949, 811.43 National Council for the Arts, Sciences and Professions (hereafter NCASP)/2-549; J. Edgar Hoover to Harry Vaughan, 5 January 1949, Truman MSS, PSF, Box 167; Hoover to Vaughan, 12 December 1947, ibid., Box 168; Dorothy Thompson to Acheson, 18 March 1949, 800.00B/3-1849; Memorandum, J. W. Amshey to D. L. Nicholson, 27 February 1949, 811.42761/2-2149.

50. Memorandum, Francis Colligan to Johnstone, 25 February 1949, 811.43 NCASP/2-549; Memorandum, Johnstone to Hulten, 1 March 1949, FW811.43 NCASP/2-549; Memorandum, George Allen to Dean Rusk, 811.00B/6-149; Telegram 615 from Moscow, 10 March 1949, 800.00B/3-1049; Memorandum, John Peurifoy and George Allen to Acheson, 18 March 1949, FRC70A4521, Lot 587, Box 404; Memorandum, Hulten to James Webb, 1 March 1949, FW811.42761/2-2149.

51. Memorandum, Acheson to Truman, 14 March 1949, Acheson Papers, Truman Library, Box 64; Memorandum, Peurifoy and Allen to Acheson, 10 March 1949, FRC70A4521, Lot 587, Box 404; "Visas Authorized for Communist Representatives," *DOSB* 20 (27 March 1949):392. Cf. Max Lerner's distinction between the *"instrumental* approach to ideas and the *manipulative* approach," in Max Lerner, *Ideas Are Weapons: The History and Uses of Ideas* (New York: Viking Press, 1939), p. 10.

52. Bryn Hovde to Norman Cousins, 8 April 1949, and Cousins to Hovde, 14 April 1949, Hovde MSS, Box 2; Enclosure to 800.00B/7.2149. For proceedings of the conference, see the *New York Times*, 24-26 March 1949, and the edited report published by the NCASP, *Speaking of Peace* (New York: Manville Broadland, 1949). The Hovde MSS, Box 3, contain clippings from the *Herald-Tribune*. See also Garry Wills's introduction to Lillian Hellman, *Scoundrel Time* (New York: Bantam Books, 1977), pp. 24-6. The State Department used the occasion to release its *Cultural Relations With the Soviet Union,* Department of State Publication 3480 (Washington, D.C.: Government Printing Office, 1949), detailing its frustrated efforts to establish cultural relations with the USSR.

53. Telegram 1129 to Paris from MacKnight, 6 April 1949, 800.00B/4-649; Telegram 1456 from Paris, 8 April 1949, 800.00B/4-849; Telegram 1161 to Paris, from Bohlen to Chipman, 12 April 1949, 800.00B/4-1249; Sidney Hook, "Report on International Day Against Dictatorship and War," *Partisan Review* 16 (July 1949):725; Donald H. McLachlan, "The Partisans of Peace," *International Affairs* 27 (January 1951):10-17. Hook's anti-Communist liberalism is briefly expounded in Sidney Hook, "Communism and the Intellectuals," *The American Mercury* 68 (February 1949):133-44.

54. Memorandum, Howland Sargeant to Robert P. Joyce, 9 June 1949, FRC70A4521, Lot 587, Box 404. On Beichman's role at the Waldorf conference, see Tom O'Connor, "News Tailored to Fit," *Nation,* 16 April 1949, pp. 438-9.

55. Memorandum by Melvin Lasky, 7 December 1947, *Der Monat* Papers, Regenstein Library, University of Chicago, Box 73; Memorandum by Lasky, *"Der Monat:* The Impact of a Democratic Magazine in Soviet Germany," undated, ibid., Box 73.

56. Lasky to William Donovan, 24 February 1950, ibid., Box 9; Sidney Hook to Lasky, 11 January 1950, ibid., Box 9; Lasky to Hook, 19 February 1950, ibid., Box 9.

57. Hook to Lasky, 16 March 1950, ibid., Box 9; Lasky to Arthur Koestler, 19 April 1950, ibid., Box 3; Lasky to William Benton, 25 March 1950, ibid., Box 4.

58. "A Congress in Berlin," *The New Republic,* 26 June 1950, p. 9; Hook to John J. McCloy, 6 November 1950, *Der Monat* MSS, Box 2; Lasky to C. J. Friedrich, 15 June 1950, ibid., Box 9; Foy Kohler to Lasky, 8 June 1950, ibid., Box 9.

59. Sidney Hook, "The Berlin Congress for Cultural Freedom," *Partisan Review* 17 (September–October 1950):715; H. R. Trevor-Roper to Lasky, 28 July 1950, *Der Monat* MSS, Box 5; the statement is in the *Manchester Guardian,* 28 June 1950; Lasky to Arthur Schlesinger, Jr., 26 July 1950, *Der Monat* MSS, Box 5. See also Christopher Lasch, "The Cultural Cold War: A Short History of the Congress For Cultural Freedom," in Barton J. Bernstein, ed., *Towards A New Past: Dissenting Essays in American History* (New York: Vintage Books, 1968), pp. 323–5. For Nabokov's account of events from the Waldorf conference to the formation of the CCF, see Nicolas Nabokov, *Bagazh: Memoirs of a Russian Cosmopolitan* (New York: Atheneum, 1975), pp. 232–46.

Conclusion: Freedom, ideology, and culture

1. See, e.g., U.S. Department of State, *The Widening Circle* (Washington, D.C.: Government Printing Office, 1957), p. 45.

2. One quickly discovers that ideology is an amorphous concept that is itself frequently used for ideological purposes. For the view of ideology as distorted thought, see Werner Stark, *The Sociology of Knowledge* (London: Routledge & Kegan Paul, 1959), pp. 46–9. Some general descriptions of the concept can be found in Harry M. Johnson, "Ideology and the Social System," *International Encyclopedia of the Social Sciences* (New York: Macmillan, 1968), ed. David Sills, vol. 7, pp. 76–85, and in Talcott Parsons, Edward Shils, Kaspar D. Naegle, and Jesse R. Pitts, *Theories of Society* (New York: Free Press, 1961), p. 992. It should be made clear that my use of ideology here differs substantially from the standard formulations of diplomatic historians, whether "New Left" or of more traditional persuasion. Specifically, both sides assume an ideological continuity to U.S. foreign policy throughout the twentieth century, whereas I view ideology as a novel ingredient that made possible the radical discontinuity in American foreign policy commonly known as the Cold War.

3. Marvin Harris, *Culture, Man, and Nature: An Introduction to General Anthropology* (New York: Crowell, 1974), p. 144; Philip K. Bock, *Modern Cultural Anthropology: An Invitation,* 2nd ed. (New York: Knopf, 1974), p. 306; Leslie A. White, *The Evolution of Culture* (New York: McGraw-Hill, 1959), p. 23; James B. Conant, "Scholarly Inquiry and the American Tradition," *The Educational Record* 31 (July 1950):282; John Simon Guggenheim Memorial Foundation, *Reports of the Secretary and Treasurer 1947 and 1948* (New York: Guggenheim Foundation, 1949), p. 18; Willard Thorp, "Iron Curtains," *DOSB* 20 (19 June 1949):799. For a classic definition of liberal idealism, see Nicholas Murray Butler, *Why War? Essays and Addresses on War and Peace* (New York: Scribner, 1940), pp. 215–16.

4. William G. Carleton, "Ideology or Balance of Power," *Yale Review* 36 (June 1947):602; Bohlen is cited in the digest of material appearing in *DOSB,* January 1949, Truman MSS, PSF, Box 188. Peter Berger and Thomas Luckman, *The Social Construction of Reality* (New York: Anchor Books, 1967), pp. 123–4, argue that "it makes little sense to use the term [ideology] if two different definitions of reality confront each other in intersocietal contact." But Talcott Parsons, *Sociological Theory and Modern Society* (New York: Free Press, 1967), pp. 467–8,

insists that the East-West conflict was ideological, as it occurred "within a pattern of order rather than a Hobbesian state of nature." I must confess that I find myself uncomfortable with both of these positions: One assumes ideology to be strictly subcultural, and the other asseverates a supracultural "pattern of order" not so obvious to all onlookers.

5. These opposing points of view can be found in Karl Mannheim, *Ideology and Utopia,* pp. 53–83, and in Edward Shils, "Ideology," in Shils, *The Intellectuals and the Powers and Other Essays* (Chicago: University of Chicago Press, 1972), pp. 23–41.

6. "Chill Wind in Chicago," *Time,* 17 January 1949, p. 60; "Flagstad, Voice and Issue," *Newsweek,* 28 April 1947, p. 88; "Gieseking Gets the Gate," *LIFE,* 7 February 1949, pp. 43–4; Paul Moore, "The Artist As Citizen," *Theatre Arts* 33 (April 1949): 38–40.

7. Robert A. Corrigan, "Ezra Pound and the Bollingen Prize Controversy," *Midcontinent American Studies Journal* 8 (Fall 1967):43–50; William Van O'Connor and Edward Stone, eds., *A Casebook on Ezra Pound* (New York: Crowell, 1959), pp.30–2; U.S. Library of Congress, Press Release No. 520, 17 February 1949.

8. Robert Hillyer, "Treason's Strange Fruit," *Saturday Review of Literature,* 11 June 1949, pp. 9–11; Hillyer, "Poetry's New Priesthood," ibid.; Allen Tate to Archibald MacLeish, 11 September 1949, MacLeish MSS, Box 19.

9. Editorial, "Ezra Pound and the Bollingen Award," *Saturday Review of Literature,* 11 June 1949, p. 20; William Rose Bénet to Hayden Carruth, 3 December 1949, Papers of *Poetry* Magazine, University of Chicago, Regenstein Library, Series 1, Box 2, Folder 3; Norman Cousins to Luther Evans, 24 August 1949, Library of Congress Central File, File "Poetry 6"; Alfred Kazin, *On Native Grounds* (New York: Reynal & Hitchcock, 1942), p. 435; Stanley E. Hyman, *The Armed Vision* (New York: Knopf, 1948), p. 261; Robert Penn Warren, *A Plea in Mitigation* (Macon, Ga.: Southern Press, 1962), p. 5; Robert Gorham Davis, "The New Criticism and the Democratic Tradition," *The American Scholar* 19 (Winter 1949–50):10–19; Peter Viereck, "Pure Poetry, Impure Politics and Ezra Pound," *Commentary* 11 (1951):340–6. The Pound affair was also an important, if unrecognized, harbinger of the disputes that would erupt in the 1970s over "elitist" versus "populist" control of art policy.

10. T. S. Eliot, "The Metaphysical Poets," in *The Achievement of American Criticism,* ed. Clarence A. Brown (New York: Ronald Press, 1954), p. 619. Radio Moscow is cited in Michael Reck, *Ezra Pound: A Close-Up* (New York: McGraw-Hill, 1967), p. 90.

11. Ninkovich, "The Currents of Cultural Diplomacy," pp. 230–1; Matthews, "Art and Politics in Cold War America," pp. 762–87. To the extent that such things are possible at all, I would hold that liberal-capitalist societies can be ideologically transparent, a proposition that Marxists would adamantly deny.

12. See Alonzo Hamby, *Beyond the New Deal: Harry S. Truman and American Liberalism* (New York: Columbia University Press, 1973), pp. 281–2, and Richard Hofstadter, *Anti-Intellectualism in American Life* (New York: Vintage Books, 1963), p. 394, for intimations of the trend to conservatism. MacLeish defends Pound in his *Poetry and Opinion* (Urbana: University of Illinois Press, 1950), passim.

13. David Caute, *The Great Fear* (New York: Touchstone Books, 1978), p. 144, in a perplexed reference to "genuinely liberal liberals" points to the discrepancy between liberalism as ideal and its ideological conservatism in the 1950s.

14. NSC 68, 14 April 1950, Modern Military Branch, National Archives.
15. Clifford Geertz, "Ideology as a Cultural System," in Geertz, *The Interpretation of Cultures*, esp. pp. 218–20; Parsons, *Sociological Theory and Modern Society*, pp. 163–4; Morton Fried, *The Evolution of Political Society* (New York: Random House, 1967), p. 26.
16. Hearings Before a Subcommittee of the Senate Committee on Foreign Relations on S. Res. 243, 81st Cong., 2nd sess., p. 44 (1950).
17. Quoted in Robert K. Merton, *The Sociology of Science* (Chicago: University of Chicago Press, 1973), p. 262.

Epilog

1. American Council on Education, 1950 Report on "Improving the Service of Research and Information Concerning International Exchange Activities," FRC63A217, Lot 52-86, Box 299. For a modern functionalist affirmation of the relationship between interdependence and political institutions, see Steven Muller, "A New American University?" *Daedalus* 107 (Winter 1978): 43.
2. Current expressions of this view can be found in Norman Daniel, *The Cultural Barrier: Problems in the Exchange of Ideas* (Edinburgh: Edinburgh University Press, 1975), pp. 133, 176; George Shuster, "The Nature and Development of Cultural Relations," in Braisted, *Cultural Affairs and Foreign Relations*, p. 36; Frankel, *The Neglected Aspect of Foreign Affairs*, p. 62. For a modern anthropological attempt to transcend culture, see Edward T. Hall, *Beyond Culture* (Garden City, N.Y.: Anchor Books, 1977), pp, 162, 212, 220–2.
3. Melville Herskovits, *Cultural Anthropology* (New York: Knopf, 1966), p. 545.
4. See Clifford Geertz, "The Impact of the Concept of Culture on the Concept of Man," in Geertz, *The Interpretation of Cultures*, pp. 33–43. On Enlightenment rationalism, see Arthur O. Lovejoy, *Essays in the History of Ideas* (Baltimore: Johns Hopkins Press, 1948), pp. 79–88, and Ernst Cassirer, *The Philosophy of the Enlightenment* (Princeton: Princeton University Press, 1951), pp. 13, 44–5, 218–21.

Bibliography

A note on sources

Of the archival collections consulted in the course of doing research for this study, those found in the Washington, D.C., area proved to be the most important. The official documents housed in the National Archives provided a logical starting point for investigation. Of these, the Department of State's Decimal Files were essential. Unfortunately, because the Department of State has indiscriminately destroyed the bulk of its general records pertaining to the cultural programs, these needed to be heavily supplemented by other sources. Vital for this purpose were the War History Branch records, the records of the various interdepartmental committees on cooperation with the American Republics, the Conference Records, and the Office of American Republic Affairs Lot Files. The Harley Notter Files were useful for studying the department's postwar planning in cultural relations.

The Department of State Lot Files in Suitland, Maryland, were another rich source of information. Most important were the Files of the Assistant Secretary for Public Affairs, the William Benton Files, and the records of the UNESCO Relations Staff. The quality of the remaining materials was disappointing, although here and there intriguing pieces of information were discovered. The Department of State Post Files provided only fragmentary data on the cultural programs. In the office of the historian for the International Communication Agency, formerly the USIA, I found copies of documents not available elsewhere.

At the Library of Congress, the papers of the American Council of Learned Societies proved indispensable to this study, providing numerous insights into the theory and practice of cultural relations. They also contain copies of important State Department documents that are not to be found elsewhere. Although the Waldo Leland Papers were on the whole disappointing, they were useful for UNESCO's early years. The other collections in the Manuscript Division were of marginal utility, occasionally illuminating specific episodes. The library's Central Services Division has interesting materials on the Bollingen Prize controversy.

At the Harry S Truman Library, the Bryn Hovde Papers were a welcome surprise. Although lacking in materials dealing with Hovde's State Department service, they were extremely helpful in documenting early American reactions to the Soviet ideological offensive. For all their bulk, the remaining manuscript collections were thin on cultural materials.

In New York City, the Papers of The Carnegie Endowment for International Peace, housed in Columbia University's Butler Library, were a basic source for reconstructing the philanthropic origins of cultural policy. The James T. Shotwell Papers documented his involvement with the U.S. National Committee on Intellectual Cooperation, but little else. The contents of the Nicholas Murray Butler Papers were dismayingly meager for my purposes. At the Institute of International Education, the microfilmed records proved to be useful for the 1920s and the mid-1940s.

A visit to the American Library Association Papers in Urbana, a large collection, helped to elucidate librarians' cultural views and activities.

In Chicago, the privately held papers of William Benton, which should be available to all researchers in the not too distant future, were a valuable complement to the Benton materials found in the State Department files. They are especially useful in documenting the early days of Rockefeller's CIAA, the art fiasco, and Benton's UNESCO activities. At the University of Chicago's Regenstein Library, the Robert Redfield Papers were extremely helpful in a number of unexpected areas. The Papers of the International Association for Cultural Freedom were less valuable for my purposes than I had expected. The *Der Monat* Papers, part of the larger IACF collection, were indispensable to an understanding of the origins of the Congress for Cultural Freedom. The remaining collections were of only incidental importance, although the *Poetry* collection has a much broader relevance to the study of cultural politics than evinced in this study.

It would be nice to report that the oral histories consulted provided some essential information or insights. Some were interesting. A few were even useful. Beyond that, I can say little on their behalf.

Archives and manuscript collections

Chicago, Illinois. Papers of William Benton. Privately held.
Chicago, Illinois. University of Chicago. Regenstein Library.
    Papers of the International Association for Cultural Freedom
    Charles Merriam Papers
    Der Monat Papers
    Papers of *Poetry* Magazine
    Robert Redfield Papers
    Quincy Wright Papers
Independence, Missouri. Harry S Truman Library.
    Dean Acheson Papers
    George V. Allen Papers
    Bryn Hovde Papers
    Charles Hulten Papers
    Charles Patterson Papers
    Harry S Truman Papers
    U.S. Senate. Committee on Foreign Relations
New York, New York. Columbia University. Butler Library.
    Nicholas Murray Butler Papers
    Papers of the Carnegie Endowment for International Peace
    James T. Shotwell Papers
New York, New York. Institute of International Education. Historical Files.
Suitland, Maryland. Federal Records Center. Department of State Lot Files.
    Lot 21. Division of Cultural Relations
    Lot 52-84. Richard Heindel Files
    Lot 52-86. Private Organizations

Lot 52-202. Files of the Assistant Secretary for Public Affairs
Lot 52-249. Archibald MacLeish Correspondence
Lot 53D339. Bryn Hovde Files
Lot 54D374. Correspondence. Private Channels
Lot 65D423. Records of the UNESCO Relations Staff
Lot 587. William Benton Files
Suitland, Maryland. Washington National Records Center. Department of State Post Files. Record Group 84.
Urbana, Illinois. University of Illinois Archives. Papers of the American Library Association.
Washington, D.C. Library of Congress. Central Files.
Washington, D.C. Library of Congress. Manuscript Division.
  Carl Ackerman Papers
  Papers of the American Council of Learned Societies
  Norman Davis Papers
  Samuel Guy Inman Papers
  Waldo Leland Papers
  Archibald MacLeish Papers
  Leo Pasvolsky Papers
  Elihu Root Papers
  Henry Wallace Papers (microfilmed)
Washington, D.C. National Archives.
  Department of State Conference Records. Record Group 43.
  Department of State Decimal Files. Record Group 59.
  Harley Notter Files. Record Group 59.
  Office of American Republic Affairs Lot Files. Record Group 59.
  Leo Pasvolsky Files. Record Group 59.
  Records of the Interdepartmental Committee on Cooperation with the American Republics. Record Group 353.
  Secretary's Staff Committee Minutes. Record Group 353.
  U.S. Senate. Committee on Foreign Relations. Record Group 46.
  War History Branch Records. Record Group 59.
Washington, D.C. International Communication Agency (USIA). Office of the Historian. Historical Files.

Official documents and publications

Addresses and Statements by the Honorable Cordell Hull in Connection With His Trip to South America to Attend the Inter-American Conference for the Maintenance of Peace at Buenos Aires, Argentina, December 1–23, 1936. Department of State Publication 1019, Conference Series No. 31. Washington: Government Printing Office, 1937.

Boal, Pierre De L. *The Substance of Foreign Relations.* Department of State Publication 2034. Washington: Government Printing Office, 1945.

Colligan, Francis J. *Twenty Years After: Two Decades of Government-Sponsored Cultural Relations.* Department of State Publication 6689. Washington: Government Printing Office, 1958.

Greene, Dorothy. *Cultural Centers in the Other American Republics.* Department of State Publication 2503. Washington: Government Printing Office, 1946.

Hanson, Haldore, comp. *The Cultural Cooperation Program, 1938–1943.* Department of State Publication 2137. Washington: Government Printing Office, 1944.

McClure, Wallace M. *International Law of Copyright.* Department of State Publication 1179. Washington: Government Printing Office, 1938.

MacMahon, Arthur W. *Memorandum on the Postwar International Information Program of the United States.* Department of State Publication 2438. Washington: Government Printing Office, 1945.

Messersmith, George M. *Some Observations on the Work and Needs of the Department of State.* Department of State Publication 1120. Washington: Government Printing Office, 1938.

Notter, Harley. *Postwar Foreign Policy Preparation, 1939–1945.* Department of State Publication 3580. Washington: Government Printing Office, 1949.

Office of the Coordinator of Inter-American Affairs. *Guide to the Inter-American Cultural Programs of Non-Government Agencies in the United States.* Washington: CIAA, 1943 (mimeographed).

Office of Inter-American Affairs. *History of the Coordinator of Inter-American Affairs.* Washington: Government Printing Office, 1947.

Report of the Delegation of the United States of America to the Inter-American Conference for the Maintenance of Peace, Buenos Aires, Argentina, December 1–23, 1936. Department of State Publication 1088, Conference Series 33. Washington: Government Printing Office, 1937.

Rosenthal, Albert H. *Administrative Problems in the Establishment of the United Nations Educational, Scientific and Cultural Organization.* Washington: Department of State, 1946 (mimeographed).

Sayre, Francis B. *The American Adventure.* Department of State Publication 1254. Washington: Government Printing Office, 1938.

Shaw, G. Howland. *Cultural Cooperation Program of the Department of State.* Department of State Publication 2130. Washington: Government Printing Office, 1944.

The State Department and Its Foreign Service in Wartime. Department of State Publication 2020. Washington: Government Printing Office, 1943.

Turner, Ralph E., and French, Hope Sewell. *Conference of Allied Ministers of Education.* Department of State Publication 2221, Conference Series 59. Washington: Government Printing Office, 1944.

U.S. Advisory Commission on Educational Exchange. *Semiannual Reports on Educational Exchange Activities,* 1949–50.

U.S. Committee on Public Information. *Complete Report of the Chairman of the Committee on Public Information, 1917:1918:1919.* Washington: Government Printing Office, 1920.

U.S. Congress. *Congressional Record.* 1938–50.

U.S. Congress. House. Committee on Appropriations. *Hearings, Department of State Appropriation Bill.* 76th–81st Cong., 1939–51.

Official Trip of Examination of Federal Activities in South and Central America: Report of a Subcommittee on Appropriations, December 4, 1941. 77th Cong., 1st sess., 1941.

U.S. Congress. House. Committee on Education and Labor. Task Force on International Education. *International Education: Past, Present, Problems and Prospects: Selected Readings to Supplement H.R. 14643.* Washington: Government Printing Office, 1966.

226   *Bibliography*

U.S. Congress. House. Committee on Foreign Affairs. *Hearings, H.R. 3342.* 8oth Cong., 1st and 2nd sess., 1947.
Interchange of Knowledge and Skills Between the People of the United States and Peoples of Other Countries. Hearing Before the House Committee on Foreign Affairs on H.R. 4368. 79th Cong., 1st and 2nd sess., 1946.
International Office of Education. Hearings on H. Res. 215. 79th Cong., 1st sess., 1945.
Membership and Participation by the United States in the United Nations Educational, Scientific and Cultural Organization. Hearings on H.J. Res. 305. 79th Cong., 2nd sess., 1946.
United States Information and Educational Exchange Act of 1947. Hearings Before a Special Subcommittee. 8oth Cong., 1st sess., 1947.
U.S. Congress. House. *Report No. 336.* 8oth Cong., 1st sess., 1948.
U.S. Congress. Senate. Committee on Foreign Relations. *Expanded International Information and Education Program. Hearings on S. Res. 243.* 81st Cong., 2nd sess., 1950.
Nominations for Under Secretary of State and Assistant Secretaries of State, December 12, 1944. 78th Cong., 2nd sess., 1944.
Promoting the Better Understanding of the United States Among the Peoples of the World and to Strengthen Cooperative International Relations. S. Rept. 811 to accompany H.R. 3342, 8oth Cong., 2nd sess., 1948.
United States Information and Educational Exchange Act of 1947: Hearings on H.R. 3342. 8oth Cong., 1st sess., 1947.
U.S. Congress. Senate. *Senate Report No. 855,* Parts 1 and 2. 8oth Cong., 2nd sess., 1948.
U.S. Department of State. *Building the Peace.* Department of State Publications 2288–93.
Bulletin. 1939–50.
Cooperation in the Americas. Department of State Publication 2971, International Information and Cultural Series 1. Washington: Government Printing Office, 1948.
Cultural Relations Between the United States and the Soviet Union. Department of State Publication 3480, International Information and Cultural Series 4. Washington: Government Printing Office, 1949.
The Defenses of Peace. Parts I and II. Department of State Publications 2457 and 2475, Conference Series 80 and 81. Washington: Government Printing Office, 1946.
Foreign Relations of the United States. Annual volumes, 1943–5. Washington: Government Printing Office.
List of Persons Compiled in Connection With the Four Conferences on Inter-American Cultural Relations, Washington, D.C., October and November 1939. Washington: Department of State, 1940 (mimeographed).
Office Of Intelligence Research. *Communist Offenses Against the Integrity of Education, Science and Culture.* Washington: Department of State, 1951 (mimeographed).
Press Releases. 1929–39
The Widening Circle. Department of State Publication 6642. Washington: Government Printing Office, 1957.
Welles, Sumner. *The Accomplishments of the Inter-American Conference for the Maintenance of Peace.* Department of State Conference Series No. 26. Washington: Government Printing Office, 1937.

Pan-American Cooperation. Department of State Publication 712. Washington: Government Printing Office, 1935.
The Practical Accomplishments of the Buenos Aires Conference. Department of State Conference Series No. 29. Washington: Government Printing Office, 1937.
Present Aspects of World Peace. Department of State Publication 1042. Washington: Government Printing Office, 1937.
The Roosevelt Administration and Its Dealings With the Republics of the Western Hemisphere. Department of State Publication 692. Washington: Government Printing Office, 1942.
The United Nations: Their Creed for a Free World. Department of State Publication 1848. Washington: Government Printing Office, 1942.
The Way to Peace on the American Continent. Department of State Publication 877. Washington: Government Printing Office, 1936.

Oral histories

Columbia Oral History Collection. Columbia University. Butler Library.
Allen, George V.
Benton, William
Carr, William G.
Davis, Malcolm
Evans, Luther
Kandel, Isaac
Leland, Waldo
Shotwell, James T.
Truman Library Oral History Collection
Block, Ralph
Clubb, O. Edmund
Riley, Russell A.

Reports

Carnegie Corporation of New York. *Annual Report.* 1921–50.
Carnegie Endowment for International Peace. *Annual Report.* 1911–50.
Institute of International Education. *Annual Report.* 1920–50.
Report of the Conference of College and University Administrators and Foreign Student Advisers, April 29–May 1, 1946, Chicago, Illinois. New York: The Institute, 1946.
Report of the Conference of Foreign Student Advisers, April 28–30, 1942, Cleveland, Ohio. New York: The Institute, 1942.
John Simon Guggenheim Memorial Foundation. *Report of the Secretary and Treasurer.* 1925–50.
National Council for the Arts, Sciences and Professions. *Speaking of Peace.* New York: Manville-Broadland, 1949.
Rockefeller Foundation. *Annual Report.* 1913–50.
World Conference of the Teaching Profession, Endicott, New York, 1946. Proceedings, August 17–30, 1946. Washington: World Organization of the Teaching Profession, 1947.

Zook, George. *Report of the Annual Meeting of the International Committee on Intellectual Cooperation, Geneva, Switzerland, July 17–22, 1939.* Washington, 1939.

Journals and periodicals

Arbaiza, Genaro. "Are the Americas Safe?" *Current History* 47 (December 1937): 29–34.
Ascher, Charles S. "The Development of UNESCO's Program." *International Organization* 4 (1950): 12–26.
Barrow, John. "American Institutions of Higher Learning in China." *Higher Education* 4 (February 1948): 121–4.
Bernal, J. D. "A Permanent International Scientific Commission." *Nature* 156 (10 November 1945): 557–8.
Blaisdell, Alan. "Educational Relationships With the Far East." Institute of International Education *News Bulletin* 25 (June 1950): 5–6ff.
  "New Crisis in Cultural Relations." Institute of International Education *News Bulletin* 23 (January 1948): 3–9.
Bonnet, Henri. "UNESCO, Spearhead of the United Nations." *American Association of University Professors Bulletin* 32 (Winter 1946): 610–14.
Bostwick, Arthur E. "Reports of Arthur E. Bostwick's Mission to China as ALA Delegate." American Library Association *Bulletin* 20 (January 1926): 35–48.
Brickman, William W. "Historical Framework of International Student Interchange." *International Educational and Cultural Exchange* (Winter 1968): 27–35.
Bronk, Detlev W. "International Relations Among Scientists." *Proceedings of the American Philosophical Society* 90 (1946): 304–8.
Brown, Elsie. "A Center of Argentine–American Friendship." *Bulletin of the Pan American Union* 73 (January 1939): 27–30.
Brunauer, Esther Caukin. "Power Politics and Democracy." *The Annals* 216 (July 1941): 109–16.
"Building a Barricade of Sneers." *Newsweek,* 6 September 1948, p. 28.
Butler, Hugh. "Our Deep Dark Secrets in Latin America." *Reader's Digest* 43 (December 1943): 21–5.
Butler, Nicholas Murray. "The Carnegie Endowment for International Peace." *The Independent* 76 (27 November 1913): 396–400.
  "The International Mind: How to Develop It." *Proceedings of the Academy of Political Science* 8 (July 1917): 16–20.
  "World Conditions We Are Facing." *International Conciliation* 350 (May 1939): 275–83.
Butts, Marie. "The International Bureau of Education." *The Annals* 235 (September 1944): 10–16.
Byrnes, Robert F. "Academic Exchange With the Soviet Union." *Russian Review* 21 (July 1962): 215–35.
Calder, Ritchie. "Science and World Government." *New Statesman and Nation* 30 (3 November 1945): 294.
Cantril, Hadley. "The Human Sciences and World Peace." *Public Opinion Quarterly* 12 (Summer 1948): 236ff.
Carleton, William G. "Ideology or Balance of Power." *Yale Review* 36 (Summer 1947): 590–602.

Carr, William G. "Five Years of UNESCO." NEA *Journal* 39 (October 1950): 530–1.
"The London Conference on Education and Cultural Organization." NEA *Journal* 34 (October 1945): 124.
"The NEA at the San Francisco Conference." NEA *Journal* 34 (October 1945): 123.
Chen Li-Fu. "Chinese Universities During the War." *The Educational Record* 24 (April 1943): 130–5.
Cherrington, Ben. "The Division of Cultural Relations of the Department of State." Institute of International Education *News Bulletin* 8 (May 1939): 5–6.
"Ten Years After." *Association of American Colleges Bulletin* 34 (December 1948): 500–22.
"Chill Wind in Chicago." *Time*, 17 January 1949, p. 60.
Chin, Theodore Hsi-En. "All Is Not Lost in China." *The Educational Record* 30 (October 1949): 478–86.
"China Turns Disaster Into Triumph." *School and Society* 57 (19 June 1943): 684.
Conant, James B. "Scholarly Inquiry and the American Tradition." *The Educational Record* 31 (July 1950): 275–82.
"A Congress in Berlin." *The New Republic,* 26 June 1950, p. 9.
Cooper, John M. "Problems of International Understanding." *Proceedings of the American Philosophical Society* 90 (1946): 314–17.
Corrigan, Robert A. "Ezra Pound and the Bollingen Prize Controversy." *Midcontinent American Studies Journal* 8 (Fall 1967): 43–50.
Craemer, Alice R. "Intellectual Solidarity." *Current History* 12 (1947): 230–5.
Curts, Henry S. "Education for a Permanent Peace." *School and Society* 58 (17 July 1943): 33–5.
Davies, Thurston J. "The Arts and the Crisis." *The Educational Record* 23 (January 1942): 30–4.
Davis, Robert Gorham. "The New Criticism and the Democratic Tradition." *The American Scholar* 19 (Winter 1949–50): 10–19.
Davis, Roy Tasco. "American Private Schools in Latin America." *The Educational Record* 25 (October 1944): 327–36.
Dexter, Byron. "UNESCO Faces Two Worlds." *Foreign Affairs* 25 (April 1949): 388–407.
"Yardstick for UNESCO," *Foreign Affairs* 28 (October 1949): 56–66.
Doyle, Michael Frances, ed. "The Inter-American Conference For the Maintenance of Peace." *International Conciliation* 328 (March 1937): 193–289.
Duggan, Laurence. "Fellowships For International Reconstruction." Institute of International Education *News Bulletin* 22 (February 1947): 3–4.
Duggan, Stephen. "The Kyoto Conference." Institute of International Education *News Bulletin* 5 (October 1929): 1–2.
"Moral Disarmament and International Education." Institute of International Education *News Bulletin* 9 (November 1933): 3–4.
"Sovereignty." Institute of International Education *News Bulletin* 17 (November 1941): 3–5.
"Education and the People's Peace." NEA *Journal* 32 (September 1943): 165–8.
Elliott, A. Randle. "Inter-American Educational Activities in the United States." Institute of International Education *News Bulletin* 19 (December 1943): 6–8.
"Embarrassment of a Confucian." *Time*, 24 April 1944, pp. 34–6.

"Ezra Pound and the Bollingen Award." *Saturday Review of Literature,* 11 June 1949, p. 20.

Faber, Maurice. "The Study of National Character." *Journal of Social Issues* 11 (1955): 52–6.

Fenwick, Charles G. "The Buenos Aires Conference: 1936." *Foreign Policy Reports* 13 (1 July 1937): 89–99.

Feuer, Lewis S. "Travellers to the Soviet Union, 1917–1932." *American Quarterly* 14 (Summer 1962): 119–49.

"Flagstad, Voice and Issue." *Newsweek,* 28 April 1947, p. 88.

Fletcher, John M. "Human Nature and World Peace." NEA *Journal* 34 (May 1945): 101–4.

Galambos, Louis. "The Emerging Organizational Synthesis in Modern American History." *Business History Review* 44 (Autumn 1970): 279–90.

"Gieseking Gets the Gate." *Life,* 7 February 1949, pp. 43–4.

Goldenweiser, Alexander. "Diffusionism and Historical Ethnology." *American Journal of Sociology* 31 (July 1925): 19–38.

Greene, Dorothy E. "The Informal Diplomats." *The American Foreign Service Journal* 23 (October 1946): 7–10.

Haines, Gerald K. "Under the Eagle's Wing: The Franklin Roosevelt Administration Forges an American Hemisphere." *Diplomatic History* 1 (Fall 1977): 373–88.

Hawley, Claude E. "Education For International Understanding." *American Association of University Professors Bulletin* 35 (Autumn 1949): 530–8.

Hawley, Ellis. "Herbert Hoover, the Commerce Secretariat, and the Vision of an 'Associative' State, 1921–1928." *Journal of American History* 61 (June 1974): 116–40.

Heindel, Richard J. "Understanding the United States Abroad." *Social Education* 11 (February 1947): 55–7.

Hillyer, Robert. "Poetry's New Priesthood," *Saturday Review of Literature,* 18 June 1949, pp. 7–9ff.

"Treason's Strange Fruit." *Saturday Review of Literature,* 11 June 1949, pp. 9–11ff.

Hodges, Charles. "The World Union of Intellectual Forces." *Current History* 24 (1926): 411–15.

Hoffman, Stanley. "The American Style: Our Past and Principles." *Foreign Affairs* 46 (January 1968): 362–77.

Holland, Kenneth. "Fear of the 'Little Hot War.'" Institute of International Education *News Bulletin* 26 (October 1950): 8.

"The Program of the Inter-American Educational Foundation." *The Educational Record* 27 (January 1946): 80–7.

Hook, Sidney. "Berlin Congress for Cultural Freedom." *Partisan Review* 17 (September 1950): 715–22.

"Communism and the Intellectuals," *The American Mercury* 68 (February 1949): 133–44.

"Encounter in Berlin." *The New Leader* 33 (14 October 1950): 16–19.

"Report on the International Day against Dictatorship and War." *Partisan Review* 16 (July 1949): 722–32.

Hovde, Bryn J. 'UNESCO." *Social Research* 14 (oMarch 1947): 26.

"UNESCO from the Point of View of Political Science." *The School Executive* 66 (October 1946): 82.

Hubbard, Ursula P. "The Cooperation of the United States with the League of Nations and with the International Labour Organization." *International Conciliation* 274 (November 1931): 675–825.

Hull, Cordell. "For Closer Cultural Contacts." *Think* 4 (December 1938): 6ff.

Hunt, Michael. "The American Remission of the Boxer Indemnity: A Reappraisal." *Journal of Asian Studies* 31 (May 1972): 539–59.

Huxley, Julian. "The Future of UNESCO." *Discovery* 7 (February 1946): 72–3.

"Science and the United Nations." *Nature* 156 (10 November 1945): 553–6.

"Ideologies." *Time*, 2 December 1946, pp. 27–8.

Jacob, Philip. "Floating Seminars, 1947: Training for International Understanding." *Social Education* 12 (January 1948): 23–7.

Johnson, Richard A. "The Origins of the United Nations Educational, Scientific and Cultural Organization." *International Conciliation* 424 (October 1946): 441–9.

Kandel, Isaac L. "Education and the Postwar Settlement." *International Conciliation* 389 (April 1943): 368–75.

"Educational Utopias." *The Annals* 235 (September 1944): 41–8.

Kefauver, Grayson. "Peace Aims Call for International Action in Education." *New Europe* 3 (May 1943): 15–19.

Kellogg, Vernon. "American National Committee on Intellectual Cooperation." *The Educational Record* 8 (January 1927): 17–27.

Kennan, George F. "International Exchange in the Arts." *Perspectives USA* 16 (1956): 6–14.

Kharlamov, M. "The Beginning of a Great World Movement." *Soviet Literature* 12 (1948): 152–6.

Kirkendall, Lester A. "Education and the Postwar World." *The Educational Record* 24 (January 1943): 44–57.

Kotschnig, Walter. "International Education." *The Educational Record* 22 (October 1941): 491–505.

"Toward an IOEDC: Some Major Issues Involved." *The Educational Record* 25 (July 1944): 259–87.

Krill de Capello, H. H. "The Creation of the United Nations Educational, Scientific and Cultural Organization." *International Organization* 24 (Winter 1970): 4.

Laves, Walter H. C. "The Reorganization of the Department of State." *American Political Science Review* 38 (April 1944): 289–301.

Leland, Waldo. "The Background and Antecedents of UNESCO." *Proceedings of the American Philosophical Society* 90 (1946): 295–9.

"The International Union of Academies and the American Council of Learned Societies." *International Conciliation* 154 (September 1920): 442–57.

"The Role and Work of the United Nations Educational, Scientific and Cultural Organization." *American Association of University Professors Bulletin* 35 (Summer 1949): 274–97.

Lerner, Max. "American Leadership in a Harsh Age." *The Annals* 216 (July 1941): 117–24.

"Libraries and the War: A Statement of Policy." American Library Association *Bulletin* 36 (January 1942): 3–4.

Lord, Milton E. "Postwar Relationships and International Cultural Relations." American Library Association *Bulletin* 36 (September 1942): 13–16.

McAfee, John. "Student Exchange and the Dollar Shortage." Institute of International Education *News Bulletin* 24 (November 1948): 5–12.

MacIver, Robert M. "The Fundamental Principles of International Order." *International Postwar Problems* 1 (December 1943): 17–30.

"Intellectual Cooperation in the Social Sciences." *Proceedings of the American Philosophical Society* 90 (1946): 309–13.

McKeon, Richard, "The Pursuit of Peace Through Understanding." *The Yale Review* 38 (December 1948): 253–69.

"UNESCO In Its Second Year." *The Educational Record* 29 (April 1948): 137–44.

McLachlan, Donald H. "The Partisans of Peace." *International Affairs* 27 (January 1951): 10–17.

MacLeish, Archibald. "How Can We Contribute To Peace?" *American Association of University Professors Bulletin* 34 (Autumn 1948): 539–45.

"Toward An Intellectual Offensive." American Library Association *Bulletin* 36 (July 1942): 423–8.

"UNESCO: UNESCO's Task." *American Association of University Professors Bulletin* 32 (Winter 1946): 605–10.

Mann, C. R. "International Educational Relations." *The Educational Record* 9 (January 1928): 26–31.

Marshall, James. "Citizen Diplomacy." *American Political Science Review* 43 (February 1949): 83–90.

"What About an International Office for Education?" *The Annals* 235 (September 1944): 33–40.

Matthews, Jane DeHart. "Art and Politics in Cold War America." *American Historical Review* 81 (October 1976): 762–87.

Messer, Robert L. "Paths Not Taken: The United States Department of State and Alternatives to Containment, 1945–1946." *Diplomatic History* 1 (Fall 1977): 297–319.

Moe, Henry Allen. "The John Simon Guggenheim Memorial Foundation." *The Educational Record* 6 (July 1925): 264–8.

Moore, Paul. "The Artist As Citizen." *Theatre Arts* 33 (April 1949): 38–40.

Morton, Louis. "National Security and Area Studies: The Intellectual Responses to the Cold War." *Journal of Higher Education* 34 (March 1963): 142–7.

Mundt, Karl. "The United States and Russia – World Leaders." *NEA Journal* 35 (October 1946): 390–1.

Murray, Gilbert. "Intellectual Cooperation." *The Annals* 235 (September 1944): 1–9.

Nabokov, Nicolas. "Russian Music After the Purge." *Partisan Review* 16 (August 1949): 842–51.

Needham, Joseph. "The Place of Science and International Scientific Co-operation in Post-War World Organization." *Nature* 156 (10 November 1945): 558–61.

Niebuhr, Reinhold. "The Illusion of World Government." *Foreign Affairs* 25 (April 1949): 379–88.

"Peace Through Cultural Cooperation." *Christianity and Crisis,* 17 October 1949, pp. 131–3.

"The Theory and Practice of UNESCO." *International Organization* 4 (1950): 3–11.

Ninkovich, Frank. "The Currents of Cultural Diplomacy: Art and the State Department, 1938–1947." *Diplomatic History* 1 (Summer 1977): 215–37.

Norton, John K. "Keystone For the Peace Treaty." *Nation's Schools* 29 (March 1942): 51–2.

O'Connor, Tom. "News Tailored to Fit." *Nation,* 16 April 1949, pp. 438–9.

Pendergast, William R. "The Political Uses of Cultural Relations." *Il Politico* 38 (December 1973): 682–96.

"UNESCO and French Cultural Relations, 1945–1970." *International Organization* 30 (Summer 1976): 453–80.

Redfield, Robert, Linton, Ralph, and Herskovits, Melville J. "Memo On the Study of Acculturation." *American Anthropologist* 38 (1936): 149–52.

Rippy, J. Fred. "The Conference of Buenos Aires: A Retrospective View." *World Affairs* 100 (March 1937): 46–9.

Rivera, Rodolfo A. "The A.L.A. and Latin America." American Library Association *Bulletin* 34 (December 1940): 671–3.

Robertson, David A. "International Educational Relations." *The Educational Record* 7 (January 1926): 46–58.

"International Educational Relations of the United States." *The Educational Record* 6 (January 1925): 91–150.

Root, Elihu. "A Requisite for the Success of Popular Diplomacy." *Foreign Affairs* 1 (September 1922): 3–10.

Sanders, William. "International Copyright Protection." *Bulletin of the Pan American Union* 73 (July 1939): 418–28.

Sharp, Walter R. "The Role of UNESCO: A Critical Evaluation." Academy of Political Science *Proceedings* 24 (1950–1): 249–62.

Shotwell, James T. "Foundation of Good Will." *THINK* 4 (December 1938): 9ff.

Shotwell, James T. and Ware, Edith E. "Intellectual Cooperation." *International Conciliation* 369 (April 1939): 337–45.

Snyder, Harold E. "The Commission for International Educational Reconstruction." *American Association of University Professors Bulletin* 33 (Summer 1947): 371–80.

"Soviet-American Cultural Exchanges: A Review Since 1917." Institute of International Education *News Bulletin* 32 (October 1956): 16–22.

Spender, Stephen. "Impressions of the First General Conference." *Britain Today* 131 (March 1947): 14–18.

"United Nations: Cultural Division." *Commentary* 3 (April 1947): 336–40.

Stoddard, George D. "Fresco, UNESCO, and Mr. Wierblowski." *School and Society* 67 (6 March 1948): 177–80.

Sweetser, Arthur. "The Non-Political Achievements of the League." *Foreign Affairs* 19 (October 1940): 179–92.

Thomas, S. B. "Recent Educational Policy in China." *Pacific Affairs* 23 (March 1950): 21–33.

Thompson, C Mildred. "United Nations Plan for Post-War Education." *Foreign Policy Reports* 20 (1 March 1945): 310–19.

Thomson, Charles A. "Intellectual Freedom as a Basis for World Understanding." *International Conciliation* 383 (October 1942): 423–9.

"The Role of Government in UNESCO." *Proceedings of the American Philosophical Society* 90 (1946): 300–3.

Tripp, Brenda H. M. "UNESCO in Perspective." *International Conciliation* 497 (March 1954): 323–85.

Turner, Ralph E. "The Conference of Allied Ministers of Education." *The School Executive* 63 (March 1944): 35–8.

"The United States and World Organization During 1935." *International Concili-ation* 321 (June 1936): 277–323.

Viereck, Peter. "Pure Poetry, Impure Politics and Ezra Pound." *Commentary* 11 (1951): 340–6.

Vitray, Laura. "UNESCO: Adventure in Understanding." *Free World* 12 (No-vember 1946): 24–8.

Wilcox, Francis O. "The Libraries and the War Effort of the Americas." Ameri-can Library Association *Bulletin* 36 (September 1942): 3–6.

"The State Department Continues Its Reorganization." *American Political Sci-ence Review* 39 (April 1945): 309–16.

Wilson, Howard E. "Education as an Instrument of International Cooperation." *International Conciliation* 415 (November 1945): 705–45.

"National Programs of International Cultural Relations." *International Concili-ation* 462 (June 1950): 297–336.

Woody, Thomas. "Faults and Futures in American–Soviet Cultural Relations." *School and Society* 64 (28 September 1946): 209–13.

Yang, Y. C. "Education in Wartime China." *Association of American Colleges Bulle-tin* 29 (March 1943): 60–9.

Zimmern, Alfred. "Nationalism and Internationalism." *Foreign Affairs* 1 (June 1923): 115–26.

Zook, George F. "The Interplay of Cultures." *International Conciliation* 369 (April 1939): 246–57.

Dissertations

Allbee, Lewis. "Education as an Implement of U.S. Foreign Policy, 1938–1948." Ph.D. dissertation, Yale University, 1948

Bennett, Alvin L. "The Development of Intellectual Cooperation under the League of Nations and the United Nations." Ph.D. dissertation, University of Illinois, 1950.

Camery, Lura G. "American Backgrounds of the United Nations Educational, Scientific and Cultural Organization." Ph.D. dissertation, Stanford Univer-sity, 1949.

Daniel, Robert L. "From Relief to Technical Assistance, A Case Study: Near East Relief and Near East Foundation." Ph. D. dissertation, University of Wis-consin, 1953.

Greco, John. "A Foundation for Internationalism: The Carnegie Endowment for International Peace, 1931–1941." Ph.D. dissertation, Syracuse University, 1971.

Halpern, Stephen M. "The Institute of International Education: A History." Ph.D. dissertation, Columbia University, 1969.

Jaenke, Sylvan F. "A Study of the Origin, Growth and Development of the United Nations Educational, Scientific and Cultural Organization." Ph.D. dissertation, University of Illinois, 1948.

Karp, Basil. "The Development of the Philosophy of UNESCO." Ph.D. disserta-tion, University of Chicago, 1951.

Ludden, Howard L. "The International Information Program of the United States: State Department Years, 1945–1953." Ph.D. dissertation, Prince-ton University, 1966.

Schulman, Lawrence D. "United States Government Educational, Literary and

Artistic Cultural Exchange Programs, 1948–1958, as a Technique of American Diplomacy." Ph.D. dissertation, New York University, 1967.

Scott, Donald H. "The Cultural Institute in Mexico City as an Example of United States Policy in Cultural Relations." Ph.D. dissertation, University of Southern California, 1959.

Tuppert, Esther Elizabeth. "International Intellectual and Cultural Cooperation between Two Wars: A Study of the Development of the Concept and Its Propagation under the Auspices of the League of Nations." Ph.D. dissertation, Yale University, 1946.

Books

Aiken, Henry D., comp. *The Age of Ideology.* New York: Mentor Books, 1956.

The American Assembly, Columbia University. *The Representation of the United States Abroad.* New York: American Assembly, 1956.

American Library Association, Board on Resources of American Libraries and International Relations Board. *Conference on International Cultural, Educational and Scientific Exchanges, November 25–26, 1946.* Chicago: American Library Association, 1947.

Appreciations of Frederick Paul Keppel by Some of His Friends. Preface by Charles Dollard and biographical note by Florence Anderson. New York: Columbia University Press, 1951.

Ascher, Charles S. *Program-Making in UNESCO, 1946–1951. A Study in the Processes of Internal Administration.* Chicago: Public Administration Service, 1951.

Bacon, Robert. *For Better Relations With Our Latin American Neighbors: A Journey to South America.* Washington: Carnegie Endowment for International Peace, 1915.

Bacon, Robert, and Scott, James Brown, eds. *Latin America and the United States: Addresses by Elihu Root.* Cambridge: Harvard University Press, 1917.

Men and Policies: Addresses by Elihu Root. Cambridge: Harvard University Press, 1925.

Bard, Harry Edwin. *Intellectual and Cultural Relations Between the United States of America and the Other Republics of America.* Washington: Carnegie Endowment for International Peace, 1914.

Barghoorn, Frederick C. *The Soviet Cultural Offensive: The Role of Cultural Diplomacy in Soviet Foreign Policy.* Princeton: Princeton University Press, 1960.

Soviet Foreign Propaganda. Princeton: Princeton University Press, 1964.

The Soviet Image of the United States: A Study in Distortion. New York: Harcourt Brace Jovanovich, 1950.

Barrett, Edward W. *Truth Is Our Weapon.* New York: Funk & Wagnalls, 1953.

Beals, Carleton. *The Coming Struggle for Latin America.* New York: Halcyon House, 1940.

Beals, Carlton, et al. *What the South Americans Think of Us: A Symposium.* New York: R. M. McBride, 1945.

Beaulac, Willard L. *Career Ambassador.* New York: Macmillan, 1951.

Bemis, Samuel Flagg. *The Latin American Policy of the United States.* New York: Norton, 1967.

Ben-David, Joseph, and Clark, Terry, eds. *Culture and Its Creators: Essays in Honor Of Edward Shils.* Chicago: University of Chicago Press, 1977.

Benedict, Ruth. *Patterns of Culture.* New York: Houghton Mifflin, 1934.
Berger, Peter L., and Luckman, Thomas. *The Social Construction of Reality: A Treatise in the Sociology of Knowledge.* Garden City, N. Y.: Anchor Books, 1967.
Berman, Maureen R., and Johnson, Joseph E., eds. *Unofficial Diplomats.* New York: Columbia University Press, 1977.
Bernstein, Barton J., ed. *Towards A New Past: Dissenting Essays in American History.* New York: Random House (Vintage Books), 1969.
Besterman, Theodore. *UNESCO: Peace in the Minds of Men.* London: Methuen, 1951.
Blakey, George T. *Historians on the Homefront.* Lexington: University Press of Kentucky, 1970.
Blau, Peter M. *Bureaucracy in Modern Society.* New York: Random House, 1956.
Bloomfield, Lincoln P. *The United Nations and the U.S. Foreign Policy.* Boston: Little, Brown, 1960.
Blumenthal, Henry. *American and French Culture, 1800–1900: Interchanges in Art, Science, Literature and Society.* Baton Rouge: Louisiana State University Press, 1977.
Bogart, Leo. *Premises for Propaganda: The United States Information Agency's Operating Assumptions in the Cold War.* New York: Free Press, 1976.
Borkenau, Franz. *World Communism.* Ann Arbor: University of Michigan Press, 1962.
Brady, Ivan A., and Isaac, Barry L., eds. *A Reader in Culture Change.* Vol 1: *Theories.* Cambridge, Mass.: Schenkman, 1975.
Braisted, Paul, ed. *Cultural Affairs and Foreign Relations.* Rev. ed. Washington: Columbia Books, 1968.
Brett, George P., Jr., et al. *The Role of Books in Inter-American Relations.* New York: Book Publishers Bureau Inc. and the American Textbook Publishers Institute, 1943.
Briggs, Ellis O. *Farewell To Foggy Bottom.* New York: McKay, 1964.
Butler, Nicholas Murray. *Across the Busy Years.* 2 vols. New York and London: Scribner, 1940.
   The International Mind: An Argument for the Judicial Settlement of International Disputes. New York: Scribner, 1912.
   Why War? Essays and Addresses on War and Peace. New York: Scribner, 1940.
Byrnes, Robert F. *Soviet-American Academic Exchanges, 1958–1975.* Bloomington: Indiana University Press, 1976.
Cantril, Hadley. *The Human Dimension.* New Brunswick, N.J.: Rutgers University Press, 1967.
   Tensions That Cause Wars. Urbana: University of Illinois Press, 1950.
Carnegie, Andrew. *Autobiography of Andrew Carnegie.* Garden City, N.Y.: Doubleday, 1933.
   The Gospel of Wealth and Other Timely Essays. Garden City, N.Y.: Doubleday, 1933.
Carnegie Endowment for International Peace. Division of International Law. *The International Conferences of American States, 1889–1928.* New York: Oxford University Press, 1931.
   The International Conferences of American States: First Supplement, 1933–1940. Washington: Carnegie Endowment for International Peace, 1940.

Proceedings of the Inter-American Educational and Cultural Conference Held at the Institute of Inter-American Affairs of the University of Florida, Gainesville, April 14–17, 1940. St. Petersburg, Fla.: Petersburg Printing Company, 1940.

Carr, William G. *Only By Understanding: Education and International Organization.* New York: Foreign Policy Association, 1945.

Carroll, Wallace. *Persuade or Perish.* Boston: Houghton Mifflin, 1948.

Cassirer, Ernst. *The Philosophy of the Enlightenment.* Princeton: Princeton University Press, 1951.

Caute, David. *The Great Fear.* New York: Touchstone Books, 1978.

Cheng, Chi-Pao, ed. *Chinese-American Cultural Relations.* Taiwan: n.p., 1965.

Cherrington, Ben M. *Methods of Education in International Relations.* New York: Teachers College, Columbia University, 1934.

The Social Science Foundation of Denver, 1926–1951: A Personal Reminiscence. Denver: Social Science Foundation, 1973.

Chiang Kai-shek. *China's Destiny & Chinese Economic Theory.* New York: Roy Publishers, 1947.

Clark, Reginald W. *The Huxleys.* New York: McGraw-Hill, 1968.

Claude, Innis L., Jr. *Swords Into Plowshares: Problems and Progress of International Organization.* New York: Random House, 1956.

Coffin, Tristram. *Senator William Fulbright: Portrait of a Public Philosopher.* New York: Dutton, 1966.

Coombs, Philip H. *The Fourth Dimension of Foreign Policy.* New York: Harper & Row, 1964.

Crabbs, Richard F. *United States Higher Education and World Affairs: A Partially Annotated Bibliography.* New York: Praeger, 1967.

Creel, George. *How We Advertised America.* New York: Harper & Row, 1920.

Cremin, Lawrence A. *Isaac Leon Kandel, 1881–1965, A Biographical Memoir.* New York: National Academy of Education, 1966.

Curti, Merle. *American Philanthropy Abroad: A History.* New Brunswick, N.J.: Rutgers University Press, 1963.

Peace or War: The American Struggle, 1636–1936. New York: Norton, 1936.

Curti, Merle, and Birr, Kendall. *Prelude to Point Four – American Technical Missions Overseas, 1838–1948.* Madison: University of Wisconsin Press, 1954.

Curtis, James E., and Petras, John W., eds. *The Sociology of Knowledge: A Reader.* New York: Praeger, 1970.

Daniel, Norman. *The Cultural Barrier: Problems in the Exchange of Ideas.* Edinburgh: Edinburgh University Press, 1975.

Davies, John Paton. *Dragon By the Tail.* London: Robson Books, 1974.

Davis, Harriet Eager, ed. *Pioneers in World Order: An American Appraisal of the League of Nations.* New York: Columbia University Press, 1944.

Dennett, Raymond, and Johnson, Joseph E., eds. *Negotiating With the Russians.* Boston: World Peace Foundation, 1951.

Deutsch, Karl W. *Nationalism and Its Alternatives.* New York: Knopf, 1969.

Nationalism and Social Communication: An Inquiry Into the Foundations of Nationality. 2nd ed. Cambridge, Mass.: M.I.T. Press, 1975.

Divine, Robert A. *Second Chance: The Triumph of Internationalism in America During World War II.* New York: Atheneum, 1971.

Dizard, Wilson P. *The Strategy of Truth: The Story of the U.S. Information Service.* Washington: Public Information Press, 1961.

Duggan, Laurence. *The Americas: The Search for Hemisphere Security.* Foreword by Herschell Brickell. New York: Holt, Rinehart and Winston, 1949.

Duggan, Stephen P. *A Critique of the Report of the League of Nations' Mission of Educational Experts to China.* New York: Institute of International Education, 1933.

Latin America. Boston: World Peace Foundation, 1936.

A Professor at Large. New York: Macmillan, 1943.

Duggan, Stephen P., and Drury, Betty. *The Rescue of Science and Learning.* New York: Macmillan, 1948.

Duggan, Stephen P., and Mussey, Henry R., eds. *The Foreign Relations of the United States.* New York: Academy of Political Science, Columbia University, 1917.

Dunn, Frederick S. *War and the Minds of Men.* New York: Harper & Row, 1950.

Elder, Robert W. *The Foreign Leader Program: Operations in the United States.* Washington: Brookings Institution, 1961.

Eliot, Charles W. *Some Roads Toward Peace: A Report to the Trustees of the Endowment on Observations Made in China and Japan in 1912.* Washington: Carnegie Endowment for International Peace, 1914.

Espinosa, J. Manuel. *Inter-American Beginnings of U.S. Cultural Diplomacy, 1938–1948.* Bureau of Educational and Cultural Affairs, Historical Studies: Number 2. Department of State Publication 8854. International Information and Cultural Series 110. Washington: Government Printing Office, 1976.

Fairbank, John King. *The United States and China.* Rev. ed. New York: Viking Press, 1962.

Fairbank, John King, ed. *The Missionary Enterprise in China and America.* Cambridge: Harvard University Press, 1974.

Fairbank, Wilma. *America's Cultural Experiment in China, 1942–1949.* Bureau of Educational and Cultural Affairs, Historical Studies: Number 1. Department of State Publication 8839. International Information and Cultural Series 108. Washington: Government Printing Office, 1976.

Fenner, Mildred S. *NEA History.* Washington: National Education Association, 1945.

Field, James A., Jr., *America and the Mediterranean World, 1776–1882.* Princeton: Princeton University Press, 1969.

Filene, Peter G. *Americans and the Soviet Experiment, 1917–1933.* Cambridge: Harvard University Press, 1967.

Fisher, Glen H. *Public Diplomacy and the Behavioral Sciences.* Bloomington: Indiana University Press, 1972.

Fisher, Harold H., ed. *American Research on Russia.* Bloomington: Indiana University Press, 1959.

Flexner, Abraham. *Henry S. Pritchett: A Biography.* New York: Columbia University Press, 1943.

Fosdick, Raymond. *Adventure in Giving: The Story of the General Education Board.* New York: Harper & Row, 1962.

Chronicle of a Generation: An Autobiography. New York: Harper & Row, 1958.

John D. Rockefeller, Jr.: A Portrait. New York: Harper & Row, 1966.

Letters on the League of Nations. Princeton: Princeton University Press, 1966.

The Old Savage in the New Civilization. Garden City, N.Y.: Doubleday, 1928.

The Story of the Rockefeller Foundation. New York: Harper & Row, 1952.

Frank, Waldo. *South American Journey.* New York: Duell, Sloan and Pearce, 1943.

Frankel, Charles. *The Neglected Aspect of Foreign Affairs.* Washington: Brookings Institution, 1966.

Fraser, Steward, ed. *Governmental Policy and International Education.* New York: Wiley, 1965.

Frazier, E. Franklin. *Race and Culture Contacts in the Modern World.* Boston: Beacon Press, 1957.

Fried, Morton. *The Evolution of Political Society: An Essay In Political Anthropology.* New York: Random House, 1967.

Frost, S. E., Jr. *Is American Radio Democratic?* Chicago: University of Chicago Press, 1937.

Geertz, Clifford. *The Interpretation of Cultures: Selected Essays.* New York: Basic Books, 1973.

Glick, Philip M. *The Administration of Technical Assistance: Growth in the Americas.* Chicago: University of Chicago Press, 1957.

Graham, Loren R. *Science and Philosophy in the Soviet Union.* New York: Knopf, 1972.

Gray, George W. *Education On An International Scale: A History of the International Education Board, 1923–1938.* New York: Harcourt Brace Jovanovich, 1941.

Greaves, H. R. G. *The League Committees and World Order.* London: Oxford University Press, 1931.

Griffin, Charles C., ed. *Concerning Latin American Culture.* New York: Columbia University Press, 1940.

Guerrant, Edward O. *Roosevelt's Good Neighbor Policy.* Albuquerque: University of New Mexico Press, 1950.

Hall, Edward T. *Beyond Culture.* Garden City, N.Y.: Anchor Books, 1977.

Hamby, Alonzo. *Beyond the New Deal: Harry S. Truman and American Liberalism.* New York: Columbia University Press, 1973.

Hamilton, William B., ed. *The Transfer of Institutions.* Durham: Duke University Press, 1964.

Harley, John E. *International Understanding: Agencies Educating for a New World.* Stanford, Cal.: Stanford University Press, 1931.

Harris, Marvin. *The Rise of Anthropological Theory.* New York: Crowell, 1968.

Hatch, Elvin. *Theories of Man and Culture.* New York: Columbia University Press, 1973.

Hawley, Ellis R. *The New Deal and the Problem of Monopoly.* Princeton: Princeton University Press, 1966.

Heald, Morrill, and Kaplan, Lawrence. *Culture and Diplomacy.* Westport, Conn.: Greenwood Press, 1978.

Heindel, Richard H. *The American Impact on Great Britain, 1898–1914.* New York: Octagon Books, 1968.

American Library in London. London: Reproduction Section, OWI, 1945.

Hellman, Lillian. *Scoundrel Time.* New York: Bantam Books, 1977.

An Unfinished Woman. New York: Bantam Books, 1970.

Henderson, John W. *The United States Information Agency.* New York: Praeger, 1969.

Hendrick, Burton J. *The Life of Andrew Carnegie.* Vol. II. Garden City, N.Y.: Doubleday, 1932.

Herman, Sondra R. *Eleven Against War: Studies in American Internationalist Thought 1898–1921*. Stanford, Cal.: Hoover Institution Press, 1969.

Herring, Hubert. *Good Neighbors*. New Haven: Yale University Press, 1940.

Herskovits, Melville J. *Acculturation: The Study of Culture Contact*. Gloucester, Mass.: Peter Smith, 1938.

Cultural Anthropology. New York: Knopf, 1966.

Franz Boas: The Science of Man in the Making. New York: Scribner, 1953.

Hofstadter, Richard. *Anti-Intellectualism in American Life*. New York: Vintage Books, 1963.

Hogan, Michael. *Informal Entente: The Private Structure of Cooperation in Anglo-American Economic Diplomacy, 1918–1928*. Columbia: University of Missouri Press, 1977.

Hook, Sidney. *Heresy, Yes – Conspiracy, No!* New York: John Day, 1953.

Hoyt, Edwin P. *The Guggenheims and the American Dream*. New York: Funk & Wagnalls, 1967.

Huszar, George Bernard de, ed. *The Intellectuals*. New York: Free Press, 1960.

Huxley, Julian. *Memories II*. London: George Allen and Unwin, 1973.

UNESCO: Its Purpose and Its Philosophy. Washington: Public Affairs Press, 1947.

Hyman, Sidney. *The Lives of William Benton*. Chicago: University of Chicago Press, 1969.

Inman, Samuel Guy. *Building an Inter-American Neighborhood*. New York: National Peace Conference, 1937.

Inter-American Conferences, 1826–1954: History and Problems. Edited, with a preface by Harold Eugene Davis. Gettysburg, Pa.: Times & News Publishing Company, 1965.

Latin America: Its Place In World Life. Chicago and New York: Willett, Clark, 1937.

Some Latin American Views on Post-War Reconstruction. New York: Foreign Policy Association, 1944.

Institute of Latin American Studies. *Inter-American Intellectual Cooperation*. Austin: University of Texas Press, 1943.

International Institute of Intellectual Co-operation. *The Reorganisation of Education in China*. Paris: League of Nations Institute of Intellectual Co-operation, 1932.

Iriye, Akira. *Across the Pacific: An Inner History of American-East Asian Relations*. New York: Harbinger Books, 1967.

From Nationalism to Internationalism: U.S. Foreign Policy to 1914. London: Routledge & Kegan Paul, 1977.

Jessup, Philip C. *Elihu Root*. Vol. 2: *1905–1937*. New York: Dodd, Mead, 1938.

Johnson, Haynes, and Gwertzman, Bernard. *Fulbright the Dissenter*. Garden City, N.Y.: Doubleday, 1968.

Johnson, Walter, and Colligan, Francis J. *The Fulbright Program: A History*. Chicago: University of Chicago Press, 1965.

Josephson, Harold, *James T. Shotwell and the Rise of Internationalism in America*. Cranbury, N.J.: Associated University Presses, 1975.

Kandel, Isaac L. *The Impact of the War Upon American Education*. Chapel Hill: University of North Carolina Press, 1949.

Intellectual Cooperation: National and International. New York: Teachers College, Columbia University, 1944.

United States Activities in International Cultural Relations. Washington: American Council on Education, 1945.

Karl, Barry D. *Charles E. Merriam and the Study of Politics.* Chicago: University of Chicago Press, 1974.

Kaufman, Burton I. *Efficiency and Expansion: Foreign Trade Organization in the Wilson Administration, 1913–1921.* Westport, Conn.: Greenwood Press, 1974.

Kellerman, Henry I. *Cultural Relations As An Instrument of Foreign Policy: The Educational Exchange Program Between the United States and Germany, 1945–1954.* Bureau of Educational and Cultural Affairs, Historical Studies: Number 3. Department of State Publication 8931. International Information and Cultural Series 114. Washington: Government Printing Office, 1978.

Keohane, Robert O., and Nye, Joseph S., Jr., eds. *Transnational Relations and World Politics.* Cambridge: Harvard University Press, 1972.

Keppel, Frederick P. *American Philanthropy and the Advancement of Learning: Address Before the Graduate Convocation June 16, 1934, Brown University.* Providence: The University, 1934.

The Foundation: Its Place In American Life. New York: Macmillan, 1930.

Philanthropy and Learning. New York: Columbia University Press, 1936.

Kiger, Joseph E. *American Learned Societies.* Washington: Public Affairs Press, 1963.

King-Hall, Stephen. *Chatham House.* London: Oxford University Press, 1937.

Kitasawa, Sukeo. *The Life of Dr. Nitobe.* Tokyo: Hokuseido Press, 1953.

Klineberg, Otto. *International Exchanges in Education, Science and Culture: Suggestions for Research.* Paris: Mouton, 1966.

Kolasa, Jan. *International Intellectual Cooperation: The League Experience and the Beginnings of UNESCO.* Warsaw: Zaklad Narodowy um Ossolinskich, 1962.

Kolbe, Park R. *The Colleges in Wartime and After.* New York: Prentice-Hall, 1919.

Kotschnig, Walter M. *Slaves Need No Leaders.* New York: Oxford University Press, 1943.

Kroeber, A. L., ed. *Anthropology Today.* Chicago: University of Chicago Press, 1953.

Kuehl, Warren F. *Hamilton Holt: Journalist, Internationalist, Educator.* Gainesville: University of Florida Press, 1960.

Lasswell, Harold D. *Propaganda Technique in the World War.* New York: Peter Smith, 1938.

Lauren, Paul Gordon. *Diplomats and Bureaucrats: The First Institutional Responses to Twentieth-Century Diplomacy in France and Germany.* Stanford, Cal: Hoover Institution Press, 1976.

Laves, Walter H., ed. *Inter-American Solidarity.* Chicago: University of Chicago Press, 1941.

Leland, Waldo. *International Cultural Relations: Historical Considerations and Present Problems.* Denver: Social Science Foundation, 1943.

The International Role of American Scholarship: Address Before the Graduate School Convocation, June 15, 1940, Brown University. Providence, R.I.: The University, 1940.

Lepawsky, Albert, ed. *Administration: The Art and Science of Organization and Management.* New York: Knopf, 1949.

Lerner, Daniel, and Lasswell, Harold, eds. *The Policy Sciences.* Stanford, Cal.: Stanford University Press, 1950.

Lerner, Max. *Ideas Are Weapons: The History and Uses of Ideas.* New York: Viking Press, 1939.

Lester, Robert M. *Forty Years of Carnegie Giving.* New York: Scribner, 1941.

Levermore, Charles Herbert. *Samuel Train Dutton.* New York: Macmillan, 1922.

Lévi-Strauss, Claude. *Tristes Tropiques.* Trans. John and Doreen Wightman. New York: Pocket Books, 1977.

Lindzey, Gardner, ed. *The Handbook of Social Psychology.* Vol. IV. Menlo Park, Cal.: Addison-Wesley, 1969.

Liu, Kuang-Ching. *Americans and Chinese: A Historical Essay and Bibliography.* Cambridge: Harvard University Press, 1963.

Lloyd, Craig. *Aggressive Introvert: Herbert Hoover and Public Relations Management, 1912–1932.* Columbus: Ohio State University Press, 1972.

Locke, Alain, and Stern, Bernhard J., eds. *When Peoples Meet: A Study in Race and Culture Contacts.* Rev. ed. New York: Hinds, Hayden & Eldredge, 1946.

Lomask, Milton. *Seed Money: The Guggenheim Story.* New York: Farrar, Straus & Giroux, 1964.

Lovejoy, Arthur O. *Essays In The History of Ideas.* Baltimore: Johns Hopkins Press, 1948.

Lynch, Frederick. *Personal Recollections of Andrew Carnegie.* New York: Revell, 1920.

Mabie, Hamilton Wright. *Educational Exchange With Japan.* Washington: Carnegie Endowment for International Peace, 1914.

McKale, Donald R. *The Swastika Outside Germany.* Kent, Ohio: Kent State University Press, 1977.

McKeon, Richard, ed. *Democracy in a World of Tensions.* Chicago: University of Chicago Press, 1951.

McMurry, Ruth E., and Lee, Muna. *The Cultural Approach.* Chapel Hill: University of North Carolina Press, 1947.

Maier, Charles. *Recasting Bourgeois Europe.* Princeton: Princeton University Press, 1975.

Malinowski, Bronislaw. *The Dynamics of Culture Change: An Inquiry Into Race Relations In Africa.* New Haven: Yale University Press, 1945.

Mannheim, Karl. *Ideology and Utopia.* Trans. Louis Wirth and Edward Shils. New York: Harvest Books, n.d.

Marshall, James. *The Freedom To Be Free.* New York: John Day, 1943.
Swords and Symbols: The Technique of Sovereignty. New York: Oxford University Press, 1939.

Matthews, Roderic D., and Akrawi, Matta. *Education in Arab Countries of the Near East.* Washington: American Council on Education, 1949.

May, Henry F. *The Enlightenment in America.* New York: Oxford University Press, 1976.

Merton, Robert K. *Social Theory and Social Structure.* Rev. ed. New York: Free Press, 1957.
The Sociology of Science: Theoretical and Empirical Investigations. Chicago: University of Chicago Press, 1973.

Merton, Robert K., Gray, Ailsa P., Hockey, Barbara, and Selvin, Hanan C., eds. *Reader In Bureaucracy,* Glencoe, Ill.: Free Press, 1952.

Metraux, Guy S. *Exchange of Persons: The Evolution of Cross-Cultural Education.* Social Science Research Council, Pamphlet No. 9. New York: The Council, 1952.

Metzger, Thomas A. *Escape From Predicament: Neo-Confucianism and China's Evolving Political Culture.* New York: Columbia University Press, 1977.

Meyer, Karl E., ed. *Fulbright of Arkansas: The Public Positions of a Private Thinker.* Washington: Robert B. Luce, 1963.

Michels, Robert. *Political Parties: A Sociological Study of the Oligarchical Tendencies of Modern Society.* Trans. Eden and Cedar Paul. New York: Free Press, 1968.

Mock, James R., and Larson, Cedric. *Words That Won The War: The Story of the Committee on Public Information, 1917–1919.* Princeton: Princeton University Press, 1939.

Morgenthau, Hans J. *Politics Among Nations.* 4th ed. New York: Knopf, 1967.

Murray, Gilbert. *From The League to the U.N.* New York: Oxford University Press, 1948.

Nabokov, Nicholas. *Bagazh: Memoirs of a Russian Cosmopolitan.* New York: Atheneum, 1975.

National Education Association. Committee on International Relations. *Education for International Understanding in American Schools. Suggestions and Recommendations.* Washington: National Education Association, 1948.

National Society for the Study of Education. *International Understanding Through the Public School Curriculum.* Bloomington, Ill.: Public School Publishing Company, 1937.

Nevins, Allan. *John D. Rockefeller: The Heroic Age of American Enterprise.* New York: Scribner, 1940.

Nitobe, Inazo. *The Works of Inazo Nitobe.* Vol. II: *The Japanese Nation: Its Land, Its People, and Its Life.* Tokyo: University of Tokyo Press, 1972.

Northrop, Filmer S. C. *The Taming of the Nations: A Study of the Cultural Basis of International Policy.* New York: Macmillan, 1952.

O'Connor, Harvey. *The Guggenheims: The Making of an American Dynasty.* New York: Covici, Freide, 1937.

Parinni, Carl. *Heir To Empire: United States Economic Diplomacy, 1916–1923.* Pittsburgh, Pa.: University of Pittsburgh Press, 1973.

Parsons, Talcott. *Sociological Theory and Modern Society.* New York: Free Press, 1967.

Patterson, David F. *Toward A Warless World: The Travail of the American Peace Movement, 1887–1914.* Bloomington: Indiana University Press, 1976.

Peters, William. *Passport to Friendship.* New York: Lippincott, 1957.

Pritchett, Henry S. *A Plan For An Exchange of Teachers Between Prussia and the United States.* New York: Carnegie Foundation for the Advancement of Teaching, 1908.

Reinsch, Paul. *Public International Unions.* Boston: Ginn and Co., 1911.

Remmling, Gunter W. *The Sociology of Karl Mannheim.* Atlantic Highlands, N.J.: Humanities Press, 1975.

Rippy, J. Fred. *Latin America In World Politics: An Outline Survey.* 3rd ed. New York: F. S. Crofts, 1938.

Romasco, Albert. *The Poverty of Abundance: Hoover, the Nation, the Depression.* New York: Oxford University Press, 1965.

Rosenau, James N. *Linkage Politics: Essays on the Convergence of National and International Systems.* New York: Free Press, 1969.

Rourke, Francis E. *Bureaucracy and Foreign Policy.* Baltimore: Johns Hopkins Press, 1969.

Rowe, Leo S., et al. *Latin America in World Affairs, 1914–1940.* Philadelphia: University of Pennsylvania Press, 1941.

Sahlins, Marshall. *Culture and Practical Reason.* Chicago: University of Chicago Press, 1976.

Sahlins, Marshall, and Service, Elman R., eds. *Evolution and Culture.* Ann Arbor: University of Michigan Press, 1960.

Sathyamurthy, T. V. *The Politics of International Cooperation: Contrasting Conceptions of U.N.E.S.C.O.* Geneva: Droz, 1964.

Schaller, Michael. *The U.S. Crusade in China, 1938–1945.* New York: Columbia University Press, 1979.

Schmeckebier, Lawrence F. *International Organizations in Which the United States Participates.* Washington: Brookings Institution, 1936.

Schoenrich, Otto. *Former Senator Burton's Trip to South America.* Washington: Carnegie Endowment for International Peace, 1915.

Schuman, Frederick L. *The Commonwealth of Man.* New York: Knopf, 1952.

Schurz, William Lytle. *Latin America: A Descriptive Survey.* New York: Dutton, 1941.

This New World: The Civilization of Latin America. New York: Dutton, 1954.

Scott, James Brown, ed. *President Wilson's Foreign Policy: Messages, Addresses, Papers.* New York: Oxford University Press, 1918.

Robert Bacon: Life and Letters. Garden City, N.Y.: Doubleday, 1923.

Selznick, Philip. *Leadership in Administration.* New York: Harper & Row, 1957.

Sewell, James P. *UNESCO and World Politics: Engaging in International Relations.* Princeton: Princeton University Press, 1975.

Shils, Edward. *The Intellectuals and the Powers & Other Essays.* Chicago: University of Chicago Press, 1972.

Shotwell, James T. *Autobiography.* Indianapolis: Bobbs-Merrill, 1961.

The Great Decision. New York: Macmillan, 1949.

The Origins of the International Labor Organization. New York: Columbia University Press, 1934.

Shuster, George N. *UNESCO: Assessment and Promise.* New York: Harper & Row, 1963.

Smith, Grafton Elliott. *Culture: The Diffusion Controversy.* New York: Norton, 1927.

Smith, Robert Freeman. *The United States and Revolutionary Nationalism in Mexico, 1916–1932.* Chicago: University of Chicago Press, 1972.

Sorensen, Thomas C. *The World War: The Story of American Propaganda.* New York: Harper & Row, 1968.

Spykman, Nicholas John. *America's Strategy in World Politics: The United States and the Balance of Power.* New York: Harcourt Brace Jovanovich, 1942.

Stark, Werner. *The Sociology of Knowledge.* London: Routledge & Kegan Paul, 1958.

Stephens, Oren. *Facts to a Candid World: America's Overseas Information Program.* Stanford, Cal.: Stanford University Press, 1955.

Steward, Jane C., and Murphy, Robert F., eds. *Evolution and Ecology: Essays on Social Transformation by Julian H. Steward.* Urbana: University of Illinois Press, 1977.

Steward, Julian. *Theory of Culture Change.* Urbana: University of Illinois Press, 1955.

Thomas, Jean. *U.N.E.S.C.O.* Paris: Gallimard, 1962.
Thomson, Charles A. H. *Overseas Information Service of the United States Government.* Washington: Brookings Institution, 1948.
Thomson, Charles A., and Laves, Walter H. C. *Cultural Relations and U.S. Foreign Policy.* Bloomington: Indiana University Press, 1963.
UNESCO: Purpose, Progress, Prospects. Bloomington: Indiana University Press, 1957.
Thwing, Charles F. *The American Colleges and Universities in the Great War, 1914–1918.* New York: Macmillan, 1920.
Tryon, Ruth. *Investment in Creative Scholarship, 1890–1956.* Washington: American Association of University Women, 1957.
Tsou, Tang. *America's Failure in China, 1941–1950.* Chicago: University of Chicago Press, 1963.
Tunstall, Jeremy. *The Media Are American: Anglo-American Media in the World.* New York: Columbia University Press, 1977.
Turner, Ralph E. *America in Civilization.* New York: Knopf, 1925.
The Great Cultural Traditions: The Foundations of Civilization. New York: McGraw-Hill, 1941.
Varg, Paul A. *Missionaries, Chinese and Diplomats: The American Protestant Missionary Movement in China, 1890–1952.* Princeton: Princeton University Press, 1958.
Wall, Joseph. *Andrew Carnegie.* New York: Oxford University Press, 1970.
Ware, Edith. *International Relations in the United States, 1934–1937.* New York: Columbia University Press, 1938.
Weaver, Warren, et al. *U.S. Philanthropic Foundations.* New York: Harper & Row, 1967.
Weber, Max. *The Theory of Social and Economic Organization.* Edited with an introduction by Talcott Parsons. New York: Free Press, 1964.
Welles, Sumner. *An Intelligent American's Guide to the Peace.* New York: Dryden Press, 1945.
Seven Decisions That Shaped History. New York: Harper & Row, 1951.
We Need Not Fail. Boston: Houghton Mifflin, 1948.
Where Are We Heading? New York: Harper & Row, 1946.
The World of the Four Freedoms. New York: Columbia University Press, 1943.
The World We Can Make. Cambridge, Mass.: Riverside Press, 1945.
Wertenbaker, Charles. *A New Doctrine For the Americas.* New York: Viking Press, 1941.
Wesley, Edgar B. *NEA: The First Hundred Years.* New York: Harper & Row, 1957.
Wheeler, W. Reginald, King, H. Henry, and Davidson, Alexander B., eds. *The Foreign Student in America.* New York: YMCA Press, 1925.
Whitaker, Arthur P., ed. *Inter-American Affairs.* New York: Columbia University Press. Annual volumes 1942–5.
White, Leonard D. *The Future of Government in the United States: Essays in Honor of Charles E. Merriam.* Chicago: University of Chicago Press, 1942.
White, Leslie A. *The Concept of Cultural Systems: A Key to Understanding Tribes and Nations.* New York: Columbia University Press, 1975.
The Evolution of Culture. New York: McGraw-Hill, 1959.
White, Llewelyn. *Peoples Speaking to Peoples: A Report on International Mass Communications From the Commission on the Freedom of the Press.* Chicago: University of Chicago Press, 1946.

White, Lyman C. *International Non-Governmental Organizations*. New Brunswick, N.J.: Rutgers University Press, 1951.

Wilson, Howard E. *American Higher Education and World Affairs*. Washington: American Council on Education, 1963.

  Universities and World Affairs. New York: Carnegie Endowment for International Peace, 1951.

Wilson, Joan Hoff. *American Business and Foreign Policy 1920–1933*. Boston: Beacon Press, 1971.

  Herbert Hoover: Forgotten Progressive. Boston: Little, Brown, 1975.

Wilson, Margaret Barclay. *A Carnegie Anthology*. New York: by the author, 1915.

World Organization. A Symposium of the Institute on World Organization. Washington: Council on Public Affairs, 1942.

Wright, Quincy, ed. *A Foreign Policy for the United States*. Chicago: University of Chicago Press, 1947.

Yergin, Daniel. *Shattered Peace: The Origins of the Cold War and the National Security State*. Boston: Houghton Mifflin, 1977.

Zimmern, Sir Alfred. *The Intellectual Foundations of International Cooperation*. Paris: International Institute of Intellectual Cooperation, n.d.

Index